U.S. Regulation of Ocean Transportation
Under the Shipping Act of 1984

U.S. Regulation of Ocean Transportation Under the Shipping Act of 1984

by Gerald H. Ullman

Cornell Maritime Press
Centreville, Maryland

"Cargoes" by John Masefield, which appears on page 2, is reprinted with the permission of The Society of Authors as the literary representative of the Estate of John Masefield.

Library of Congress Cataloging-in-Publication Data

Ullman, Gerald H.
    U.S. regulation of ocean transportation under the Shipping Act of
1984 / Gerald H. Ullman
        p.   cm.
    Includes index.
    ISBN 0-87033-470-0 (hc)
    1. Maritime law—United States.   2. Carriers—Law and legislation
—United States.   3. Ocean freight forwarders—United States.
I. United States. Shipping Act of 1984.   II. Title
KF2606.U45   1995
343.7309′62—dc20
[347.303962]   95–14074

Manufactured in the United States of America
First edition

To Michael and Jerry

TABLE OF CONTENTS

FOREWORD

Gerry Ullman has written a much needed and very practical guide to the rights and responsibilities of all parties involved in ocean transportation. He examines the Shipping Act of 1984 in detail, giving, where needed, the logic, the history and the legislative intent behind the Act and related statutes, and his own very pragmatic interpretations of the law.

His book is a "must" reference work for all shippers, ocean carriers, NVOCCs, marine terminal operators, and freight forwarders. It tells you what you *must* do, what you *can* do, and what you *are* due. It provides non-maritime lawyers with quick answers and ready citations.

In my view, Gerry Ullman is truly a clients' lawyer. He is approachable, attentive, sharp, persevering, relentless, perceptive, and very, very knowledgeable. In his forty-odd years of maritime practice, he made it a point to know and to work closely with all of the players on the maritime field—including the legislators, jurists, and regulators who create, enforce, and interpret the governing laws and regulations.

One of the best things about this book is that it enables non-lawyers to ask the right questions, and to get needed answers fast. The book includes a user-friendly appendix which contains not only useful forms, but also the complete text of the Shipping Act of 1984. The detailed index makes it simple to locate the information that you need when you need it.

As a non-lawyer who welcomes plain talk and the opportunity to confirm for myself the legal advice I am given, I strongly recommend this book.

> Leslie Kanuk
> Former Commissioner and Acting Chairman
> Federal Maritime Commission

PREFACE

My 1967 work, *The Ocean Freight Forwarder, The Exporter & The Law* set forth in detail the statutory and regulatory responsibilities of ocean freight forwarders under the U.S. shipping laws and their legal relationships with exporters and ocean common carriers. Not long thereafter I realized that a comparable treatise delineating the legal responsibilities of the other major participants in ocean transportation—vessel operators, terminals, shippers, and NVOCCs—could serve a worthwhile purpose.

I was, however, sidetracked until my retirement in 1990 by a busy and fascinating maritime law practice representing all segments of the industry involved in ocean transportation. In addition, believing that the 50-Mile Rule was an insidious and onerous impediment to our export-import commerce, I became heavily involved through the years in legislative hearings, lengthy dockets, and appeals involving the Rule. As lead counsel in the litigation, it was gratifying for me to help accomplish the nullification in 1989 of this gross blight on our oceanborne foreign trade.

In a way it was fortuitous that I was occupied through the years in my practice with no opportunity to write another work. The Shipping Act of 1984 substantially changed the 1916 Act and had I produced another work prior to 1984, it would have soon become outdated. The extensive citations in this book of the decisions and regulations of the Federal Maritime Commission and the rulings of the courts will, I hope, provide a current and ready reference to the statutory and regulatory responsibilities of those involved in the sale, processing, and transportation of export cargo. In addition, attorneys not closely familiar with maritime law may find this volume to be a quick and timesaving guide to the 1984 law and the cases thereunder.

Not being able wholly to restrain the advocate in me, I have in this work from time to time taken issue with Congress when its language is unclear or its intent unwise, and with the courts and agencies when I believed that their decisions were of doubtful merit. Further, based upon the many practical problems encountered through the years, suggestions on how to avoid legal difficulties and civil penalties have been offered.

I acknowledge gratefully the devoted services of Sandy Farber, my faithful amanuensis through the years, in the production of this work.

U.S. Regulation of Ocean Transportation
Under the Shipping Act of 1984

CARGOES

Quinquireme of Nineveh from distant Ophir,
Rowing home to haven in sunny Palestine,
With a cargo of ivory,
And apes and peacocks,
Sandalwood, cedarwood, and sweet white wine.

Stately Spanish galleon coming from the Isthmus,
Dipping through the Tropics by the palm-green shores,
With a cargo of diamonds,
Emeralds, amethysts,
Topazes, and cinnamon, and gold moidores.

Dirty British coaster with a salt-caked smoke stack,
Butting through the Channel in the mad March days,
With a cargo of Tyne coal,
Road-rails, pig-lead,
Firewood, iron-ware, and cheap tin trays.

—John Masefield

CHAPTER I

HISTORY OF U.S. OCEAN SHIPPING REGULATION

Early civilizations, such as the Phoenicians, regularly exchanged goods carried by water with their trading partners. This sea commerce fostered comity and peaceful relations between societies. People who trade with each other do not war with each other. The benefits of this trade between nations were recognized almost two hundred years ago by a maritime writer:

> . . . the establishment of commerce and exchange, is the necessary consequence of the creation of mankind, whose wants obliged them to maintain a close and mutual intercourse with each other, and to form connexions of friendship.[1]

With the advent of rail and steamer transportation, England early recognized the need to protect shippers from unfair transportation practices by land and water carriers. An 1854 act provided that railway companies could not

> make or give any undue or unreasonable preference or advantage to or in favour of any particular person or company, or any particular description of traffic in any respect whatsoever. Nor are they to subject any particular person or company, or any particular description of traffic, to any undue or unreasonable prejudice or disadvantage in any respect whatsoever.[2]

This Act was amended by providing that its ban on undue preferences and unreasonable prejudice applied also to "traffic by sea in any vessels belonging to or chartered or worked by any railway company."[3]

The protection of shippers from unfair treatment under English law was initially adopted in the United States in the Shipping Act of 1916 (the 1916 Act)[4] almost verbatim and later carried over into the Shipping Act of 1984 (the 1984 Act).[5] Thus, approaching the twenty-first century, we are substantially guided by statutory language protective of ocean shippers drafted by English lawmakers in the mid-nineteenth century.

The replacement of sail by steam-powered vessels in the latter part of the nineteenth century revolutionized the relationship among ocean transporters of cargo. English vessel operators found themselves engaging in rate wars and other improper practices resulting in rebating and unfair discrimination. The industry was in chaos. In 1875, a leading British vessel operator, Sir Samuel Cunard, persuaded his competitors to form a "conference" of steamship lines in the trade between Calcutta and England that would fix rates and practices among the member lines, and establish sailing schedules and cargo sharing pools. In 1909 a British Royal Commission, after weighing the pros and cons, approved the use of the conference system to regulate the competition among the lines.

In the early 1900s steamship lines in the United States were involved in the same kind of rate wars and cutthroat competition earlier experienced by the English. In an effort to achieve stability, some U.S. lines adopted the English conference idea of agreeing upon rates and practices only to find themselves indicted by the Department of Justice for violations of antitrust laws. Upon an urgent appeal for help by the lines to Congress, a unit of the House Committee of Merchant Marine and Fisheries, known as the Alexander Committee, after two years of study, concluded that the advantages of the conference system significantly outweighed its disadvantages (H.R. Doc. No. 805, 63d Cong., 2d Sess., 1914) and, as a result, Congress passed the 1916 Act. Conference line members could thereafter agree to the joint fixing of rates and practices with antitrust law immunity upon approval under section 15 of the act by a newly established regulatory agency.[6]

The 1916 Act has been substantially amended through the years. In 1968 dual-rate contracts, declared unlawful by the U.S. Supreme Court,[7] were legalized.[8] These contracts, sometimes known as "loyalty" or "merchant rate" agreements, permit a shipper to obtain lower rates by committing all or a fixed portion of its cargo to conference members. Common carriers were required to file tariffs with the Federal Maritime Commission (FMC) showing their rates and practices. A second review standard under section 15 was adopted. An agreement that was "contrary to the public interest" could not be approved by the FMC. Conference lines were required to establish adequate provisions for policing the obligations of their members and reasonable procedures for promptly dealing with shipper requests and complaints.

The "contrary to the public interest" standard, the lines asserted through the years, created problems. In *Svenska,* the U.S. Supreme Court approved an FMC ruling that the public interest requirement gave rise to a presumption that concerted conference action interfered with U.S. antitrust laws and, as a result, the lines were required to establish that a filed agreement was necessary by "a serious transportation need, necessary to secure important public benefits, or in furtherance of a valid regulatory purpose of the Shipping Act."[9] The *Svenska* doctrine imposed a heavier burden of proof on the lines since antitrust law policy had to be considered by the FMC in the approval process. With the antitrust division of the Department of Justice regularly intervening before the FMC opposing approval of many filed conference agreements, the carriers also complained of the great delays, costs, and uncertainty in obtaining approval of what they considered to be efficient and necessary arrangements between them.

The lines' problems were further intensified in the late 1960s with the advent of the so-called "container revolution," said to be the most radical change in ocean transportation since the substitution of steam for sail. Instead of packages being individually loaded into a net at the pier, hoisted aboard the vessel, and then unloaded into a hatch, cargo is loaded (stuffed) at a facility away from the pier, either at a public or private warehouse, into a metal container usually 20 or 40 feet long, 8 feet high, and 8 feet wide, with a maximum load of 44,000 or 60,000 pounds respectively. The container is then delivered to a pier and loaded into a cellular vessel called a "containership." Vast sums of money were expended for such vessels, containers, terminal facilities, and storage yards. Because the "wonder boxes" could be carried below and on deck, vessel capacity was dramatically increased and loading and unloading could be accomplished in a fraction of the time formerly required.[10] At destination the container was discharged for delivery to the consignee's warehouse away from the terminal and unloaded (stripped). The stuffing at origin and the stripping at destination of containers resulted in tremendous savings to all segments of U.S. foreign commerce.

The lines claimed that the full economies of containerization could not be achieved unless shippers were offered a through transportation service with a single rate from origin point to overseas destination. The law was unclear as to whether such a service could be furnished by the carriers without the risk of prosecution under antitrust laws. As a result, the adoption of a through transportation service and rate, most valuable to the shipping public, was being impeded.

After approximately five years of study and hearings, Congress finally responded to the carriers' concerns with the passage of the 1984 Act.[11] A most important change in the law was the elimination of FMC prior "approval" of agreements among carriers under section 15 of the 1916 Act. Instead, a filed agreement, unless rejected as defective in form, became "effective" the forty-fifth day after filing or the thirtieth day after notice of the filing was published in the Federal Register, whichever day was later, or forty-five days after the FMC received requested information.[12] The lines were no longer required to prove a negative, that is, that the proposed agreement was not "detrimental to the commerce of the United States" or "contrary to public interest."

To remove the ever-present risk of an antitrust violation if the lines could not satisfactorily show that an action taken by them was clearly authorized in the conference agreement, the 1984 Act provided that the antitrust laws would not apply to any activity or agreement entered into by the lines if they had a "reasonable basis" to conclude that their action was pursuant to an agreement on file with the commission and in effect when the activity took place.[13] Point-to-point rates and through transportation routes were recognized,[14] and a joint venture or consortium of two or more common carriers operating as a single entity would be treated as a single common carrier, thereby avoiding the time and expense of a filing with the FMC.[15]

Congress in the new law also sought to protect the interests of the shipping public. Less-than-container-load (LCL) shippers extensively used non-vessel-operating common carriers (NVOCCs) generally providing lower rates. While the NVOCC concept had long been recognized in FMC decisions,[16] to avoid any doubt as to its status, this type of common carrier was statutorily defined.[17] Time-volume rates and service contracts, offering the opportunity for lower freight costs, were permitted,[18] shippers' associations were recognized,[19] and carriers, either alone or with others, might not refuse to negotiate with such groups.[20] A new era in the U.S. regulation of ocean transportation had begun.

CHAPTER II

OCEAN COMMON CARRIERS

Treated below are those sections of the 1984 Act pertaining to common carriers.[1]

Section 2—Declaration of Policy [2]

As indicated in the Conference Report on the 1984 Act,[3] the House version of the 1984 Act did not contain a statement of policy; the Senate bill recited an extensive list of purposes. The conferees concluded that such a list was unnecessary because it duplicated language contained in the operative sections of the bill. Accordingly, the conferees agreed to a broad declaration establishing three principal goals of regulation: minimal intervention in a nondiscriminatory regulatory process; an efficient and economic transportation system that, insofar as possible, is consistent with international practices; and development of an efficient U.S. liner fleet meeting national needs.

Section 2(1) provides that one of the purposes of the Act is "to establish a nondiscriminatory regulatory process for the common carriage of goods by water in the foreign commerce of the United States with a minimum of government intervention and regulatory costs."[4] This language bears some analysis.

At the outset it should be noted that the term "common carriage" is not defined in section 3, Definitions.[5] The FMC has held that "common carriage" should be defined for the purposes of a tariff filing as a commercial activity establishing a clear intention to move cargo under the proffered tariff within a commercially reasonable period of time subsequent to filing.[6] Common carriage is undertaken by a "common carrier" defined in section 3(6) as a person holding himself out to the general public to provide transportation by water of cargo between the United States and a foreign country for compensation that (A) assumes responsibility for the transportation from a port or point of receipt to the port or point of destination, and (B) utilizes, for all or part of that transportation, a vessel operating on the high seas or the Great Lakes between a port in the United States and a port in a foreign country.[7] The statutory definition is in accord with the long held view of the FMC. When a carrier assumes complete responsibility for the safe transportation and

7

delivery of goods entrusted to it from the time of receipt from the ship-per until the goods arrive at the ultimate destination, it is a common car-rier by water.[8]

The term "foreign commerce" in section 2(1) is likewise undefined in the 1984 Act. To qualify under this section, a carrier must use a U.S. port at some point on its own route or a through route in which it participates. Thus, if an NVOCC moves cargo by motor carrier from an inland U.S. point to a Canadian port and then overseas, it is not a common carrier by water in the foreign commerce of the United States.[9] An extraordinary "single shot" undertaking does not, standing alone, change an enterprise engaged in an aspect of the shipping business into a "common carrier" required by law to file a tariff.[10] Where the transpor-tation of property to and from the United States is accomplished by a transshipment arrangement, the movement is in the foreign com-merce of the United States, a stop at a transshipment point being only incidental to the movement, and that does not change its character.[11]

Section 2(2) states that one of the purposes of the law is to provide "an efficient and economic transportation system in the ocean com-merce of the United States that is, insofar as possible, in harmony and responsive to, international shipping practices."[12] In determining what such a system would be, Congress has stated:

> The Committee believes that preservation of the Conference system is essential not only to the maintenance of a strong U.S. merchant fleet but for the reliable and efficient flow of trade in the U.S. foreign commerce. This does not mean the Conference will necessarily be the best choice of carrier or shipper, but merely that it should be permitted where commercial considerations warrant its use.[13]

The final purpose stated by Congress in section 2(3) was "to encour-age the development of an economically sound and efficient United States-flag liner fleet capable of meeting national security needs."[14] In that connection Congress indicated that

> [a]t the very least our regulatory law has to set all carriers serving our trade on a par and permit U.S. carriers to compete without handicaps preordained by their own nation's law. Otherwise no amount of promotional aid will persuade private individuals to invest in the U.S. maritime industry: We would be "marching up the hill and marching right down again."[15]

The Declaration of Policy is not a substantive provision to be enforced by the FMC and complied with by persons subject to the Act. Rather, it is an expression of congressional intent to serve as a guide to the agency and the shipping public.

Section 3—Definitions [16]

Section 3 sets forth twenty-seven definitions of terms used in the law. Most of these definitions are clear and need no treatment, but some do merit comment.

As noted above, in section 3(6) a "common carrier" is a person holding himself out to the general public to provide transportation of cargo between the U.S. and a foreign country for compensation by assuming responsibility for the transportation from a point of receipt to a point of destination, and utilizing a vessel operating on the high seas or the Great Lakes between a port in the U.S. and a foreign port.[17] While this section states what a "common carrier" does, it does not distinguish between a common carrier or other types of carriers not subject to regulation. Thus, it becomes necessary to determine what acts of the carrier constitute common carriage as distinguished from noncommon (or contract) carriage. The distinction is vital, since a common carrier is regulated by the FMC while a contract carrier is not.

The term "common carrier" is not an unyielding dictionary definition. Rather, it is a flexible regulatory concept. In brief, a common carrier is "one who holds himself to carry for hire the goods of those who choose to employ him."[18] Common carriage arises out of a contract or undertaking, express or implied, during some stage of the process of transportation.[19] In a leading case, *Containerships*,[20] the requirements for a common carrier status were outlined. The line in this case had originally filed tariffs with the FMC, but thereafter notified the agency that it was ceasing common carrier operations and cancelling its tariffs because its policy was to limit its services on its vessel to three or four shippers per voyage, and it had entered into contracts with consignees of vehicles providing for very substantial space. The line did not advertise its service or publish sailing schedules, conducting its solicitation in the form of negotiation of long-term contracts with desirable shippers.

The FMC held that a common carrier status is not lost by the carrier's failure to publish sailing schedules or advertise.[21] The carriage of cargo pursuant to special contracts also is not determinative of status. The movement of cargo is subject to some contract or agreement of transportation. One operating as a common carrier maintains that status even if it uses a shipping contract other than a bill of lading or if it attempts to disclaim liability by an express exemption in the bill of lading or contract of affreightment.[22]

While the FMC in *Containerships* did not establish any hard and fast rules as to what constitutes common carriage, it expressed general guidelines on the subject. It will consider a variety of factors, such as type of cargo carried, number of shippers, type of solicitation utilized, regularity of service and port coverage, responsibility of the carrier towards the cargo, issuance of bills of lading or other standardized contracts of carriage, and the method of establishing and charging rates.[23]

A common carrier holds itself out to the general public to provide transportation when it accepts goods from whomever offered to the extent of its ability to carry.[24] A carrier who serves a trade "by inducement only," that is, if a sufficient amount of cargo makes it worthwhile for a carrier to serve a port, is not a common carrier.[25] A common carrier status does not arise solely from the issuance of a document labeled a bill of lading.[26] One engaged in a lighterage and brokerage business is not a common carrier by water.[27] The incorporators of a corporation do not personally become common carriers merely because they have formed a new company.[28]

Section 3(6) excepts from the definition of common carrier an ocean tramp or chemical parcel-tanker and a ferryboat on a regular route. How does a tramp differ from a common carrier? A tramp transports on any one voyage cargo supplied by a single shipper only under a single charter party or contract of affreightment. A tramp is a "free-lance" operator and earns its name from its gypsylike existence. In addition to having no regular time of sailing, it has no fixed route and is ever seeking those ports where profitable cargo is most likely to be found.[29] The basic distinction between a tramp and a liner vessel is that the liner has fixed routes and regularity of service; the tramp does not.[30]

May a carrier serve as both a common and contract carrier on the same vessel and voyage? Early on, the FMC held in the negative.[31] Later, the FMC reconsidered, stating that the "better approach" is that a mixture of common and contract carriage on one vessel is permissible, but may not be used to evade regulation and must not result in a carrier's avoidance of its common carrier obligations to respect the fair, nonpreferential, and nondiscriminatory treatment of shippers.[32] A carrier with a dual operation may discriminate against shippers in the legitimate furtherance of its business, so long as the discrimination is not unjust or undue, a factual question.[33]

Conferences

In section 3(7) of the 1984 Act a "conference" means an association of ocean common carriers permitted, pursuant to an approved or effective agreement, to engage in concerted activity and to utilize a common tariff;

but the term does not include a joint service, consortium, pooling, sailing, or transshipment arrangement.[34] A shipping conference is a voluntary association of ocean common carriers operating on a particular trade route between two or more countries. The purpose of a shipping conference is the self-regulation of price competition, primarily through the establishment of uniform freight rates and terms and conditions of service among the member shipping lines. By operating within an internally regulated conference, carriers seek mutual restraint from the pursuit of sharp business practices and rate tactics that result in unstable economic consequences. By setting a common tariff, rate levels are more stable and predictable by minimizing price competition.[35] Under section 4(a) of the Act, ocean common carriers are permitted to enter into agreements covering various activities.[36] In return, before becoming effective, such agreements must be filed with the FMC under section 5(a) and must contain various provisions as set forth in section 5(b).[37]

Non-Vessel-Operating Common Carriers (NVOCCs)
This term is defined in section 3(17) of the Act.[38] An NVOCC is a common carrier that does not operate the vessels by which the ocean transportation is provided, and is a shipper in its relationship with the ocean common carrier. As noted above in Part I, *supra*, the NVOCC concept was decisionally recognized by the FMC under the 1916 Act. The 1984 Act conferred upon the NVOCC statutory recognition as a type of carrier that acts as an intermediary between the vessel operator and shipper of less-than-container loads. The NVOCC also has the status of a shipper and is statutorily protected as such.[39]

Shippers
A shipper is defined in section 3(23) as an owner or person for whose account the ocean transportation of cargo is provided or the person to whom delivery is to be made.[40] According to the U.S. Department of Commerce, in 1987 approximately 100,000 manufacturing firms were involved in exporting. Only 2 to 3 percent of the firms were large shippers with annual exports of $10,000 or more.

In its section 18 Report to the Congress, the Advisory Commission on Conferences in Ocean Shipping (ACCOS) adopted definitions of small, medium, and large shippers. A small shipper is defined as a firm which annually ships 100 TEUs (twenty-foot equivalent units) or less; a medium shipper is one who ships between 101 TEUs and 2,000 TEUs yearly; and a large shipper is one whose total shipments are over 2,000 TEUs annually.[41]

Shippers' Associations

Section 3(24) states that a "shippers' association" means a group of shippers that consolidates or distributes freight on a nonprofit basis for the members of the group in order to secure carload, truckload, or other volume rates or service contracts.[42] Such associations were given recognition for the first time in the 1984 Act.

According to ACCOS, since the enactment of the Act, two types of shippers' associations have been operating in the U.S. export liner trade. The first type negotiates only rates and service contracts with conferences on behalf of the participating members. The members own the cargo and pay the ocean transportation costs directly to the carrier.

The second type is a full-service shippers' association, a cooperative which obtains transportation under a service contract or tariff rates. This type acts as the shipper in its relation with the common carrier and is named as such in the transportation documents. The association is responsible to the carrier for the freight charges to the carrier and is reimbursed by the members. A full-service association may also own its own terminal and warehouse facility to consolidate and distribute the members' freight. In this regard, it has some of the characteristics of an NVOCC.[43]

Section 4—Agreements Within Scope of Chapter [44]

Section 4(a) itemizes the kinds of agreements covered in the 1984 Act. When read in conjunction with sections 5, 6, and 7,[45] the effect is to remove such agreements from the reach of the antitrust laws as defined in the Act.

Under section 4(a) the law applies only to agreements by vessel operators who:

1. fix, discuss, or regulate transportation rates;
2. pool or apportion traffic;
3. allot ports or restrict the number and character of sailings;
4. limit the volume or character of cargo;
5. engage in exclusive, preferential, or cooperative working arrangements among themselves or with one or more marine terminal operators or non-vessel-operating common carriers;
6. control, regulate, or prevent competition in international ocean transportation; and
7. regulate or prohibit the use of service contracts.[46]

From its many years of experience in processing agreements filed under the former section 15 of the 1916 Act, the FMC has dealt with a variety of issues involving the need to file. No filing is required unless two or more common carriers by water reach an agreement or a meeting of minds.[47] Even if oral, a memorandum of any agreement reached is required to be filed. However, a cooperative "spirit" does not quite achieve the status of an agreement or a cooperative working arrangement that would be capable of being filed.[48] A mere agreement to agree or to negotiate an agreement does not make it capable of being filed.[49]

Routine or interstitial agreements between the member lines that would not require action by the FMC are those which are limited to the "pure regulation of intraconference competition."[50] Conventional rate changes are such routine agreements.[51] An agreement relating to transportation to be performed within or between foreign countries is not one which may be filed.[52]

As noted above, section 4(a)(1) applies to agreements regulating transportation rates and other conditions of service. A rate is a carrier's compensation for the performance of a transportation service.[53] Charges are the segregated items of expense which are to be demanded by the carrier for any service in connection with transportation.[54] The division of the total ocean charge into a basic tariff rate and a surcharge does not remove either part of the total from the general category of freight charges where both parts must necessarily be paid for the transportation of the items of cargo.[55] Wharfage, dockage, and wharf demurrage are "transportation rates" in section 4(a).[56] The "regular rate" for the transportation of a commodity is the rate appearing in the carrier's tariff and none other. If a carrier discounts the rate or absorbs any charges which would normally be payable by the shipper, such discount or absorption must appear in the carrier's filed tariff.[57]

Section 4(a)(2) applies to agreements to pool or apportion traffic, revenues, earnings, or losses. A "pooling agreement" means an agreement between ocean common carriers which provides for the division of cargo carryings, earnings, or revenue and/or losses between the members in accordance with an established formula or scheme.[58] Such an agreement has long been held not to be per se unlawfully discriminatory.[59] But an agreement to pool traffic that allocates the percentage or any portion thereof on the basis of flag or national interest has been held to be discriminatory.[60] Nor may a pooling agreement embody discriminatory or unfair quotas dictated by government fiat.[61] The approval by the FMC of a mandatory arbitration clause in a pooling agreement is not a waiver by the FMC of any right to review disputes arising from the agreement and does not deprive the agency of jurisdiction to hear a complaint that the agreement had been modified through an arbitration decision.[62] A "sailing agreement" means an agreement between ocean common carriers which provides for the rationalization of service by establishing a schedule of ports which each carrier will serve and/or the frequency of each carrier's calls at those ports.[63]

Section 4(a)(5) covers agreements among liner vessels to engage in "cooperative working arrangements" among themselves or with one or more marine terminal operators or non-vessel-operating common carriers. The section raises questions as to scope. The term "cooperative working arrangement" was not defined in either the 1916 or 1984 Acts, but has been extensively dealt with by the Commission through the years. The Commission has said that it could not lay down any "hard and fast rules" concerning the type of agreements within this category. The facts and circumstances under which the agreement came into being and its aims and purposes must be considered.[64] The Supreme Court has held that under the principle of "ejusdem generis" (of the same kind) the term "cooperative working arrangements" was intended by Congress as a catch-all provision to include various types of agreements similar to those enumerated in this section.[65]

Section 4(a)(6) allows carrier agreements that control, regulate, or prevent competition in international ocean transportation. Substantially similar authority was included in section 15 of the 1916 Act.[66] This provision having long been applied to the regulation of ocean shipping, Congress in passing the 1984 Act thought it unnecessary to expand upon its language. The legislative history of the 1984 Act thus dealt briefly with the language used. The new law was intended to allow U.S. carriers and shippers to conduct ocean commerce in a stable, efficient, and competitive manner.[67] The intent of the section is to state what may be done by carriers. It does not control what effect the actions of the agreeing carriers may have on carriers not party to the agreement. It is recognized that one of the effects of limiting or preventing competition between conference members will be the improvement of the conference's competitive position in relationship to nonconference carriers. Nevertheless, the legislation does not prohibit agreements that have this effect. Nor is it intended to preclude a conference or conference members from meeting the competition of an independent carrier by any lawful means.[68]

Section 4(a)(7) authorizes carriers to regulate or prohibit their use of service contracts.[69] The 1916 Act did not contain a similar authorization to conference lines. It appears that few, if any, conferences totally prohibit the use of service contracts, but a survey conducted by ACCOS showed that "no conference in the U.S. foreign trades permits its member lines to engage independently in service contract activity."[70]

While the conferences have maintained that section 4(a)(7) is necessary to preserve the integrity of their rate structure, shippers have complained that under the power to "regulate" service contracts difficulties have arisen. A member line of a conference which cannot meet a shipper's service requirements is permitted to veto a proposed contract for such shipper. This is said to be not only harmful to the shipper but also denies to other conference members the opportunity to carry that cargo. The complaint is that it is unreasonable for a carrier to block a service contract when it cannot itself address a shipper's needs.[71]

It appears questionable whether a conference should use its power to "regulate" service contracts to permit a disinterested line to veto a particular service contract request. In its lengthy consideration of the 1984 Act, Congress attempted to strike a bargain between the interests of carriers and shippers. As pointed out in Part I above, the lengthy approval process for filed agreements has been eliminated, the "detriment to commerce" and "contrary to public interest" standards of proof are deleted and the antitrust exemption for carriers is considerably broadened. As the quid pro quo to shippers, time-volume rates, shippers' associations, and a limited use of a loyalty contract were authorized. Probably most important of all to shippers was the authority given to the lines to offer service contracts to shippers. The concern of Congress was that "service contracts not be employed so as to discriminate against all who rely upon the common carriage tradition of the lines system."[72]

Service contracts are being extensively used in our inbound and outbound foreign trades. Approximately one-third to two-thirds of the total tonnage of conferences, mostly larger shippers, presently move under such contracts.[73] When a conference allows a disinterested line to use its veto power to deny a service contract to a shipper lacking bargaining strength, the conference may be engaging in an unduly prejudicial or an unreasonable practice, an area of concern to the Congress.[74]

Section 4(b) provides that the Act applies to agreements involving ocean transportation in the U.S. foreign commerce "among marine terminal operators and among one or more terminal operators and one or more ocean common carriers" to (1) fix rates and conditions of service and (2) engage in exclusive, preferential, or cooperative working arrangements.[75] A similar provision was contained in the 1916 Act.[76] The section permits two types of agreement: one between terminals themselves and another between terminals and ocean common carriers. In the predecessor bill, H.R. 1878, the House Merchant Marine Committee stated:

> Subsection (b) extends the coverage of the bill to certain agreements among marine terminal operators and between marine terminal operators and ocean common carriers.[77]

Neither sections 4(a) or (b) authorize forwarders or NVOCCs to regulate competition among themselves or make agreements with carriers.[78]

Section 4(c)—Acquisitions

This section provides that the 1984 Act "does not apply to any acquisition by any person, directly or indirectly of any voting security or any other person's assets."[79] "Voting security" ordinarily means the purchase of all of the issued and outstanding shares of a corporation or at least a majority thereof (a "stock deal") or all of the assets (an "assets deal") of the seller. This exclusion is limited. In a 1983 legislative predecessor to the 1984 Act, S.504, the Senate Commerce Committee noted that this section "is intended to make clear that this Act does not remove mergers and acquisitions in the maritime area from the normal antitrust oversight which might otherwise be conducted by the various agencies of the executive branch."[80]

The question as to whether the FMC had jurisdiction to approve merger agreements between carriers, thus providing antitrust immunity, was exhaustively litigated under the provisions of section 15 of the 1916 Act.[81] The issue was whether under the term "agreement" in section 15, a merger was "controlling, regulating, preventing, or destroying competition." In the *Seatrain* case,[82] the Supreme Court held that the Commission had jurisdiction over mergers, but only if the agreement, or portions of the agreement, created ongoing relationships and responsibilities which necessitated continuous supervision. In the *American Mail Line* case it was held that there were no ongoing responsibilities merely because the two lines to be merged were subsidiaries of the same corporate parent.[83] The language in section 4(c) would seem to end the uncertainty in this area. If a purchaser of the stock or assets gains control of a line to be merged, the FMC no longer has jurisdiction. Part 572.202(a) of the FMC rules repeats the statutory language.

Section 5—Agreements [84]

Section 5(a) provides that a true copy of every agreement entered into with respect to an activity described in section 4(a) or (b) of the Act shall be filed with the Commission. The word agreement is defined in section 3(1) as "an understanding, arrangement, or association (written or oral) and any modification or cancellation thereof, but the term does not include a maritime labor agreement.[85] In its rules the FMC substantially repeats the Act's definition.[86] The agreement must involve an activity described in section 4(a) or (b) of the Act. Since such agreements relate solely to ocean common carriers and marine terminal operators, as noted above, agreements among NVOCCs or ocean freight forwarders, previously authorized under the 1916 Act,[87] are excluded, the Commission no longer having jurisdiction over such agreements.

Exercising the exemption authority in section 16 of the Act, [88] the FMC has exempted from filing various types of agreements: nonsubstantive agreements, such as one dealing with the procurement of office facilities or reflecting changes in the name of a geographic locality stated in the agreement;[89] husbanding agreements; agency agreements; equipment interchange agreements; nonexclusive transshipments and certain marine terminal agreements; agreements between wholly owned subsidiaries; and miscellaneous modifications to agreements.[90] Section 5(a) excludes from filing agreements related to transportation to be performed within or between foreign countries and agreements among carriers to establish, operate, or maintain a marine terminal in the United States. If an agreement is oral, a complete memorandum specifying in detail the substance of the agreement shall be filed.

This section also authorizes the agency to prescribe the form and manner in which an agreement shall be filed and the additional information and documents necessary to evaluate the agreement. Congress has said that this authority is limited so that petitioners before the Commission "will be asked only for information relevant to the Commission evaluation of an agreement rather than for information based upon broad standards unrelated to that agreement."[91]

Since ocean common carrier agreements are confined to those providing transportation by water between the United States and a foreign country,[92] questions have arisen as to whether an agreement need be filed when one or more of the parties thereto do not operate in the U.S. trade. One case involved a joint service and chartering agreement between four signatories. Two lines were noncarriers in the U.S. trade, and two lines were such carriers. Since the agreement contained at least two signatory carriers in the U.S. trade, the FMC held that jurisdiction existed.[93] A more complicated question arose in a case where the agreement was between two lines, one being a common carrier in the U.S. foreign trade, the other not. However, the latter carrier was part of a "group" consisting of a number of companies providing shipping services, among which two were common carriers by water in the U.S. foreign trade. The issue was whether the U.S. common carrier status of the affiliates in the U.S. trade may be "imputed" to the non-U.S. carrier signatory. An administrative law judge held (and the FMC agreed) that the preponderance of credible evidence showed that the agreement was intended to apply to members of the group. Hence, the affiliates being common carriers under the Act made the agreement subject to FMC jurisdiction.[94]

As earlier mentioned, an agreement need not be filed unless there is an actual meeting of minds between two or more carriers subject to the Act.[95] A cooperative "spirit," standing alone, fails to achieve the status of an agreement ready to be filed.[96] Routine or interstitial activities, such as conventional rate making, cannot be filed.[97] However, an agreement authorizing the fixing or regulating of compensation to be paid by the carriers to ocean freight forwarders may be filed.[98] A "mixed agreement" is one that includes transportation between foreign ports, contains both regulated and unregulated activities, and inasmuch as the FMC does not have subject matter jurisdiction over the unregulated activity, such an agreement cannot be filed in its entirety.[99] The Commission will not allow the statutory purposes of the Act to be frustrated through the use of separate corporate entities. Thus, the agency will not disregard the fact that petitioners are subsidiaries of common carriers in deciding their status under the law.[100]

An agreement filed must be the complete agreement among the parties and shall specify in detail the substance of the understanding of the parties.[101] With respect to conference agreements, section 5(b)(1) requires that the document must "state its purpose." Thus, the agreement should be in accord with the congressional intent of granting to the Commission the authority to deal with agreements of a continuing nature.[102] The central purpose of the Act is to provide for industry self-regulation through agreements among carriers under the aegis of the FMC, that is, to review agreements with an eye to preventing certain practices deemed unjustly or unfairly discriminatory.[103]

Section 5(b)(2) requires a conference agreement to provide reasonable and equal terms and conditions for admission and readmission to conference membership for any common carrier willing to serve the particular trade or route.[104] The legislative purpose of this language is to mandate the "open conference system."[105] One of the areas upon which ACCOS was required to make a recommendation to the Congress was whether "the Nation would be best served by prohibiting conferences, or by closed or open conferences."[106] As noted in the treatment below of section 18, ACCOS made no such recommendation. Each conference agreement is required to provide for admission to conference membership any carrier operating vessels of the United States willing to serve the particular trade or route. This insures that any membership limitations cannot be exercised in a manner that would discriminate against U.S. carriers.[107]

Early in the administration of our shipping laws, the FMC's predecessors rejected unfair restrictions upon admission to conference membership. Thus, it was held to be unjustly discriminatory and unduly prejudicial to deny membership on the grounds that the additional tonnage would tend to demoralize the trades, rejecting the argument that the member lines had more than adequate tonnage available and that granting the application would be contrary to the best interest of the trade.[108] Also rejected was the argument that the test of admission should be similar to the authority of the Interstate Commerce Commission to issue a certificate of public convenience and necessity. The delegation of power by Congress was so clear that there was no possible ambiguity or doubt as to its intent.[109]

Nor would the agency sanction a refusal of admission on the grounds that a conference could limit membership to carriers actually engaged in operating vessels in the trade.[110] However, a conference is not entirely without discretion in determining admission. It may adopt "reasonable and equal terms and conditions for admission" under section 5(b)(2). The mere fact of an application does not assure a carrier's admission to the conference: "The determination that a particular condition of membership is reasonable or unreasonable is necessarily a factual one."[111]

Section 5(b)(3) requires that a conference agreement permit any member to withdraw from conference membership upon reasonable notice without penalty. This is true even if the member line withdrawing intends to operate an independent service in the trade being served by the conference.[112] The withdrawal by a line of its membership does not deny to the conference the right to proceed against the former member for breaches of the agreement or malpractices engaged in during the period of membership.[113]

Section 5(b)(4) obligates a conference at the request of any member to establish "an independent neutral body to police fully the obligations of the conference and its members."[114] This language does not impose a flat requirement for such a body in all cases, but only if a member line of a conference requests it. Earlier versions of the 1984 Act did not confer such an option on a member line. The requirement in predecessor bills was that "independent neutral policing bodies must be engaged by each conference. . . ."[115] In the legislative history of this section it was stated that neutral body self-policing has the advantage of minimizing the need for FMC intrusion into the commercial affairs of ocean carriers and conferences and avoids the awkward government-to-government confrontations that arise when the FMC seeks access to commercial information abroad that is protected by a foreign blocking statute.[116] The neutral body can obtain access to this necessary "compliance" information by contract with the conference and its members on a purely commercial basis.[117]

the agreement. The agency may then initiate on its own motion an investigation to determine whether there has been a violation of the Act.[129] It may not issue a preliminary cease and desist order, since it has no authority to do so as part of the administrative process.[130] The FMC may issue such an order only after a hearing and upon a finding of a violation of the Act.[131] Nor does the Commission have the authority itself to issue an interlocutory or temporary injunction.[132] But the agency is authorized under section 6(g) and (h) to seek appropriate injunctive relief, even if the agreement has become effective, if it determines that it is likely to reduce competition in the trade, resulting in an unreasonable reduction in service or an unreasonable increase in cost. An application would be made to the U.S. District Court for the District of Columbia to enjoin the operation of the agreement. Should the FMC fail to act in a timely fashion, the Department of Justice could take action since "an enforcement vacuum has occurred."[133]

As noted above, the FMC and the Department of Justice may not act simultaneously. The conferees consider this to be "double jeopardy." However, if the FMC action has not yet gone to judgment, query whether Justice may proceed under the antitrust laws. As noted above, Congress has indicated that the FMC "retains principal and initial authority to enforce all prohibitions in the Act. And so long as the FMC is "actively pursuing a matter," antitrust agencies should "as a matter of discretion, defer to the FMC."[134]

Section 5(b)(6) requires each conference agreement to provide for a consultation process designed to promote (A) partial resolution of disputes, and (B) cooperation with shippers in preventing and eliminating malpractices.[135] In the legislative consideration of a predecessor bill, S.1593, the Senate Commerce Committee noted that:

> Conferences must . . . establish processes for consulting and communicating with shippers and responding to their requests and complaints; this requirement assures that carriers cannot hide behind a collective organization and refuse to be responsive to those who rely on their services.[136]

In a rulemaking proceeding designed to ease the regulatory burden of record keeping and filing of required reports, the Commission deleted a rule requiring an annual statistical report furnishing detailed information as to requests by shippers for consultations. Instead, its new rule states that the minutes of conference meetings should set forth any consultations with shippers and shippers' associations and indicate the action taken.[137]

Section 5(b)(7) requires a conference agreement to contain a provision which establishes procedures for promptly and fairly considering shippers' requests and complaints.[138] As in the case of the consultation process in section 5(b)(6), conferences may inform the FMC of shippers' requests and complaints and the action taken thereon in their filed minutes. The requests and complaints must, of course, relate to ocean common carriers as defined in the 1984 Act. A complaint involving a common carrier by water not within the definition in the Act may not be considered by the FMC, since it lacks jurisdiction to do so.[139]

Section 5(b)(8) provides that any member of a conference may take independent action on any rate or service item required to be filed in a tariff under section 8(a) of this Act upon not more than ten calendar days after the notice to the conference. The conference will include the new rate or service item in its tariff for use by that member, effective no later than ten calendar days after receipt of the notice. Any other member may use the rate or service item if it notifies the conference that it has elected to adopt such item on or after its effective date in lieu of the existing conference tariff provision for that rate or service item.[140]

A conference must permit independent action on time-volume rates, since such rates must be filed in a conference tariff under section 8(a) of the Act. However, a conference may limit the right of independent action on service contracts under section 4(a)(7), since they need not be filed under section 8(a). A conference agreement may not prohibit the exercise of independent action on a tariff rate or service item during the pendency of service contract negotiations affecting these items.[141] A conference may not withdraw any adopting independent action by a member line whenever the originating independent action is withdrawn, the adopting independent action standing on its own unless the adopting member line voluntarily advises otherwise.[142]

Under section 8(a)(1)(C) a common carrier is required to state the level of ocean freight forwarder compensation, if any, by a carrier or conference.[143] Since such compensation must be included in the tariff, may a conference prohibit independent action in this area? The FMC concluded that the term "rate or service item" was a single concept, which embraces two integrally related activities, namely the rate established or the transportation services provided by a common carrier to a shipper. Hence, the service performed by a forwarder for a carrier for which compensation is paid is not "a rate or service item" within the Act. That phrase applies only to carrier services to shippers and not to forwarder services for carriers. A member line may not, therefore, take independent action on forwarder compensation.[144] This holding was

3. upon a finding in accordance with the above paragraph, the FMC shall make assessment adjustments based upon prospective credits or debits to future assessments;
4. where a complainant has ceased activities subject to an assessment, the FMC may award reparations.

This subsection treats differently those injured by unjustly discriminatory provisions of an assessment agreement while still in business as compared to those who are not. In the case of the former, the FMC "shall" remedy the injury by prospective credits, etc. However, in the case of the complainant that has ceased activity the FMC "may," but need not, award reparations. Under section 11(g) of the Act,[153] reparations shall include actual injury, loss of interest at commercial rates, plus reasonable attorney's fees.

Subsection 5(d) continues the present law on the subject.[154] The remedies and regulatory standards applicable to assessment agreements are intended to be exclusive.[155] Subsequent to 1980 it was no longer necessary to obtain affirmative approval of an assessment agreement from the FMC. Such an agreement became effective by operation of law and could be challenged only upon a complaint of a private party and not on the Commission's own motion.[156]

Section 5(d) specifically identifies the entities protected, namely "carriers, shippers or ports." One who neither directly nor indirectly paid an assessment and alleges only a secondary competitive injury has no standing to file a complaint. Thus, an off-dock consolidation or freight station not utilizing ILWU (International Longshoremen's & Warehousemen's Union) labor for container handling has no basis to claim relief.[157]

Subsection 5(e) relates to maritime labor agreements.[158] It provides that the 1984 Act does not apply to maritime labor agreements except for "any rates, charges, regulations or practices of a common carrier that are required to be sent forth in a tariff, whether or not those rates . . . arise out of, or are otherwise related to, a maritime labor agreement." This is the so-called "tariff matter" exception. Initially included in the Maritime Labor Agreements Act (Public Law 96-325), according to the FMC this law "demarcated clearly between labor and shipping concerns, and removed the confusion and uncertainty that had existed previously."[159] The purpose was "to preserve the essential principal that a common carrier cannot alter its statutory common carrier obligations at the bargaining table."[160] Accordingly, even though certain rules on containers were incorporated into a collective bargaining agreement between the employers and the union, the FMC retained jurisdiction to review the rules under the 1984 Act.[161]

Section 6—Action on Agreements [162]

As mentioned in Chapter I, this section was the response of Congress to the substantive and procedural difficulties experienced by conferences in meeting their burden of proof to establish that a proposed agreement was not "detrimental to the commerce of the United States" or "contrary to public interest," as required by section 15 of the 1916 Act. Under the *Svenska* doctrine, the lines were required to establish that the agreement was necessary by a serious transportation need, necessary to secure important public benefits, or in furtherance of a valid regulatory purpose of the Shipping Act. In its discussion of a predecessor bill, S.504, the Senate Commerce Committee stated:

> It is the intent of Committee to overrule legislatively *Federal Maritime Commission v. Svenska Amerika Linen*, 390 U.S. 238 (1968). Neither the burden of proof nor the burden of persuasion shall be shifted solely on the grounds that the agreement would, absent approval, violate the antitrust laws or have significant anticompetitive effects. The burden of proof shall remain throughout the proceedings on the opponents of an agreement.[163]

In their report the conferees of the 1984 Act stated:

> The model for FMC review of agreements is the portion of the Hart-Scott-Rodino Act governing premerger clearance of proposed acquisitions and mergers (15 U.S.C. §18a). Agreements are to be reviewed promptly—unless special problems are encountered, the FMC will be allowed only a forty-five day period—and they will take effect automatically unless the Commission takes affirmative action under subsection (b) or (h).[164]

Under section 6(a), within seven days after an agreement is filed, the Commission shall transmit a notice of its filing to the Federal Register for publication. The Commission is required under section 6(b) to reject any agreement filed under section 5(a) of the Act that, after preliminary review, does not meet the requirements of section 5(a). "This power of rejection, however, does not extend to agreements that violate the competition standard. With respect to such violations, the Commission's sole remedy is to seek a temporary or permanent injunctive relief in the United States District Court for the District of Columbia."[165]

Under section 6(c), unless rejected by the Commission under section 6(b), agreements other than assessment agreements shall become effective (1) on the forty-fifth day after filing, or on the thirtieth day after

quality of service. There are two distinct aspects to this requirement. The first is whether the harm to shippers is "unreasonable" in a commercial context. Unreasonableness refers to the cost of transportation to the shipper or the availability or quality of service. The Commission may not determine that rate increases or service reductions are "per se" impermissible results of agreements. Rate increases or decreases in the frequency or variety of service may be necessary to achieve other benefits of the Act.[173]

The second aspect of the unreasonableness requirement is that the negative impact upon shippers may be offset by the benefits of an agreement. For example, the competitive harm ensuing from conferences, already diminished by the statutory limitations on their activity, can and often will be offset by the significant benefits of such activity.[174] Another possible benefit that the Commission should consider is the impact of agreements, such as a revenue or cargo-sharing pools, and their effect on U.S. foreign policy and international comity. Participation in such agreements may be necessary for U.S. flag parties to compete for the reserved cargo. After giving due consideration to the maritime and trade policy views of the United States, the Commission may conclude that the agreement is necessary in order to maintain a viable U.S. flag service, a decision that the agency has reached in the past under such circumstances.[175]

Should the Commission conclude that a filed agreement violates the standards in section 6(g), section 6(h) authorizes a suit by the FMC in the U.S. District Court for the District of Columbia to enjoin operation of the agreement. The court may issue a temporary restraining order or preliminary injunction and upon a showing that the agreement is likely to violate section 6(g), the court may enter a permanent injunction. The Commission has the burden of proof before the court and no third party may intervene with respect to this litigation.

The conferees believed that even when an agreement raised potential issues under the general standard, the procedural framework for application of that standard would give carriers maximum flexibility. They will be able to obtain a prompt ruling from the Commission and if the Commission objects, the filing party may withdraw it, modify it, or force the Commission to make its showing in court. And, even after such a court proceeding is initiated, the filing party retains the option of withdrawing or settling the matter with the Commission.[176] Under section 6(i), if a person filing the agreement fails substantially to comply with the request for the submission of additional information or documentary material, the D.C. District Court may, at the request of the Commission:

1. order compliance;
2. extend the period for the furnishing of the information; or
3. grant such other equitable relief as the court in its discretion determines necessary or appropriate.

Section 6(j) provides that except for an agreement filed under section 5 of the Act, information and documentary material filed with the FMC under section 5 or 6 is exempt from disclosure and may not be made public except as may be relevant to an administrative or judicial action or proceeding. This section does not, however, prevent disclosure to either body of Congress or to a duly authorized committee or subcommittee thereof.

Section 6(k) provides that upon notice to the Attorney General, the Commission may represent itself in the District Court proceedings under section 6(h), Injunctive Relief; 6(i), Compliance With Informational Needs; and section 11 (h), authorizing the agency to bring suit to enjoin conduct in violation of the Act. The conferees concluded that, in sum, "the general rules of operation and approval of agreements have been developed by the Congress with full awareness of the realities of international ocean carriage; a general standard has been retained to provide the necessary flexibility to deal with the unusual or severe cases not addressed by other prohibitions in the Act."[177]

While the 1984 Act is a substantial improvement over its predecessor, the 1916 Act, there would appear to be serious shortcomings in the review procedure before the FMC and the role of the District Court thereafter. A basic and worthwhile purpose of reducing the time and cost of the filing procedure has been accomplished. However, there is still the potential for substantial delay if the party filing the agreement is unable to reach an understanding with the FMC staff on some of its provisions. District courts are known to have congested calendars and overworked judges, very few of whom are knowledgeable in maritime matters. Thus, absent the granting of a priority by the court, which is not assured, it appears difficult to predict how long the injunction proceeding will last. Faced with substantial delay, it seems clear that on occasions the proponents of an agreement may be compelled to agree with the FMC's suggested modifications even when considered lacking in merit or legal basis. In its consideration of this matter, ACCOS has noted that the FMC has had section 6(g) concerns regarding a number of agreements filed by the carriers since the Act, and has negotiated to modify agreements to avoid the possibility that such agreements would produce substantially anticompetitive situations. Thus, ACCOS noted that the FMC has not found it necessary to seek court action,[178] but this may be

tise of the FMC in its traditional administrative role, and (2) allowing parties their due process right to protect their interests before the agency and the courts.

Section 7—Exemption from Antitrust Laws[187]

Allowing conferences concertedly to fix rates and practices was first authorized in section 15 of the 1916 Act.[188] However, as noted in Chapter I above, in the administration of that section conferences faced uncertainties as to the scope of the antitrust immunity conferred and lengthy and costly delays in obtaining FMC approval of filed agreements commonly occurred. In its consideration of S.504, the Senate Commerce Committee noted that although the 1916 Act was originally designed to validate the conference system and insulate it from our antitrust laws, the combined impact of subsequent case law on section 15's antitrust protection for the conference system had rendered the antitrust exemption largely illusory. Conferences could act only at their peril as the FMC and the courts placed severe limitations upon their ability to take joint action.[189]

In an attempt to eradicate the administrative and interpretive problems arising under section 15, section 7(a)(2) of the 1984 Act provides that the antitrust laws do not apply to any activity or agreement within the scope of the Act, whether permitted under or prohibited by the Act, undertaken or entered into with a "reasonable basis to conclude" that (A) it is pursuant to an agreement on file with the Commission and in effect when the activity took place, or (B) it is exempt under section 16 of the Act from any filing requirement. This section, however, confers no immunity on secret or covert conduct or on agreements that are not filed.[190]

The conferees chose the "reasonable basis to conclude" formulation of section 7(a)(2) from the Senate bill; the House bill would have keyed immunity to "a reasonable belief." It was felt that the test—a "reasonable basis to conclude"—was objective. The actual belief of the parties at the time of the conduct would, generally, not be controlling. At the same time, if parties to concerted conduct are shown to have believed that their conduct was outside the scope of an effective agreement and not exempted from the filing requirements, this would "tend to demonstrate" that no reasonable basis to conclude is present.[191]

The "reasonable basis to conclude" test has not as yet been litigated. A somewhat similar exemption from the antitrust laws existed by case law under the 1916 Act, the Supreme Court having held that courts were precluded from awarding treble damages in actions against shipping companies under the antitrust laws when the conduct was "arguably lawful" under that Act.[192] The legislative history does not offer any guide as to whether the reasonable basis would be one of fact or law, or perhaps a combination of both. Conceivably, if a conference is advised by an attorney competent in the field that a proposed action is authorized by the agreement, this could be construed as a reasonable basis for the action taken.

In its comments on S.504 the Senate Commerce Committee indicated that once the requirements of sections 5 and 6 had been met, activities pursuant to such agreements were subject solely to the 1984 Act. Only the standards, remedies, and penalties of this legislation would apply. Carriers operating in the U.S. foreign commerce would no longer face the "chilling effect, the uncertainties, and the inefficiencies forced by antitrust exposures."[193]

Section 7(a)(3) states that the antitrust laws do not apply to any agreement or activity that relates to transportation services within or between foreign countries, whether or not via the United States, unless that agreement or activity has a direct, substantial, and reasonably foreseeable effect on the commerce of the United States. The policy objective of this provision is to harmonize U.S. shipping regulation more closely with that of our trading partners.[194] The new provision parallels language of Title IV of the Export Trading Company Act of 1984 and is intended to limit the extraterritorial reach of the U.S. antitrust laws.

Section 7(a)(4) provides that the antitrust laws do not apply to any agreement or activity concerning the foreign inland segment of through transportation that is part of the transportation provided in the U.S. import or export trade. It appears that the purpose of this provision is to make it clear that when carriers are offering a point-to-point intermodal service from the United States, the portion thereof representing the movement from a foreign port of discharge to an inland destination point, or from an overseas inland origin point to the foreign port of dispatch to the United States is not subject to antitrust prosecution.

Section 7(a)(5) confers antitrust law immunity for any agreement or activity to provide or furnish wharfage, dock, warehouse, or other terminal facilities outside the United States. However, under section 7(b)(3), carriers do not have antitrust immunity for any agreement among them to establish, operate, or maintain a marine terminal in the United States.

Under section 7(a)(6) concerted action by the lines have antitrust immunity, subject to section 20(e) of the Act, for any agreement, modification, or cancellation approved by the Commission before the effective date of the 1984 Act under section 15 of the 1916 Act or permitted under section 14(b) of that Act and any properly published tariff, rate, fare or charge, classification, rule, or regulation explanatory thereof

tween points of origin and destination, either or both of which lie beyond port terminal areas, for which a through rate is assessed and which is offered or performed by one or more carriers, at least one of which is a common carrier between a U.S. point or port and a foreign point or port." A "through rate" means the single amount charged by a common carrier in connection with through transportation.[211]

While section 8(a)(1) states that cargo excepted (or exempted) need not be filed in a carrier's tariff, the FMC has stated that a carrier or conference may voluntarily file tariff provisions covering exempt transportation. If there is such a filing, then all statutory provisions, including the requirement to adhere to the filed tariff provisions, apply.[212] In 1985 the Commission reviewed its provision accepting tariffs on exempted commodities filed on a voluntary basis and concluded that the authority given to carriers and conferences to do so would continue to be recognized.[213] In 1992 the Commission again revisited this issue, soliciting comments as to whether it should adopt rules to no longer accept the voluntary filing of tariffs and service contracts covering excepted commodities.[214] In that same year the agency concluded that it "saw no reason to change its regulations to no longer accept the voluntary filings of tariffs and service contracts covering excepted commodities."[215]

Section 8(a)(1)(E) requires carriers to include sample copies of any loyalty contract, bill of lading, contract of affreightment, or other document evidencing the transportation agreement. A bill of lading is both a receipt and contract and under particular circumstances it may also constitute documentary evidence as to which party has title to the goods.[216] The bill of lading, being a contract of adhesion, must be strictly construed against the carrier.[217] An overriding stamp that is printed on a bill of lading supersedes the printed form if there is a conflict between the two.[218]

The terms and conditions set forth in a carrier's tariff may not be waived or changed by private agreement with shippers.[219] The only lawful rate that a carrier may charge a shipper is that appearing in a carrier's filed tariff.[220] A line may cancel its foreign commerce tariff immediately if the effect of the cancellation is to eliminate a service and not to raise the cost of that service.[221] When a carrier publishes and files a tariff, it has an obligation to serve the ports and places included therein, and if the carrier has the space available at the time it refuses to book cargo for the reason that more profitable bookings are available elsewhere, such a practice is not permitted under our shipping laws.[222]

Every transportation service or a service in connection therewith must be clearly set forth in a tariff before a line may lawfully render such service, and this applies with equal force to services for which a charge is made as well as to services where the line makes no charge.[223] For example, if a carrier offers a lighter loading and unloading service, the filed tariff must inform the shipping public of such services and the exact charges for them.[224] A carrier must include in its tariff all of its applicable rates, such as rates for tollage, wharfage and handling, regardless of whether it is the carrier or terminal operator collecting the charge.[225] Upon acceptance of a tariff by the FMC for filing, the tariff is valid and binding between the shipper and carrier even if subsequently found to violate provisions of the Shipping Act or the agency's rules; the tariff is not void ab initio.[226] A carrier serving a trade "by inducement only" is not a common carrier by water for the purpose of publishing a tariff covering a particular trade.[227]

Suppose a carrier fails to file a tariff. Does this omission automatically result in an award of reparations? The FMC has answered in the negative. A shipper is not entitled to reparations in this situation unless the sum it paid amounts to an unjust or unreasonable exaction for the service rendered.[228] The fact that a carrier has filed its tariffs properly does not mean it has gained any measure of protection from a subsequent challenge under the substantive proscriptions of the Act merely because the agency has accepted the tariff for filing. A tariff filing is not an adjudicatory proceeding nor does it finally determine the individual rights and privileges of the parties. The fact that a carrier must adhere to its tariff does not mean that the contents are in any other respect lawful.[229] If the Act is violated even though the carrier acted without fault, arguments as to good intentions, lack of knowledge, etc., may, however, be considered in fixing the amount of penalties.[230] A filed tariff provides constructive notice only of those terms which are required by law to be filed.[231] Demanding and collecting a greater compensation than specified in a filed tariff is unlawful.[232]

A carrier may not by a statement of policy, no matter how widely the line may publish it, establish a rule that would be binding on shippers unless the rule was first filed with the Commission. Potential shippers are entitled to know what changes are to be expected.[233] The use of untariffed rates in violation of the Act deprives a shipper of the benefits of the tariff filing requirements and this causes injury for which reparations may be granted.[234]

Tariffs are to be interpreted according to a reasonable construction of their language. Neither the intent of the framers of the tariffs nor the practice of the carrier controls, for the shipper cannot be charged with the knowledge of such intent or with the carrier's cannons of construc-

Act.[258] In its notice the Commission stated that if the current regulatory scheme for military rates resulted in unfair or prejudicial treatment to the MSL, U.S. flag carriers, or any other party, the agency could remove format exemptions and require military rates to be published in exactly the same manner and format as commercial rates, i.e., in tariffs and service contracts. Upon consideration of the various comments filed, the FMC concluded that the proceedings should be discontinued without further rulemaking. It was satisfied that there was no factual basis in the record which would support a proposed exemption for military rates on the filing requirements of section 8 or the prohibited conduct in section 10 of the Act or to have a requirement that contracts for military cargo be filed as service contracts.[259]

In a 1991 docket the FMC dealt with its foreign tariff and service contract filing regulations pertaining to the publication of free time and detention charges applicable to carrier-provided equipment interchanged with inland carriers, consignees, and shippers.[260] The agency had previously exempted from the filing requirements of the Act equipment-interchange agreements (EIAs) between common carriers and inland carriers, where such agreements were not referred to in the carrier's tariffs and did not affect the tariff rates, charges, or practices of the carriers.[261] In amending its rules[262] the agency promulgated a final rule that: (1) requires publication of an EIA standard free days and charges; (2) allows carriers and conferences to publish separately the free days and charges in those instances where they differ from the standard; (3) provides guidelines for filing and governing EIA tariffs; (4) permits the referencing of EIA tariffs by individual rate tariffs; (5) clarifies that conferences can file EIA provisions in an existing rate and EIA tariff; and (6) clarifies the filing requirements for service contracts. The filing rule applies to vessel-operating common carriers and non-vessel-operating common carriers and does not distinguish between foreign and domestic ports.[263]

Section 8(b), (c), and (e), Time Volume Rates, Service Contracts, and Refunds will be treated under Chapter III, Shippers.

Tariffs required to be filed must actually be received by the agency in order to comply with the Act.[264] Tariffs stand as filed and not as approved.[265]

Section 8(f), Form, provides that the Commission may by regulation describe the form and manner in which the tariffs required by this section shall be published and filed. The Commission may reject a tariff not filed in conformity with this section and its regulations. Upon rejection by the Commission, the tariff is void and its use is unlawful.[266]

Suppose a bill of lading included in a carrier's tariff pursuant to section 8(a)(1)(E) contains a limitation of liability provision not in conformity with the Carriage of Goods by Sea Act (COGSA),[267] or the bill of lading fails to provide a place for a shipper to declare the value of the goods and obtain an increase in the liability limit by paying a higher rate.[268] Under these circumstances, the courts have held that the COGSA limitation may not be applicable. This being so, may the FMC under section 8(f) reject the tariff under these circumstances?

It would appear that the agency has no such authority. Its power to reject a tariff is limited in section 8(f) to violations of its tariff filing regulations prescribing the "form or manner" of publishing or filing tariffs. Accordingly, the FMC may not reject a tariff on any basis other than the essentially technical requirements as set forth in the Act.[269] Thus, violations of COGSA or any other law are not a basis for rejection of a tariff.

Section 8(d) provides that no new or initial rate or change in an existing rate that results in an increased cost to the shipper may become effective earlier than thirty days after filing with the Commission. The Commission, for good cause, may allow such a new or initial rate or change to become effective in less than thirty days.

Section 9—Controlled Carriers [270]

Section 3(8) of the 1984 Act defines a "controlled carrier" to mean an ocean common carrier that is directly or indirectly owned or controlled by a government under whose registry the vessels of the carrier operate.[271] This section carries forward without substantive change the provisions of section 18(c) of the 1916 Shipping Act.[272]

The reason for section 9 was set forth by the House Merchant Marine Committee in its consideration of a predecessor bill, H.R. 1878:

> Many U.S. ports were opened to Soviet vessels by the bilateral maritime agreement negotiated by the Nixon administration in 1972, to carry one third the cargoes the Soviet Union purchased. An unexpected result of this agreement was the extent to which Soviet ships were able to compete for other U.S. cargoes as cross traders.
>
> Soviet shipping lines proved to be aggressive and increasingly successful competitors. Their success in winning U.S. cargoes, particularly by sharp rate-cutting, soon diverted cargoes traditionally carried by other carriers. It was contended that, because of government subsidized fuel and manning, and the political nature of their merchant fleet, the tactics of the U.S.S.R. were unfair. It was also

otherwise applicable.[281] The shipper may not avail himself of a strained and unnatural interpretation of a tariff. Descriptive words therein must be construed in the sense they are generally understood and accepted commercially. The proper test is the meaning which the words used might reasonably carry to the shipper to whom they are addressed.[282] If a shipper has full information about the article shipped but consistently and continually chooses an improper description, the shipper "knowingly and willfully" obtains transportation in violation of section 10(a)(1).[283] It is not an extenuating circumstance that the shipper was meeting unfair competition or others were also misbilling their shipments.[284]

When a claim for reparation involving alleged errors of weight, measurement, or description is made, the shipper, not the carrier, has the heavy burden of proof and must establish sufficient facts to indicate with reasonable certainty or definiteness the validity of the claim. The party who commits a mistake in the description of the goods bears the burden of establishing this fact.[285] It is not the declaration on the bill of lading that governs, but rather what is actually shipped that determines the applicable rate. Whenever reasonable, a conference's tariff rule should be upheld and enforced.[286]

In general, the obligation of a carrier is to rate the goods accurately according to the descriptions available to it. The issue for determination is simply what the actual nature of the commodity shipped was and whether or not the proper tariff rate was applied to that commodity.[287] In rating a shipment the carrier is not bound by the shipper's description appearing on the bill of lading.[288] It is the shipper's duty to demonstrate what actually moved by a preponderance of the evidence, notwithstanding an incorrect description in the bill of lading originally furnished to the line. The "preponderance of the evidence" standard is traditional in administrative and most civil cases.[289] The applicable freight rate should depend upon the intrinsic nature and market value of the goods themselves rather than a shipper's representation as to the intended use of the goods.[290] Evidence of knowledge and willfulness by a shipper is relevant not only to the question of penalties but to the very violations themselves. "Knowingly and willfully" in the 1984 Act means deliberately and purposefully or intentionally and can also mean conduct which shows a continuing pattern of indifference to the requirements of law.[291] A carrier may impose a penalty charge for the purpose of deterring cargo misdescriptions, but a conference tariff rule which prescribes such penalties cannot be enforced by means of a lien against the cargo.[292]

Under section 10(a)(1) a shipper is in violation not only by reason of any false or deceptive act but also if it employs "any other unjust or unfair device or means" to obtain transportation at less than the applicable rates. "Unfair device or means" coming at the end of a list of fraudulent practices such as false billing, etc., comprehends practices of the same general class as those specifically mentioned in this section. As earlier noted, this statutory rule of construction is known as "ejusdem generis."[293] When a shipper demands a return of a portion of the freight charges on the basis of a claim it knew or should have known to be false, such conduct is an unjust or unfair device or means. This is true even though the shipper's conduct did not amount to a fraud upon the carrier. The statute is not so limited; it covers a situation where the shipper obtained a less than applicable rate in such a way that its competitors were unaware of what transpired.[294] Thus, when a shipper prepares a bill of lading without disclosing the specific classification of the paper being shipped to conceal the contents from the shipper's competitors, an unfair device or means exists since it destroyed equality of treatment between shippers.[295] However, where both the line and the competitors are aware of the shipper's conduct, the means through which the lower rate was obtained was not by fraud or concealment and there is no violation.[296]

Whether a particular arrangement results in getting transportation, directly or indirectly, at less than the applicable rates and willfully and knowingly is a question of fact.[297] Haphazard document comparisons by a carrier with a total reliance on a shipper's representations constitutes such a wanton disregard of duty as to allow the shipper to obtain transportation on its terms.[298] Agents of common carriers, as such, are not subject to the 1984 Act,[299] but the law may not be circumvented through the medium of an agent. Accordingly, whether the carrier authorized the agent to rebate or indeed even knew of such activity is not material.[300]

Section 10(a)(2) provides that no person may operate under an agreement required to be filed under section 5 of the Act that has not become effective under section 6 or that has been rejected, disapproved, or cancelled. Section 5 requires a filing with the FMC of a copy of every agreement included in section 4 as within the scope of the 1984 Act. Section 6 provides for a review of the agreement by the FMC and an effective date of forty-five days after filing or thirty days after Federal Register publication unless additional information is required from the filer by the agency. The forerunner of section 10(a)(2), although substantially changed, was section 15 of the 1916 Act.[301] The obvious purpose of these provisions is to prohibit a carrier from operating concertedly with others in our foreign trade without appropriate authority from the regulatory agency.

ation against a shipper was treated in *Isbrandtsen* by the Supreme Court. A shipper who failed to enter into an exclusive patronage (loyalty) contract was charged a 9½ percent higher rate by conference members than a contracting shipper. A contracting shipper was required to pay a liquidated damage amount equal to 50 percent of the contract rate when it failed to use a conference vessel. The court held that the imposition of a higher rate on a noncontracting shipper and the levying of a liquidated damage amount for breach of contract by a contracting shipper constituted a method of retaliation against both kinds of shippers.[322]

Section 10(b)(6) provides that except for service contracts, a carrier may not engage in any unfair or unjustly discriminatory practice in the matter of (A) rates; (B) cargo classifications; (C) cargo space accommodations or other facilities; (D) the loading and unloading of freight; or (E) the adjustment and settlement of claims.[323] In its consideration of a predecessor bill, S.504, the Senate Commerce Committee indicated that the purpose of this provision was to codify the common carrier obligations to treat similarly situated shippers and ports alike:

> The uniformity of treatment contemplated in the bill was a relative equality based upon transportation conditions only. It is not intended to prohibit carriers from treating shippers or ports differently when the transportation circumstances surrounding the service were not substantially similar. Nor is it intended that the Commission have the authority to order a carrier or conference to provide service to any point, port, or place. It is basic that the dissimilarity of circumstances and transportation conditions may warrant dissimilarity in rates and charges, services, regulations and practice.[324]

A basic purpose of section 10(b)(6)(A) was to impose upon common carriers subject to the Act the duty of charging uniform rates to all shippers receiving a similar transportation service.[325] It is not sufficient that there be mere discrimination in rates between shippers. Early in the administration of the 1916 Act it was held that the discrimination must be "undue, unreasonable, or unjust."[326] The law condemns and makes unlawful every regulation, device, or subterfuge which undertakes to give to anyone an advantage based upon conditions other than those inherent in the transportation itself.[327]

An unlawful discrimination in transportation rates or charges ordinarily requires a showing of a competitive relationship between two shippers who are assessed different rates.[328] But when dealing with a service which is absolute or an across-the-board fixed charge on all cargo carried regardless of the commodity involved, the showing of a competitive relationship is not required.[329]Varying charges for identical services are prima facie unlawful unless justified.[330] Whether a rate is unjustly discriminatory does not depend upon unlawful or discriminatory intent.[331] A carrier or group of carriers must be the common source of the discrimination. Either the carrier or group must effectively participate in both rates if an order is to be entered against them to make corrections.[332] The provisions of section 10(b)(6)(A) are not simplistic and dogmatic. Congress did not intend to adopt a rule of absolute uniformity. The existence of unjust discrimination is a factual question which depends upon more than a bare difference in rates on similar commodities. An examination of all attendant transportation circumstances is permitted.[333]

Section 10(b)(6)(B) makes unlawful an unjustly discriminatory practice involving cargo classifications. Care should be taken by carriers to make the tariff definitions clear and precisely descriptive of the commodities covered and in specifying the freight rates applicable thereto.[334] Where a commodity shipped is included in more than one commodity description in the same tariff, the description which is more specific is applicable.[335] The shipper's own sales literature and samples of the commodity itself may be relied upon in attempting to determine the true nature of the goods,[336] but the use of a product and the manufacturer's description for sales purposes need not be considered when the product clearly falls within a specific commodity description.[337]

Section 10(b)(6)(C) bans an unjustly discriminatory practice relating to cargo space accommodations or other facilities. Early on it was held that a refusal to book cargo when space was available for the sole reason that there were more profitable bookings elsewhere was not permitted.[338] A carrier's failure to arrange its vessel itineraries and apportion space in proportion to cargo offerings which were at hand and ready for loading is unlawful.[339]

Forward booking arrangements for transportation for a period not exceeding two years is reasonable provided that the available space is prorated among all qualified shippers who desire it. The practice of contracting all of a carrier's space to three shippers to the exclusion of other qualified shippers is unjustly discriminatory; it is the common carrier's duty to offer the space and give shippers the chance to devise cooperative means of using it.[340] However, the refusal of a carrier to offer refrigerated space for a two-year period following the cancellation of an agreement for good cause by the carrier was not unjustly discriminatory.[341] A container is a cargo facility and the denial of a container to an NVOCC acting as a shipper is a violation of 10(b)(6)(C) of the 1984 Act.[342] So too is a willful and persistent failure by a carrier to give notice of rates and cargo classifications to be applied.[343]

Section 10(b)(6)(D) bans unjust discrimination in the loading and unloading of freight. An ocean common carrier is required by its transportation obligation, absent a special contract, to unload the cargo onto the dock segregated by bill of lading and count, put it in a place of rest on the pier so it is accessible to the consignee, and afford the consignee a reasonable opportunity to get it.[344] Wharf demurrage may be assessed on cargo left in the possession of the terminal beyond the allowed free time period.[345] A carrier's right to collect demurrage must appear clearly in the tariff regulations, and the tariff itself must be made part of the contract of carriage, although it may be implied.[346] The duty of moving freight from the place of delivery on the dock to the ship's tackle and thence to a place on the dock at the port of delivery is a part of the duty of the carrier transporting the freight from port to port.[347]

Section 10(b)(6)(E) provides that no common carrier may engage in an unjustly discriminatory practice in the adjustment and settlement of claims. To avoid unlawful discrimination, a carrier is obligated to apply its charges carefully in accordance with its established tariff rates. Compromising claims in a manner which ignores such rates is unlawful.[348] To award damages allegedly incurred by reason of unjust discrimination, the FMC must have that degree of certainty and satisfactory conviction of the mind and judgment as is necessary under well-established principles of law in cases that form the basis for a judgment in court.[349] Damages are awardable only if there is discrimination against a complainant. Overcharges and discrimination have quite different consequences as far as reparation is concerned; a different measure of recovery applies.[350] When a failure to perform common carrier obligations is shown, the burden is then placed upon the carrier to mitigate the damages that have occurred.[351] The FMC will not entertain a claim unless unjust discrimination is established. Where there is a dispute as to whether a carrier has refused to refund money, the shipping aspects of the transaction have been completed and there is, therefore, no violation of the Act.[352]

The FMC has in the past allowed a carrier to seek reparation under section 10(a)(1) where a shipper had failed or refused to pay its freight charges. Absent any fraud or concealment, the agency has on review concluded that there is no statutory basis to entertain a reparation action by a carrier under section 10(a)(1).[353] Thus, a carrier must now seek to collect unpaid freight charges in an ordinary breach of contract action in the courts.

Section 10(b)(7) prohibits a common carrier from employing any fighting ship, a provision derived from the 1916 Act.[354] Under section 3(10) of the 1984 Act a "fighting ship" means a vessel used in a particular trade by an ocean common carrier or group of such carriers for the purpose of excluding, preventing, or reducing competition by driving another ocean common carrier out of that trade. This definition is in accord with the FMC's earlier concept of a fighting ship.[355]

The FMC's predecessor early acknowledged that the 1916 Act recognized that a carrier may reduce rates below a fair and remunerative basis with the intent of driving a competitive carrier by water out of business without such action necessarily constituting the operation of a fighting ship.[356] In its consideration of a predecessor bill, S.1593, the Senate Commerce Committee noted that section 10(b)(7) was intended to include any predatory practice intended to eliminate the participation of an independent line in that trade. Nevertheless, the committee recognized that conferences do not and should not be required to set rates in a vacuum; conferences may consider and analyze the rates and services offered by independent carriers when setting conference rates. Accordingly, while a conference may compete with independent carriers, it may not intentionally drive them out of business using unjustly predatory practices.[357]

The FMC has previously recognized that under its section 15 authority in the 1916 Act it had to be especially wary of any agreement which places restraints upon third parties. The freedom allowed conference members to agree upon terms of competition is limited to freedom to agree upon terms regulating competition among themselves.[358] But when a conference reduced its rates to a noncompensatory level to drive an independent carrier out of the trade, the FMC found that this was "detrimental to the commerce of the United States" under its section 15 authority.[359]

In addition to its section 15 authority to restrain predatory rate practices, the 1916 Act allowed the agency to "disapprove any rate or charge filed by a common carrier by water in the foreign commerce of the United States or conference of carriers which, after hearing, it finds to be so unreasonably high or low as to be detrimental to the commerce of the United States."[360] Both the "detriment to commerce" standard in section 15 and section 18(b)(5) have been eliminated in the 1984 Act. The question arises as to what authority, if any, the FMC now has to curtail destructive rate fixing for the purpose of driving an independent carrier from the trade. Under section 6(g), Substantially Anticompetitive Agreements, if, at any time after the filing or effective date of an agreement the Commission determines that the agreement is likely by a reduction in competition to produce an unreasonable reduction in transportation service, the agency may seek appropriate injunctive relief. Conceivably, a conference reduction in rates intended to eliminate a nonconference carrier authorizes section 6(g) action by the FMC.[361] In addition, as noted *infra*, section 10(c)(3) prohibits any predatory practice by carriers acting concertedly to restrict any common carrier from participation in a particular trade.

Section 10(b)(8) bans a carrier from offering or paying any deferred rebate. A "deferred rebate" is defined as the return by a common carrier of any portion of freight money to the shipper as a consideration for the shipper giving all or any portion of its shipments to that carrier, payment of which is deferred beyond the completion of the service for which it is paid.[362] A deferred rebate differs from an ordinary rebate, which is a return of a rate or charge in whole or part on or about the time of a shipment. To establish a deferred rebate payment there must be proof that the shipper complied with the rebate agreement both during the period for which the shipment payment was computed and during the period of deferment.[363] In the past the FMC has held an exclusive patronage dual rate system to be unlawful because in effect it was creating deferred rebates.[364] A repayment of a deferred rebate received from a carrier does not cure the illegality.[365]

Section 10(b)(9) provides that no common carrier may use a loyalty contract (also called "dual rate" or "exclusive patronage" system) except in conformity with the antitrust laws. A loyalty contract is defined as "a contract with an ocean common carrier or conference, other than a service contract or contract based upon time-volume rates, by which a shipper obtains lower rates by committing all or a fixed portion of its cargo to that carrier or conference."[366] While Section 10(b)(9) allows the use of a loyalty contract if in conformity with the antitrust laws, it would appear that this restriction as a practical matter would in all probability preclude the use of most, if not all, conference loyalty contracts.[367] The key statutory distinction between a loyalty contract and a service contract as defined in the 1984 Act is that a loyalty contract is stated in terms of a fixed percentage of cargo, whereas a service contract is stated in terms of a minimum quantity of cargo. As noted earlier, the Supreme Court had held that a loyalty contract was unlawful.[368] Congress in 1961 legalized such contracts,[369] and the FMC thereafter held that a loyalty contract may be used in through intermodal transportation as well as in port-to-port transportation.[370]

In 1987 the Department of Justice (DOJ) reviewed the request of the Chemical Manufacturers Association (CMA) for the issuance of a business review letter pursuant to DOJ's procedure.[371] CMA requested a statement from DOJ of its current enforcement intention with respect to a proposed loyalty contract between an individual shipper, a member of CMA, and individual ocean common carriers, individually negotiated. In its letter (June 1987) the antitrust division of DOJ noted that loyalty contracts can provide flexibility to shippers who have difficulty estimating the amount of cargo they can commit to an ocean common carrier because of unpredictable demand for U.S. exports. DOJ concluded that the loyalty contract entered into by a member of CMA would be unlikely to adversely affect competition nor would such contracts be likely to make it more difficult for carriers to enter any relevant market. Accordingly, it concluded that a loyalty contract between individual shippers and carriers did not raise any concerns under the antitrust laws and that DOJ had no current intention to challenge such contracts.

Section 10(b)(10) prohibits a carrier from demanding, charging, or collecting any rate or charge which is unjustly discriminatory between shippers or ports. The intent of this provision was set forth by the Senate Commerce Committee in its consideration of a predecessor bill, S.1593. Because section 10(b)(10) protects shippers or ports only, it is not as broad as the unjustly discriminatory standard in section 15 of the 1916 Act which prohibited unjust discrimination between "carriers, shippers, exporters, importers, or ports, or between exporters from the United States and their foreign competitors." According to the committee, the term "shipper" is broad enough so that section 10(b)(10) can reach discrimination between exporters from the United States and their foreign competitors.[372] However, the new law is not aimed at preventing unjust discrimination among carriers within a conference. Thus, an unfair allocation of pool shares between member lines would no longer be unlawful.[373]

The committee has also said that the purpose of section 10(b)(10) is to codify the common carrier obligation to treat similarly situated shippers and ports alike. The uniformity of treatment contemplated is a relative equality based upon transportation conditions only. It is not intended to prohibit carriers from treating shippers or ports differently when the transportation circumstances surrounding the services are not substantially similar. Carriers and shippers should not be required by this subsection to engage in outdated and economically unsound practices, and rates, charges, and services should not be found to be unjustly discriminatory because they result in changes in transportation patterns.[374]

Considerable litigation has ensued dealing with the practice known as "port equalization." That term means the allowance or absorption by an ocean carrier of such amount as will make the shipper's cost of overland transportation identical, or substantially so, from its inland point of origin to any one or two or more ports. Its purpose is to enable the ocean carrier to compete for cargo without calling at the port closest to, or enjoying the lowest inland transportation cost from, the point where the cargo originates.[375]

Ports were specifically protected by sections 16 and 17 of the 1916 Act against unreasonable preference and discrimination and the provisions have been carried forward in essentially identical terms in sections 10(b)(6), (10), (11), and (12) of the 1984 Act.[376] Port equalization violates the Act where it diverts traffic from a port to which the area of origin is "naturally tributary" to a port that is not naturally tributary, and is not justified in the shipper's interest.[377] The naturally tributary concept has to do with the territory locally tributary to a particular port, not with the general territory which an entire range of ports, or more than one range or seaboard, may serve competitively.[378] Neither the naturally tributary concept nor the prohibitions in the Act relating to discriminatory actions vest a port with a monopoly over local cargo. This provision merely means that improper rate making devices may not be employed to channel the flow of cargo elsewhere. Carriers and ports have a right to compete fairly for all cargo.[379]

When diversion of naturally tributary cargo occurs, the reasonableness of the particular practice is determined by:

1. the quantity and quality of cargo being diverted and whether there is substantial injury;
2. the costs to the carrier of providing direct service to the port;
3. any operational difficulties or other transportation factors that bear upon the carrier's ability to provide direct services (e.g., lack of cargo volume, inadequate facilities);
4. the competitive conditions existing in the trade; and
5. the fairness of the diversionary method employed.[380]

Equalization as such is not illegal, and the tariff that allows for equalization, therefore, is not per se illegal. It is only the application of the tariff in a particular manner that may be illegal.[381]

Section 10(b)(11) states that no carrier may, except for service contracts, make or give any or undue or unreasonable preference or advantage to any particular person, locality, or description of traffic in any respect whatsoever. This section is derived from section 16 (First) of the 1916 Act.[382] In an early decision, the FMC's predecessors held that the undue preference or advantage provision in section 16 of the 1916 Act imposed upon a common carrier the duty of charging uniform rates to all shippers receiving a similar transportation service.[383] Not all preferences and advantages were, however, condemned, but only those that were undue or unreasonable.[384] In order to sustain a finding of undue or unreasonable preference or advantage, the complainant need prove:

1. that the preferred port, cargo, or shipper is actually competitive with the complainant;
2. that the conduct complained of is the proximate cause of injury to the complainant; and
3. that such conduct was undue, unreasonable, or unjust.[385]

Good faith will not save an otherwise unjustly prejudicial practice from condemnation. The equality of treatment required is not conditioned on a carrier's intentions.[386] The prohibition against uneven treatment in section 10(b)(11) extends not only to "any particular person" but also to a "locality or description of traffic." Thus, if the shipment describes a particular kind of traffic, this section applies even if the shipper does not qualify as a "person."[387]

As previously noted in the discussion under subsection 10(b)(6)(A), to establish an unlawful discrimination in transportation charges requires a showing of a competitive relationship between two shippers assessed different rates. However, the situation is different when dealing with a service which is absolute or an across-the-board fixed charge (e.g., a surcharge) on all cargo carried regardless of the commodity involved. Here, a competitive relationship is not required, the carrier having an obligation to administer the charge equally on all commodities. The failure to do so establishes a clear situation of undue prejudice to a "description of traffic" vis-à-vis other commodities in violation of the Act.[388]

Section 10(b)(12) prohibits a common carrier from subjecting any particular person, locality, or description of traffic to an unreasonable refusal to deal or any undue or reasonable prejudice or disadvantage in any respect whatsoever.[389] On occasions, the particular facts may permit the conclusion that there may be violations of several sections of the Act. In a proceeding in 1989 the interrelationship between the various subsections of section 10(b) is demonstrated.[390] A conference in the North European trade published a Rule 7(a) providing for the payment of collect freight charges. The rule generally required that all collect charges, including all monies advanced and any charges for demurrage and detention, would be paid to the carrier before the cargo was released from the port of discharge for delivery or for subsequent movement or on-carriage. There was, however, an exception for specified shippers:

1. All conference members could extend credit up to fourteen days to shippers of wine and spirits following the receipt of a carrier's invoice by shipper; and
2. Three carriers, under independent action, taken by them, could also extend credit for up to fourteen days to shippers of chocolate

confectionery in temperature-controlled containers from ports in the Hamburg-Bordeaux range following receipt of carrier's invoice by the shipper.

In an Order to Show Cause the FMC noted that it would appear that Rule 7(a), by providing credit privileges to certain shippers to the exclusion of other shippers, constituted the giving of an undue or unreasonable preference and advantage to one class of shippers or description of traffic, and, in so doing, subjected other classes of shippers or descriptions of traffic to undue or unreasonable prejudice or disadvantage in violation of section 10(b)(11) and (12) of the 1984 Act. For these reasons, the agency stated that Rule 7(a) might also be an unjustly discriminatory practice under section 10(b)(6) and an unreasonable refusal to deal under section 10(b)(12). Upon receipt of the Order to Show Cause, Rule 7(a) was withdrawn by the conference.

Section 10(b)(13) prohibits any carrier, alone or with others, to refuse to negotiate with a shippers' association. That term is defined in section 3(24) of the 1984 Act "as a group of shippers that consolidates or distributes freight on a non-profit basis for the members of the group in order to secure carload, truckload, or other volume rates or service contracts."[391] Its inclusion in the 1984 Act constitutes the first legislative instance of a shippers' association being recognized as a separate entity in ocean transportation. The role of such an association in our foreign commerce will be treated in Chapter III, Shippers.

In its report, ACCOS noted that its record revealed that there are not as many shippers' associations operating in the marketplace today as had been anticipated, and most of them have expressed great concern that conferences were not negotiating in good faith with them and thereby undermining the role that they could play.[392] Difficulties were being experienced in negotiating service contracts with carriers, and it was urged that the provisions of the 1984 Act for carrier "refusal to deal" be strengthened. The managing director of a large conference, however, took exception, stating that his conference had not entered into service contracts because the associations refused to commit anything but a token amount of freight to a service contract.[393]

Section 10(b)(16) restricts the disclosure of confidential information by a common carrier either alone or in conjunction with any other person. Such carrier may not knowingly disclose, offer, solicit, or receive any information concerning the nature, kind, quantity, destination, consignee, or routing of any property tendered or delivered to a common carrier without the consent of the shipper or consignee if that information:

1. may be used to the detriment or the prejudice of the shipper or consignee;
2. may improperly disclose its business transaction to a competitor; or
3. may be used to the detriment or prejudice of any common carrier.

There are some exceptions to this prohibition: for example, a disclosure may be made in response to legal process to the United States or to any independent neutral body.[394]

This section is derived from section 20 of the 1916 Act.[395] There is, however, one difference between the two acts. In the 1916 Act the proscription against disclosure of confidential information applied to "any common carrier by water or other person subject to this act." Under the 1916 Act the term "other person" included marine terminal operators, NVOCCs, and ocean freight forwarders. Thus, it was unlawful for a forwarder to receive information from a carrier as to the billings of shipments consigned to another terminal.[396] The 1984 Act, however, excludes forwarders from the confidentiality requirement, but terminals continue to be included under section 10(d)(3) of the Act.

Section 10(c), Concerted Action, regulates the conduct of a "conference or group of two or more common carriers" in certain areas. At first blush, it would appear that a conference would at all times consist of two or more carriers and that the "group of two or more common carriers" language may be redundant. This is not necessarily the case, since two or more carriers may engage in concerted action even though not operating in conference form. For example, vessel operators may operate under a rate agreement where a conference structure is not used.

In its consideration of an earlier bill, H.R.1878, the House Merchant Marine Committee outlined the scope of section 10(c):

One of the important ways in which this legislation will reduce burdensome and confusing regulation and allow ocean carriers to function efficiently and with certainty is the development of specified prohibited acts which replace the vague "public interest" and "detriment to commerce" standards contained in the Shipping Act of 1916. Four of the prohibited Acts set forth in section 10(c)—group boycotts, predatory practices, restraints on intermodalism, and restraints on shipper selection of competitors—have been included in subsection 10(c) as a result of analysis of types of activities which the FMC has, in the past, prohibited pursuant to the vague standards of the 1916 Act.

However, while in terms of statutory language inclusion of these four prohibited acts is new, inclusion of these provisions does not reflect a Congressional intent to prohibit activities which are permissible today. By substituting these and other specific prohibited acts for more broadly worded standards, the bill removes FMC discretion to determine that activities other than those listed are prohibited. The bill does not direct the FMC to interpret the prohibitions against group boycotts, etc., more expansively than it has ruled against such activities to date, under the present law. Thus, the FMC is not expected to administer these four provisions in a manner inconsistent with its past decisions on these points. Activities which have not been considered unlawful as group boycotts or predatory, etc., under the present public interest and detrimental to commerce standards of the present law are therefore not intended to be prohibited by the listing of these prohibitions in a different form in this bill. Moreover, these four prohibitions are not to be interpreted in a vacuum, but in the context of the shipping industry and reasonable shipping industry practices and not give it any new meaning contrary to the general intent of the legislation to reduce regulation.[397]

Section 10(c)(1) states that no conference or group of two or more carriers may boycott or take any other concerted action resulting in an unreasonable refusal to deal. Ordinarily, in a boycott, parties refrain from commercial dealings by a concerted effort. The intent of Congress was that a group boycott or concerted refusal to deal, which fell within the unjustly discriminatory standard of section 15 of the 1916 Act, be prohibited under this subsection.[398] An example of a concerted refusal to deal was set forth by the Senate Commerce Committee in its consideration of S.504, a predecessor bill. A conference agreement prohibited any member line from paying a consolidation allowance for shipments consolidated or deconsolidated at places other than deep-sea waterfront facilities. An administrative law judge held that this agreement was a type of group boycott aimed at one segment of the consolidation industry, those performing services off-pier. He concluded that this restriction was unjustly discriminatory under section 15.[399]

Section 10(c)(2) bans concerted conduct that unreasonably restricts the use of intermodal services or technological innovations. Reference to intermodalism is intended to be by way of example. The language of this section is broad enough to prevent conferences or other agreements among carriers from becoming vehicles for restricting the development of new progressive services.[400] In a case cited by the Senate Commerce Committee, a conference agreement provided that a member line could commence individual interior point services of a type not offered by the conference only after providing 120 days' advance notice of its decision.

A current FMC rule allowed the filing of tariffs covering new services to become effective thirty days after filing. The FMC held that advance notice of 120 days was not necessary for the conference to accomplish its basic objection of ameliorating excess rate competition, nor was so long an advance notice required to permit the member lines to freely and thoroughly discuss intermodal proposals with each other.[401]

Subsection 10(c)(3) prohibits conferences from engaging in any predatory practice designed to eliminate the participation, or deny the entry, in a particular trade of a common carrier not a member of the conference, a group of common carriers, an ocean tramp, or a bulk carrier. The subject of "predatory practice" has been treated above under section 10(b)(7) dealing with the employment of fighting ships.

In section 10(c)(4) carriers may not concertedly negotiate with a nonocean carrier or group of nonocean carriers (for example, truck, rail, or air operators) on any matter relating to rates or services provided to ocean common carriers within the United States by those nonocean carriers. It will be recalled that under section 8(a)(1) common carriers shall not be required to state separately or otherwise reveal in tariff filings the inland divisions of a through rate. According to the Senate Commerce Committee, this prohibition preserves recently enacted deregulatory changes affecting inland modes of transportation within the United States.[402] This is not to say, however, that a common carrier may not individually negotiate the inland division of a through rate with a domestic carrier; section 10(c)(4) merely prohibits a conference or "group" of carriers under the 1984 Act from engaging in such negotiations. But as stated in the proviso in this section, this restriction does not prevent a conference or other carrier groups from publishing a joint through rate by a conference, joint venture, or an association of ocean commerce carriers.

Section 10(c)(5), dealing with compensation to be paid by carriers to ocean freight forwarders, will be treated in Chapter VI.

Section 10(c)(6)'s provision is new and appears not to have any legislative history in the 1984 Act. It prohibits carriers from concertedly agreeing to allocate shippers among specific carriers or prohibiting a carrier party to an agreement from soliciting cargo from a particular shipper. The apparent purpose of this provision is to preserve for a shipper the right without conference restriction to choose which member line in a conference will carry the shipper's cargo.

Section 10(d) carries forward certain prohibitions from sections 16, 17, and 20 of the 1916 Act.[403] Section 10(d)(1) provides that common carriers, forwarders, and MTOs may not enforce unreasonable regulation related to the receiving, handling, storing, or delivery of property.

Section 10(d)(2) prohibits agreements by a marine terminal operator (MTO) with another MTO or with a common carrier to unreasonably discriminate on terminal services against a common carrier or ocean tramp. Section 10(d)(3) imposes on MTOs the obligation set forth under sections 10(b)(11), (12), and (16). The latter provisions are separately treated in other parts of this work.

Section 10(e), Joint Ventures, provides that a joint venture or consortium of two or more common carriers but operated as a single entity shall be treated as a single common carrier.[404] "Joint venture" is not defined in the 1984 Act, but the FMC provides in its rules that a "joint service agreement" among carriers operates under its own name, independently fixes its own rates, publishes its own tariffs, issues its own bills of lading, and acts generally as a single carrier.[405] Since a joint venture is to be treated "as a single common carrier" it would appear that the joint service agreement need not be filed under section 5(a) of the Act.

In a predecessor bill, S.504, the Senate Commerce Committee discussed pools and joint ventures, pro and con. The committee noted that the hearings and the record available to Congress had not indicated that pools and joint ventures in existence at that time had created any of the types of problems which the bill would protect against. In the vastly overtonnaged shipping market, the public needs as many efficiency-creating devices as possible so that carriers may achieve cost savings which could be passed on to shippers and ultimately to consumers. The threshold test of an impermissible joint venture or pool would be whether the agreement has the effect of substantially reducing competition in a trade considered as a whole. Since such an agreement can enable carriers to raise necessary capital, attain economies of scale, and rationalize their services, joint ventures may result in more effective and efficient service being provided in a trade.[406]

Section 11—Complaints, Investigations, Reports, and Reparations

This section generally carries forward the provisions in section 22 of the 1916 Act pertaining to formal investigations.[407] Investigations and proceedings under this section may reach any potential violation of the Act. Although Commission investigations may reach possible violations of the general standard in section 6(g) banning substantially anticompetitive agreements, enforcement of that standard is solely by the U.S. District Court through section 6(h) of the 1984 Act.[408]

Section 11(a), Filing of Complaints, provides that any person may file with the Commission a sworn statement alleging a violation of the Act, other than section 6(g), and may seek reparation for any injury caused to the complainant by that violation. The United States is a "person" within the provisions of this section.[409] Under the FMC's Rules of Practice and Procedure, a complaint must be verified and contain a concise statement of the cause of action and a request for the relief or other affirmative action sought. If the complaint fails to indicate the sections of the Act alleged to have been violated or clearly to state facts which support the allegations, the Commission may, on its own initiative, require the complaint to be amended to supply such particulars as it deems necessary.[410] The complaint should also designate the place at which a hearing is desired. The respondent named in the complaint shall file with the FMC an answer to the complaint and shall serve it on the complainant within twenty (20) days after a copy of the complaint was served by the FMC upon the respondent.[411]

While section 11(a) permits a person filing a complaint with the agency to seek reparations, it is not necessary that a complainant request reparations. A "person" may file a complaint for a violation of section 11 without being directly affected by such violations.[412] The FMC will not approve an agreement among carriers which would interfere with the statutory right of "any person" to complain to the agency of activities which may violate the Act and which might interfere with the FMC's carrying out of its regulatory functions.[413]

The naming of a carrier's agent as respondent in a complaint which alleges a violation of the Act without naming the carrier-principal involved is jurisdictionally defective regardless of the agent's authority to act on behalf of its principal located overseas.[414] A complaint which was originally defective because it seeks an incorrect remedy but correctly states the substance or gravamen of the claim may be cured subsequently even if the period of limitations has meanwhile expired.[415] But amendments to a complaint that would substitute a different party, especially when such party is jurisdictionally indispensable, are not merely clarifying amendments but a new complaint, which should be so treated despite the possible effects of the period of limitations contained in the Act.[416]

Section 11(b), Satisfaction or Investigations of Complaints, provides that the Commission shall furnish a copy of the complaint to the person named therein who shall, within a reasonable period of time specified by the Commission, satisfy the complaint or answer it in writing. It has long been the policy of the Commission, as with the courts, to favor and encourage settlements as opposed to litigation, and both the courts and the Commission engage in presumptions that favor findings that settlements are fair, correct, and valid, and unless there is a conflict with some statutory policy, settlements are approved.[417]

The Commission's Rules of Procedure expressly encourages settlements. Rule 91(a) provides that all interested parties shall have the opportunity for the submission and consideration of facts, arguments, offers of settlements, or proposal of adjustment, without prejudice to the rights of the parties.[418] Rule 93 provides that if a respondent satisfies a complaint, a statement to that effect signed and verified by the opposing parties shall be filed with the FMC. Such statement shall show the amount of the reparation agreed upon. Satisfied complaints shall be dismissed at the discretion of the Commission.[419]

Pursuant to the provisions of the Administrative Dispute Resolution Act,[420] the FMC has amended its Rules of Practice and Procedure to require timely consideration of the use of alternative dispute resolution techniques.[421] At an early stage litigants shall be required to consider alternative methods of resolving their dispute.[422] At the request of any party or the presiding judge, the chief administrative law judge (ALJ) "may" appoint a "mediator or settlement judge" acceptable to the parties who shall submit any settlement reached to the presiding judge.[423] Such judge is required to facilitate the use of the alternative dispute resolution procedure.[424]

Under section 11(c), Commission Investigations, upon a complaint or upon its own motion, the Commission may investigate any conduct or agreement that it believes to be in violation of the Act. Unless enjoined under section 11(h), *infra,* an agreement under investigation remains in effect until the Commission issues an order under this section. The agency may by order disapprove, cancel, or modify any agreement filed under section 5(a) that violates the Act. With respect to agreements inconsistent with section 6(g), that is, agreements that are deemed to be substantially anticompetitive, the Commission's sole remedy, as noted above, is to proceed under 6(h), which authorizes the agency to seek an injunction to enjoin the operation of the agreement.

A primary purpose of the 1984 Act was to expedite proceedings before the FMC. Thus, section 11(d), Conduct of Investigation, states that within ten days after the initiation of a proceeding, the FMC shall set a date on or before which its final decision will be issued. This date may be extended for good cause by order of the Commission. Under section 11(e), Undue Delays, if the Commission determines that it is unable to issue a final decision because of undue delays by a party to the proceeding, the agency may impose sanctions including entering a decision adverse to the delaying party.

Under section 11(f), Reports, the Commission is required to make a written report of every investigation in which a hearing was held, stating its conclusions, decisions, findings of fact, and order. "Hearing" does not necessarily mean a full evidentiary proceeding and is defined to be "any oral proceeding before a tribunal"; it may be by trial or argument. A respondent is, of course, entitled to a fair hearing. But that concept means only that the party must have an opportunity to meet such facts which adversely affect its interests.[425] Where no genuine issue of fact is presented, there is no need for an evidentiary hearing.[426] The determination of questions of law does not necessarily require an evidentiary hearing. Oral argument on such a question affords a full opportunity to be heard.[427]

Section 11(g), Reparations, provides for compensation for "actual injury." The 1984 Act substantially differs from its predecessor, the 1916 Act, in this area. Under section 22 of the earlier Act, if a complaint was filed within two years after the cause of action accrued, the agency "may" direct the payment of full reparations to the complainant for the injury caused by such violation. The power vested in the FMC under the 1916 Act was, thus, permissive and discretionary, and the mere fact that a violation was found did not in itself compel a grant of reparations.[428] Under section 11(g) the FMC "shall" award reparations for "actual injury." The FMC may not grant compensation under section 22 for other than the actual damage incurred.[429]

Under section 11(g) of the 1984 Act the statute of limitations has been increased from two to three years after the cause of action accrued. The purpose of a time limitation is to give protection against stale claims.[430] The failure to file a complaint within the three year period extinguished not only the right of the complainant but also the FMC's jurisdiction.[431] The statute is not tolled during the period of negotiations between the shipper and the carrier, and the three year period does not begin when the carrier rejects the claim.[432] When a complaint is filed within the statutory period, recovery may not be barred by a conference rule requiring that a claim must be filed within a shorter period.[433]

The cause of action may accrue at the time of delivery of the cargo to the carrier, the time of shipment, or the time of payment of the freight charges, whichever is later.[434] Although the limitation period applicable to affreightment overcharge complaints is not applicable to a federal court action to recover such overcharges, an action brought in such court more than three years after the overcharges were discovered was barred by laches.[435]

Damages must be the proximate result of violations of the law. There is no presumption of damage, and the violation in and of itself without proof of pecuniary loss resulting from the unlawful act does not afford a basis for reparations.[436] The agency cannot award reparation in an investigatory proceeding, but only in a complaint case establishing actual injury.[437]

Under the 1916 Act the award of interest was discretionary on the part of the FMC.[438] The FMC recognized that interest could be denied where the principles of equity and justice so required. However, the generally accepted practice governing the allowance of interest on liquidated sums under the 1916 Act was to recognize as an element of damage loss of interest on charges unlawfully exacted, and in ordering reparation to include as part of the damages such interest from the date of payment.[439] Under section 11(g) of the 1984 Act, as part of the complainant's actual injury, it is mandatory for the FMC to include loss of interest at commercial rates compounded from the date of injury. Rule 253 states that interest awarded shall accrue from the date of injury to the date specified in the Commission order awarding reparations. The rate of interest will be derived from the average monthly secondary market rates on six-month U.S. Treasury bills compounded daily from the date of injury to the date specified in the Commission order awarding reparations.[440]

Unlike the 1916 Act, also mandatory is the requirement in section 11(g) that the complainant be awarded "reasonable attorney's fees." The conferees believed that in determining the amount of such fees, a complainant's expenses for representation before the Commission as well as in any federal court proceeding should be considered. But the conferees believed that a successful complainant is not entitled to attorney's fees for any portion of the proceeding for which it did not prevail or for procedural motions that were unsuccessful.[441]

Under the FMC's Rule 254(a), "attorney's fees" include the fair market value of the services of any person permitted to appear and practice before the Commission and may include compensation for services rendered the complainant in a related proceeding in a federal court that is useful and necessary to the determination of a reparations award in the complaint proceeding. Based upon a petition specifying the number of hours claimed supported by evidence of the reasonableness of the hours claimed and the customary fees charged by attorneys in the community, an award of fees shall be made.[442]

Section 11(g) of the 1984 Act also allows for additional reparations under certain circumstances. If the injury to the complainant was caused by an activity that is prohibited by section 10(b)(5) or (7) or section 10(c)(1) or (3) of the Act or violates section 10(a)(2) or (3), the Commission may (but is not required to) direct the payment of additional amounts; but the total recovery may not exceed twice the amount of the actual injury.[443] Further reparations are awardable if the injury is caused by any unfair or unjustly discriminatory practice in the matter of rates or cargo classifications, as prohibited by sections 10(b)(6)(A) or (B). The amount awarded shall be the difference between the rates paid by the injured shipper and the most favorable rate paid by another shipper.

Prior to the passage of the 1984 Act there was some question as to whether the FMC could stay allegedly unlawful action until a final decision was reached. The Commission could issue a cease and desist order to prevent the carrying out of an unapproved agreement on the ground that this was "a necessary corollary to the requirement that such agreements obtain approval before they may be carried out."[444] But if the allegedly unlawful action did not involve an unapproved agreement, the Commission did not have authority to issue a preliminary cease and desist order as part of the administrative process.[445]

Section 11(h)(1) and (2), Injunction, permit a court to grant injunctive relief to the FMC or a complainant upon a showing that the standards for granting such relief by courts of equity are met. If the defendant prevails in an injunction suit brought by a complainant, the court "shall" allow reasonable attorney's fees to be assessed and collected as part of the costs of the suit. The conferees of the 1984 Act believed that an automatic award of reasonable attorney's fees to a successful defendant would discourage frivolous private suits to block legitimate conduct. Such an award should cover only those fees reasonably caused by the complainant's suit for a preliminary injunction, excluding any unnecessary costs generated by a defendant's response.[446]

The 1984 Act has provided the FMC with different procedures for the adjudication of claims. The first of these is the formal proceeding which is initiated by a complaint and the remittance of a filing fee. A copy of a complaint form in a formal docket procedure is attached hereto as Appendix E. A respondent files an answer with the FMC to the complaint within twenty days after the date of service of the complaint by the FMC on him. A form for an answer to the complaint is attached hereto as Appendix F. The proceeding is ordinarily heard by an ALJ generally following the rules of procedure in our federal courts. An initial decision is issued by the ALJ subject to review by the FMC.[447]

In Subpart K, Shortened Procedure, with the consent of the parties and the approval of the FMC or the presiding officer, a complaint proceeding may be conducted without oral hearing unless ordered by the ALJ. The complaint (Appendix G) filed with the FMC shall have a memorandum of the facts, subscribed and verified, and of arguments separately stated, upon which the complainant relies. Within twenty-five days after service, a respondent, if it consents to the shortened procedure in an affidavit, will serve upon the complainant an answering memorandum of the facts and of arguments, separately stated, upon which it relies. Thereafter, a complainant may file a memorandum in reply which shall close the record for decision by the ALJ. An initial decision is served by the ALJ, which is subject to review under the same procedure with respect to proceedings under a formal hearing.[448]

In the event that the respondent elects not to consent to a determination of the claim under Subpart K, the issues shall be adjudicated by an ALJ. The respondent will serve an answer to the complaint and the complainant may file a reply memorandum accompanied by appropriate affidavits and supporting documents. Unless otherwise ordered by the ALJ, no oral hearing or argument will be allowed. The ALJ thereafter issues an initial decision which may be reviewed by the FMC on the ground that a material finding of fact or a necessary legal conclusion is erroneous or that prejudicial error has occurred. If a complaint is awarded reparations, attorney's fees shall also be awarded.[449]

If the gravamen of the complaint is that the rate charged by the carrier was "unreasonable" and that it should be disapproved and a "reasonable" rate be fixed, the FMC has held that the special docket procedure in Subpart K is not available in the foreign trades. This type of proceeding relates solely to the Commission's jurisdiction over common carriers in the contiguous domestic trades rather than in our foreign trades. Accordingly, the authority of the FMC to fix a just and reasonable maximum rate not existing in the foreign trades, the shortened procedure is not available.[450]

In Subpart S, Informal Procedure for Adjudication of Small Claims, a claim in an amount of $10,000 or less will be referred to the FMC's Informal Dockets Activity for adjudication and decision by a settlement officer without the necessity of formal proceedings under the FMC's rules. A determination under this Subpart shall be administratively final and conclusive unless reviewed at the request of an individual commissioner.[451]

A claim under Subpart S alleging violation of the 1984 Act must be filed within three years from the time the cause of action accrues together with supporting documents. The claimant may attach a memorandum or other document containing discussion, argument, or legal authority in support of its claim. Thereafter, the respondent files a response to the claim within twenty-five days, together with an indication as to whether the informal procedure is consented to. If the respondent refuses to consent to an informal adjudication of the claim, the claim will be considered as a complaint under section 502.311, as a formal procedure under Subpart T, and will be adjudicated thereunder.[452]

Section 11a.—Foreign Laws and Practices

This section was enacted as part of the Foreign Shipping Practices Act of 1988[453] and not as part of the Shipping Act of 1984. The basic purpose of section 11a. is to protect U.S. vessel operators and intermediaries from discriminatory activities by foreign flag operators and their governments.

Congressional action to prevent discriminatory practices in our ocean-borne trades is not a recent phenomenon. In the Merchant Marine Act, 1920,[454] Section 19 dealt with a similar problem.[455] That section authorizes the FMC to adopt rules affecting shipping in the foreign trade to meet general or special conditions unfavorable to shipping in such trade resulting from foreign laws or from competitive practices employed by vessel operators of a foreign country. Under its rulemaking authority, the FMC has outlined what it considers to be conditions unfavorable to shipping in the foreign trade of the United States.[456] These conditions, summarized, are:

1. imposing upon vessels in the foreign trade of the United States fees or restrictions different from those imposed on other vessels competing in the trade or which preclude vessels in the foreign trade from competing on the same basis as any other vessel;
2. reserving substantial cargoes for the national flag or other vessels and failing to provide, on reasonable terms, equal access to such cargo by vessels in the foreign trade of the United States;
3. conditions that are discriminatory or unfair as between carriers, shippers, exporters, importers, or ports or between exporters from the United States and their foreign competitors;
4. conditions that restrict or burden a carrier's intermodal movements or shore-based maritime activities;
5. conditions that are otherwise unfavorable to shipping in the foreign trade of the United States.

The FMC has used its section 19 authority through the years in an effort to correct conditions imposed by foreign vessels or nations unfavorable to shipping in the U.S. trade. In a recent (1992) proceeding the FMC acted against a Korean law that on its face was discriminatory in that it clearly establishes nationality-based requirements for non-Korean companies wishing to participate in the Korean trade and prohibits companies owned by U.S. citizens, as well as other non-Koreans, from participating in the U.S./Korea bilateral and Korean cross trades in the same manner, and with the same opportunities, as their Korean-owned competitors. Korean firms, on the other hand, were found to be free to operate in the United States without such barriers. This was the first case where U.S. intermediaries, NVOCCs, were affected rather than vessel operators.[457]

Section 11a. likewise seeks to protect U.S. firms from foreign discrimination. Under section 11a.(b) the Commission may investigate whether any rules or practice of foreign governments, or any practices of foreign carriers or other persons providing maritime or maritime-related services in a foreign country, resulted in the existence of conditions that (1) adversely affect the operation of U.S. carriers in United States ocean-borne trade; and (2) do not exist for foreign carriers of that country in the United States or are a result of acts of U.S. carriers or other persons providing maritime or maritime-related services in the United States.[458]

Under section 11a.(c) investigations may be initiated by the FMC on its own motion or by a petition of "any person" harmed by conditions unfavorable to shipping in the foreign trade of the United States. Whenever the agency determines that such conditions exist, it is authorized to issue regulations which may:

1. impose equalizing fees or charges;
2. limit sailings to and from U.S. ports or the amount or type of cargo carried;
3. suspend, in whole or in part, tariffs filed with the Commission for carriage to or from U.S. ports, including a common carrier's right to use tariffs of conferences in U.S. trades of which it is a member for any period the Commission specifies;
4. suspend, in whole or in part, an ocean common carrier's right to operate under an agreement, including any agreement authorizing preferential treatment at terminals or preferential terminal leases, whether filed with the Commission or not filed with the Commission pursuant to the exemptions granted in 46 CFR Part 572; or any agreement filed with the Commission authorizing space chartering, or pooling of cargo or revenues with other ocean common carriers;
5. impose a fee, not to exceed one thousand dollars per voyage;
6. request the collector of customs at the port or place of destination in the United States to refuse the clearance required by section 4197 of the Revised Statutes, 46 U.S.C. app. 91, to a vessel of a foreign carrier which is or whose government is identified as contributing to the unfavorable conditions described in subpart C;
7. request the collector of customs at the port or place of destination in the United States to collect any fees imposed by the Commission under paragraph (e) of this section;
8. request the secretary of the department in which the Coast Guard is operating to deny entry, for purposes of oceanborne trade, of

any vessel of a foreign carrier which is or whose government is identified as contributing to the unfavorable conditions described in subpart C, to any port or place in the United States or the navigable waters of the United States, or to detain any such vessel at the port or place in the United States from which it is about to depart for any other port or place in the United States; or

9. take any other action the Commission finds necessary and appropriate to adjust or meet any condition unfavorable to shipping in the foreign trade of the United States.[459]

The FMC has used this section to protect not only vessel operators but NVOCCs and forwarders as well. In 1992 the FMC imposed sanctions on offending Korean entities, but suspended the effective date to permit negotiations. In September 1993 the agency dismissed the proceeding when the offenders agreed to take corrective action to permit U.S. firms the right to operate trucking services, conduct warehouse activities, or provide services at a dockside agency.[460]

It appears that the above statutory provisions have served as a strong deterrent against discriminatory conditions imposed on U.S. flag operators or intermediaries and after the commencement of proceedings and sometimes after difficult negotiations, a settlement satisfactory to all sides is usually achievable. However, if a settlement is not reached and a violation is found, section 11a.(f) provides that upon the request of the FMC the collector of customs at any U.S. port shall refuse clearance to any vessel of a foreign carrier found in violation, and the vessel of such carrier shall be denied entry for the purpose of oceanborne foreign trade or shall be detained in a port of the United States from which it is about to depart for any other U.S. port.

Section 12—Subpoenas and Discovery [461]

This section in general provides that in investigations and adjudicatory proceedings various forms of discovery, such as depositions, written interrogatories, and other procedures, may be utilized by any party, with the FMC having the authority to compel the attendance of witnesses and the production of books and other evidence.

The Commission has for many years been faced with the difficult issue as to whether it could require a foreign carrier to furnish documents physically located outside the United States. The agency may lawfully order a foreign flag carrier serving in the U.S. trade to furnish documents in compliance with a lawful order.[462] In making such a demand, the FMC is not limited to information existing within our borders. However, a number of our trading nations have enacted so-called "blocking statutes" which prevent a foreign carrier from furnishing information outside the United States unless authorized by a foreign governmental agency. While our courts have recognized the claim of foreign carriers that they could not produce documents located aboard if prevented by a blocking statute, nevertheless, a District Court has ruled under the 1916 Act that the statute of a foreign government may not be used to block disclosure unless it contains criminal sanctions.[463]

The general provisions governing discovery are set forth in the FMC's Rule 201.[464] Generally, a party may be examined regarding any matter, not privileged, which is relevant to the subject matter involved in the proceeding. It is not grounds for objection that the testimony will be inadmissible at the hearing if the testimony sought appears "reasonably calculated" to lead to the discovery of admissible evidence.[465] Upon motion by a party from whom discovery is sought, and for good cause shown, the presiding officer may make any order which justice requires to protect a party from annoyance, embarrassment, oppression, or undue burden or expense.[466]

The 1916 Act authorized the FMC under section 22(b) to investigate "any violation" of that law.[467] It was argued that a fact-finding investigation was not an adjudicatory proceeding under section 22(a) to determine whether the statute was violated, and consequently, the agency could not subpoena witnesses under section 27 of that Act[468] to attend such an investigation. It was held that a fact-finding investigation could culminate in an adjudicating proceeding and, accordingly, the FMC could use its subpoena power to require attendance.[469] Congress settled all doubt in the 1984 Act by providing in section 12(a) that subpoenas and discovery applied "in investigations and adjudicatory proceedings." In its discussion of this issue in a predecessor bill, S.504, the Senate Commerce Committee made it clear that the Commission's rules on discovery may be applied in all investigations and adjudications under the bill and not simply to an investigation involving violations of the law.[470] Under the FMC's Rule 131, a subpoena for the attendance of witnesses or for the production of evidence shall be issued by a presiding officer upon request of any party without notice to any other party. The person to whom the subpoena is directed may, under Rule 132, by motion with notice to the party requesting the subpoena, petition to quash or modify the subpoena.[471]

Section 13—Penalties[472]

This section has made several changes in the 1916 Act. For a violation of certain provisions of that Act, a person would be guilty of a misdemeanor punishable by a fine not to exceed $5,000.[473] The 1984 Act has eliminated any provision for a criminal penalty. Both laws authorized civil penalties. Under the earlier act, a violation of specified provisions could result in a civil penalty of $5,000 for each violation and $1,000 for each day that any order, rule, or regulation of the FMC was violated.[474] Under section 13(a) of the 1984 Act, an unintentional violation of any of its provisions or a regulation or Commission order may result in a civil penalty not to exceed $5,000 for each violation. There is no distinction in the Act as to whether the violation involves a substantive provision of the law or a regulation or order issued thereunder.

For a violation "willfully and knowingly" committed, a civil penalty may, under section 13(a), be as much as $25,000 for each offense.[475] "Willfully and knowingly" can mean deliberately and purposefully or intentionally or it can mean conduct which shows a continuing pattern of indifference to the requirements of the law.[476] In determining the amount of a penalty, the FMC shall under section 13(c) consider the gravity of the offense, the degree of culpability of the violation, history of prior offenses, ability to pay, and such other matters as justice may require.[477]

Section 13(b)(1) provides for additional penalties. If a carrier charges more or less than as shown in the tariff; rebates, extends, or denies a privilege or facility not tariffed; allows transportation at less than tariff rates by a fraud or concealment; or offers or pays a deferred rebate, the FMC may suspend the tariff of the common carrier (either a vessel or non-vessel-operating carrier) or a vessel operator's right to use a tariff of a conference of which it is a member for a period not to exceed twelve months. Upon a failure to supply information ordered to be produced or compelled by a subpoena, the FMC may, under section 13(b)(2), after notice and an opportunity for hearing, suspend any tariff of the carrier or its right to use any conference tariff.

Section 13(b)(3) states that a common carrier accepting or handling cargo for carriage under a tariff that has been suspended, or after its right to utilize that tariff has been suspended, is subject to a civil penalty of not more than $50,000 for each shipment, the heaviest civil penalty in the law.

Section 13(b)(4) deals with a failure by a carrier to comply with a subpoena or discovery order to produce documents or information. If in defense the carrier alleges that documents or information are located in a foreign country and cannot be produced because of the laws of that country, the Commission shall immediately so notify the Secretary of State. Thereupon, the Secretary of State shall promptly consult with the government of the nation within which the documents or information are alleged to be located for the purpose of assisting the Commission in obtaining the documents or information sought.

Section 13(b)(5) deals with restrictions imposed upon a U.S. flag carrier in a "foreign-to-foreign" movement, that is, a movement between two foreign ports. If, after notice and hearing, the Commission finds that action of a common carrier, acting alone or in concert with any person or a foreign government, has unduly impaired access of a vessel documented under the laws of the United States to ocean trade between foreign ports, the Commission shall take action that it finds appropriate, including the imposition of any of the penalties authorized under paragraphs (b)(1), (2), and (3) of this section 13. Under section 13(b)(6), before an FMC order under section 13(b)(5) becomes effective, it must be submitted to the President for review. He may disapprove the order for reasons of national defense or U.S. foreign policy.

In Rule 587.2 the FMC has spelled out various facts indicating conditions which would unduly impair the access of a U.S. flag vessel, whether liner, bulk, tramp, or other vessel, to "ocean trade between foreign ports," which includes intermodal movements.[478] They include, but are not limited to, (a) imposition upon U.S. flag vessels or shippers or consignees using such vessels, fees, charges, or restrictions different from those imposed on national flag or other vessels, or which preclude a U.S. flag vessel from competing in the trade on the same basis as any other vessel; (b) reservation of a substantial portion of the total cargo in the trade to national-flag or other vessels, which results in a failure to provide reasonable competitive access to cargoes by U.S. flag vessels; (c) use of predatory practices, including but not limited to, closed conferences employing fighting ships or deferred rebates, which unduly impair access of a U.S. flag vessel to the trade; (d) any government or commercial practice that results in unequal or unfair opportunity for U.S. flag vessel access to port or intermodal facilities or services related to the carriage of cargo inland to or from ports in the trade; (e) any other practice which unduly impairs access of a U.S. flag vessel to trade between foreign ports.

Section 13(d) authorizes a person against whom a civil penalty was assessed to obtain a review thereof under Chapter 158 of Title 28, U.S. Code.

Under section 13(e), if a person fails to pay an assessment of a civil penalty, the Attorney General, at the request of the Commission, may seek to recover the amount assessed in an appropriate district court of the United States. In such action the court shall enforce the Commission's order unless it finds that the order was not regularly made or duly issued.

Section 13(f)(1) eliminates a conspiracy prosecution, a misdemeanor, for certain acts: violations of section 10(a)(1), a "person" getting a lower rate by deception or fraud; section 10(b)(1), a carrier charging a higher or lower rate than the tariff provides; section 10(b)(4), allowing a person by deception or fraud to obtain a lower than tariff rate; or defrauding the government by concealing any such violation. A conspiracy prosecution is, however, still possible for violations of other sections of the Act.[479]

Subsection 13(f)(2) provides that each proceeding to assess a civil penalty under this section shall be commenced within five years from the date the violation occurred. A question arises as to precisely when a violation does in fact occur. The FMC has held that the determination of this question for the purpose of assessing a civil penalty takes into account the last act performed in violation of the statute. Thus, a violation of the Act could occur upon the payment of ocean freight at less than the applicable rates.[480]

While the foregoing provisions of section 13 are primarily directed against common carriers, an individual or corporate entity not a common carrier may also have a penalty imposed under this section. Section 13(a) provides that "whoever" violates a provision of the Act is liable to the United States for a civil penalty. As previously noted under section 10(a)(1), "no person" may knowingly and willfully obtain transportation by a fraud or concealment at less than the applicable tariff rate. Thus, a shipper or other person within the purview of section 10(a)(1) may become subject to the penalty provisions of section 13.

Is a corporate official immune from the imposition of a civil penalty merely because the violations were made by the corporation? In a 1987 case the Commission considered whether it was empowered to impose a civil penalty for violation of our shipping laws not only upon the corporation itself, but upon the officers and possibly the directors as well. The FMC noted that it would not consider the abandonment and dissolution of a corporation as a mitigating circumstance or allow it otherwise to be used as a shield for egregious violations of law. It warned that in future cases the FMC would carefully scrutinize the record for appropriate factual and legal bases to impose individual liability for civil penalties on corporate officials engaged in illegal conduct.[481]

Following this warning, later in the same year, the FMC extended its jurisdiction by imposing, for the first time, heavy civil penalties upon the officers of an NVOCC. It noted that, based upon the number of different devices and corporate screens used and the lengthy period of time over which they continued, there was a sufficient basis to conclude that the individual officers had engaged in "knowing and willful" violations.

Under these circumstances the FMC held that it was appropriate to "pierce the corporate veil" in order to prevent such use of the corporate device to commit fraud and statutory violations.[482]

In a 1990 case the FMC appears to have retreated somewhat from its 1987 holding that corporate officers may be individually subject to civil penalties. It stated that the contention that the Commission may exercise discretion in deciding whether "nonregulated persons" are "responsible" for violations actually contradicts section 11(g), which requires the Commission to award reparations only for "actual injury" caused by violations. Equitable considerations requiring the exercise of the Commission's discretion only arise, the FMC noted, when damages beyond actual harm are sought under the special provisions of section 11(g), but nothing in the statute indicates that this discretion may be employed to "commandeer" someone outside the Act.[483]

Since the prohibitions in section 10(b) apply to "common carriers," an officer thereof not being a carrier, it would appear from the above 1990 decision that the officer, being a nonregulated person, cannot violate the 1984 Act, and accordingly may not be "commandeered" to pay a civil penalty. When Congress wishes to impose a statutory responsibility upon a corporate officer, it knows how to do it. For example, section 15(a) of the 1984 Act provides that the Commission "may require any common carrier, or any officer . . . thereof" to file a periodic report. The prohibited acts in section 10(b) apply only to a "common carrier," but impose no duty upon any officer thereof. When the penalty for a single offense may be as much as $50,000 for each shipment,[484] it seems clear that the liability of a corporate officer must be unequivocally set forth in the law and not be left to inference.

Section 14—Commission Orders [485]

This section carries forward with no substantive change the provisions contained in sections 23, 25, 29, and 30 of the 1916 Act.[486] Section 14(a) provides that orders of the Commission relating to a violation of the 1984 Act or a regulation issued thereunder shall be made upon sworn complaint or on its own motion, only after opportunity for hearing. An "order" within this section is one duly issued after hearing upon complaint and answer, or which the agency issued on its own motion after first having instituted an inquiry into the matter.[487] Where the question to be determined by the Commission is one of law, it may properly be decided without providing the respondent with a full-trial type evidentiary hearing.[488]

Subsection 14(b) states that the agency may reverse, suspend, or modify any order made by it, and upon application of any party to a proceeding it may grant a rehearing of the same or any matter determined herein. A proceeding should not be reopened except for "unusual or weighty reasons."[489] Nevertheless, it is within the province of the Commission to review its conclusions in light of a more complete and accurate understanding of the underlying facts.[490] The fact that an FMC decision is on appeal does not automatically bar the agency from reopening the proceeding.[491]

Subsection 14(c) provides that in case of a violation of an order of the Commission, or for failure to comply with a Commission's subpoena, the Attorney General, at the request of the Commission, or any party injured by the violation, may seek enforcement by a U.S. district court having jurisdiction over the parties. If, after hearing, the court determines that the order was properly made and duly issued, it shall enforce the order by an appropriate injunction or other process, mandatory or otherwise.

A district court errs when it requires a conclusive showing of the Commission's jurisdiction over an investigation before the court will enforce discovery orders of an administrative law judge; the court's function is, rather, to determine whether the discovery orders were regularly made and duly issued and, if they were, to enforce obedience by writ of injunction or other proper process.[492] The words "or other process" in section 14(c) authorizing the court to enforce obedience of an order of the FMC by an appropriate injunction or other process, mean that a federal district court may fashion its enforcement proceedings according to the nature of the specific order for which enforcement is sought.[493]

Section 14(d)(1) states that in case of a violation of a Commission order for the payment of reparation, the person to whom the award was made may seek enforcement of the order in a U.S. district court having jurisdiction of the parties. This section does not authorize the maintenance of an action in a district court against the FMC to review its decision denying reparation under this section for alleged discriminatory charges and practices. Such review is exclusively in the U.S. Court of Appeals.[494]

Section 14(d)(2) provides that in a U.S. district court the findings and order of the Commission shall be prima facie evidence of the facts therein stated. The petitioner in the district court who prevails shall be allowed reasonable attorney's fees to be assessed and collected as part of the costs of the suit. Where the findings of the FMC are supported by substantial evidence, and where no new evidence on the subject is introduced by either party at the trial, it is the duty of the court to accept and give such findings effect.[495]

Section 14(d)(3) states that all parties in whose favor the Commission has made an award of reparation by a single order may be joined as plaintiffs, and all other parties in the order may be joined as defendants in a single suit in a district court in which any one plaintiff could maintain a suit against any one defendant. Judgment may be entered in favor of any plaintiff against the defendant liable to that plaintiff.

Under section 14(e) an action seeking enforcement of a Commission order must be filed within three years after the date of the violation of the order. However, the United States is exempt from statutes of limitations and defenses of laches, unless Congress provides otherwise.[496]

Upon petition and in its discretion the FMC may issue a declaratory order "to terminate a controversy or to remove uncertainty." The matters involved must be conducted or actively regulated by the Commission under statutes administered by it, and the declaratory order procedure shall be invoked solely for the purpose of a ruling which will allow a person to act without peril upon their own view. A petition may not be filed involving an allegation of violation for which a coercive ruling or cease and desist order is sought.[497]

It is generally inappropriate for the FMC to "terminate" a controversy on a pending adjudicatory proceeding.[498] There must be a dispute which calls not for an advisory opinion upon a hypothetical basis, but for an adjudication of a present right upon established facts of sufficient immediacy and reality to warrant the issuance of a declaratory judgment.[499]

Section 15—Reports and Certificates

In its report on a predecessor bill, S.504, the Senate Commerce Committee stated that this section carries forward "without substantive change" the provisions of section 21 of the 1916 Act.[500] In the past the Commission made extensive use of its authority to request a "Section 21 Report" from carriers, terminal operators, and forwarders.[501]

Section 15(a) states that the Commission may require any common carrier, or any officer, receiver, trustee, lessee, agent, or employee thereof, to file with it any periodical or special report or any account, record, rate or charge, or memorandum of any facts or transactions appertaining to the business of that common carrier. The report, etc., shall be made under oath whenever the Commission so requires and shall be furnished in the form and within the time prescribed by the Commission.[502]

It is perhaps not entirely correct, as noted above, for Congress to note in the legislative history that section 15 of the 1984 Act carries over the section 21 provisions of the 1916 Act "without substantive change." Under section 21, the authority to demand a report included not only common carriers by water but also, importantly, "other persons" subject to the 1916 Act, which encompassed one carrying on the business of forwarding or furnishing wharfage, dock, warehouse, or other terminal facilities. Section 15(a) excludes the authority to demand a report from forwarders or terminal operators.

The FMC's Rule 288 states that the agency may issue an order requiring a person to file a report or answers in writing to specific questions relating to "any matter under investigation."[503] It has been held that section 21 of the 1916 Act may be employed to obtain information to be used in a contested matter before the agency in which it is asserted that the law has been violated,[504] and that this section is applicable when the FMC seeks information relevant to its enforcement power as well as its regulatory power.[505] But suppose that a report requested is not for "any matter under investigation," as the above Rule 288 provides, and is sought merely to gather information. It would appear that the FMC is not limited to an investigation under way as the basis to require a report, section 15(a) making it clear that the FMC's authority extends to seeking information on "any acts and transactions appertaining to the business of that common carrier."

An order issued by the FMC requiring a line to file with it a summary of its books and records does not constitute an unconstitutional search and seizure since it does not call for the production or inspection of the line's books or records.[506] The agency must, however, lay a proper foundation for an order requiring a line to file the divisions of its joint through rates.[507] An FMC order requiring a report by a carrier is fatally defective if it does not state the purpose for which the information is being demanded.[508]

Under section 15(b) the FMC shall require the chief executive officer of every common carrier (VOCC or NVOCC) and to the extent deemed feasible by the FMC, it may require any shipper, shippers' association, terminal operator, freight forwarder, or broker to file a periodic written certification under oath attesting to a policy prohibiting the payment, solicitation, or receipt of any unlawful rebate.[509] A forwarder failing to file a timely anti-rebate certification may, after notice, have its license suspended.[510] Similarly, a common carrier failing to make a timely filing will have its tariff(s) cancelled and attempted filings rejected.[511] Furthermore, if such carrier's rates are published in a conference tariff, its name will be stricken from the list of carriers participating in such tariff.[512] Where a single firm operates in more than one capacity, such as both an NVOCC and a forwarder, a single anti-rebate certificate is authorized.[513] In 1992 the FMC amended its rules from an annual to a two year filing requirement for such certifications by carriers and forwarders.[514] Although authorized by section 15(b), the FMC has not required anti-rebate certifications from shippers, shippers' associations, or terminals.

Section 15 contains another substantive change which appears not to have been treated in the legislative history. The third sentence of section 15(a) states that "[c]onference minutes required to be filed with the Commission under this section shall not be released to third parties or published by the Commission." The FMC's rules provide that with exceptions relating to particular types of rates, and purely administrative matters, a conference in its minutes must describe "all matters within the scope of the agreement which are discussed or considered" at any meeting and shall indicate the action taken.[515] Shippers, forwarders, and others who may be significantly impacted by a particular conference action thus had available under the 1916 Act information as to subject matters discussed and the basis for the action taken. By prohibiting the release of copies of the minutes or their publication, Congress in the 1984 Act has made it much more difficult for persons affected by conference action to protect their interests. Precisely why the equivalent of a military "top secret" status should be granted to the minutes of carriers enjoying antitrust immunity appears not to have been explained in the legislative history and is of dubious merit.

Section 16—Exemptions [516]

This section authorizes the Commission, upon application or on its own motion, by order or rule, to exempt for the future any class of agreements between persons subject to the 1984 Act or any specified activity of those persons from any requirement of the Act if it finds that the exemption will not "substantially impair effective regulation by the Commission, be unjustly discriminatory, result in a substantial reduction in competition, or be detrimental to commerce." The Commission may attach conditions to any exemption and may, by order, revoke any exemption. No order or rule of exemption or revocation of exemption may be issued unless opportunity for hearing has been afforded interested persons and departments and agencies of the United States.

This section carriers forward the provisions of section 35 of the 1916 Act.[517] The earlier Act was expanded in section 16 by conferring an opportunity to be heard not only to "interested persons" but also to departments and agencies of the United States, the latter not having been specifically included in the 1916 Act. In a discussion of a predecessor bill, S.504, the Senate Commerce Committee noted that the exemption power conferred in section 16 upon the Commission was consistent with the objectives of the bill to minimize government intervention in and supervision of international liner shipping whenever not inconsistent with other goals of the law. The power to exempt may also prove useful in the event of conflict of laws where a trading partner also regulates the trade regulated by the Act.[518]

The FMC may exempt "by order or rule." While the FMC must afford interested parties or government agencies an opportunity for a hearing, as previously noted, a trial-type evidentiary hearing is not always required. Where there are no disputes as to the material facts, an appropriate hearing may consist of the filing of briefs or memoranda of law. In the usual case, the Commission affords interested parties an opportunity for hearing by the publication in the Federal Register of an invitation to submit comments, protests, or requests for hearing.[519]

The 1984 Act contains two types of exemptions. One is statutory. For example, section 3(6)(b), Definitions, states that a ferry boat, ocean tramp, or chemical parcel-tanker are not covered under the definition of "common carrier." So too, section 8(a)(1) excepts from tariff filing by a common carrier of certain types of cargo, such as bulk cargo, forest products, recycled metal scrap, waste paper, and paper waste. Exemptions may also be granted by regulation. Thus, the FMC has exempted transportation of cargo between foreign countries, including transshipments from one carrier to another at a U.S. port.[520] Also exempted from the tariff filing requirement of the Act are services involving transportation between various U.S. and Canadian ports[521] and controlled common carriers meeting specified requirements.[522]

A person manifestly subject to the FMC's jurisdiction may not so segment its operation as to make part of it subject and part of it exempt when this segmentation is unjustly discriminatory.[523] A port authority is not exempt from regulation by the FMC under the Act by reason of its status as a political subdivision.[524] Marine terminal agreements (other than marine terminal conference, interconference, joint venture, and discussion agreements) are exempted from the waiting period requirement of the 1984 Act.[525]

Section 17—Regulations [526]

Section 17(a) states that the Commission "may prescribe rules and regulations as necessary to carry out" the 1984 Act. This subsection is virtually identical to the FMC's rulemaking authority in section 43 of the 1916 Act, which provided that "the Commission shall make such rules and regulations as may be necessary to carry out the provisions of this Act."[527]

Under the earlier Act, litigation ensued through the years as to the extent of the FMC's authority to regulate persons subject to the law. The issue under section 43 of the 1916 Act and currently under section 17 of the 1984 Act is whether the agency has authority to regulate the conduct of persons subject to the Act when the rule itself is not based upon a substantive provision of the law. Neither the FMC nor the courts have definitively settled this question. In an early case the FMC held that its rulemaking power was to be used "only where necessary to carry out a statutory power, duty, or function. Failing the power, duty or function, the jurisdiction to adopt rules cannot exist."[528] But the FMC's more recent view is that it is authorized under section 17 to adopt rules in subject areas or involving practices not specifically within the scope of a substantive provision of the Act.[529]

The federal appellate courts have not been consistent in interpreting the extent of the agency's rulemaking power. In 1965, the U.S. Court of Appeals for the District of Columbia Circuit, the major reviewer of administrative agency actions, held that the Commission may only adopt rules necessary for substantive regulation under the Act.[530] Two years later, however, the same court held that in carrying out its responsibility to enforce overall objectives of the law, the FMC is authorized to promulgate rules in regard to matters not specifically covered by substantive provisions in the Act.[531] To compound the confusion, in a more recent case (1978), that same circuit held that "the Commission . . . cannot expand by its own regulations the power given it by Congress . . ."[532]

In a 1990 decision involving the 50-Mile Rule, treated below, the FMC appears to have drawn back from its position that it has authority to promulgate a rule without basis in a substantive provision of the law. In response to the argument that the exercise of authority over a respondent in that proceeding need not be based upon "any affirmative grant of statutory power," the Commission said:

> This extraordinary proposal that agencies can wield any power not specifically withheld from them flouts a number of long standing tenets of administrative law. The Commission is not a court, and cannot rely . . . on the powers of a court of equity. On the contrary, the law is settled that an administrative agency can exercise only those powers conferred upon it by Congress. (citations omitted) Even if an agency is confronted by a new malpractice that it believes ought to be stopped, it may not justify reaching the malfeasor by references to its statute's general policies, if that results from a circumvention of the limits on its jurisdiction created by the statute's language and legislative history. (citation omitted). Lacunae in a statute may well be the result of a deliberate Congressional decision not to include a particular type of entity or activity, perhaps as part of the compromise process

that frequently underlies legislation. (citation omitted). Liberal, purpose-driven readings of the Shipping Acts are justified and desirable where a particular provision is broadly written, thus signifying an intention by Congress that Commission jurisdiction should not be narrowly construed. (citations omitted). But in the absence of authority grounded in the statute, the Commission may not assume that Congress, if asked, would have wished it to close a particular jurisdictional loophole (citations omitted). In sum, the decision to regulate always must be made by Congress in the first instance pursuant to its power under the Commerce Clause of the Constitution. *An agency's authority to act must be the result of a positive delegation from Congress,* (citations omitted) *and any powers not reasonably derivative from that delegation are reserved to Congress* (emphasis added).[533]

As the above forceful quotation indicates, it appears that the better view of the FMC's rulemaking authority is that it may not adopt a rule governing a particular practice of a regulated person in an area where Congress has not statutorily established the standard of conduct to be observed. Were the law otherwise, the agency would be acting as a court of equity, as noted above by the FMC, with the right to regulate any and all conduct that it deems a desirable subject of government control. An administrative agency, after all, "administers" a statute, and when it seeks to regulate conduct without a "positive delegation from Congress," it is no longer administering—it is legislating.

Recently (1992), Congress enacted the Negotiated Rulemaking Act ("Reg-Neg"),[534] which the FMC has described as "an alternate process under which the agency may establish and administer committees for the development of consensus positions regarding regulation and policies." After a review of the statute's purpose,[535] the agency added a new regulation, entitled "Negotiated Rulemaking," which provides that the FMC, either upon petition of interested persons or upon its own motion, may establish a negotiated rulemaking committee to negotiate and develop consensus on a proposed rule, if the use of such a committee is determined by the agency to be in the public interest.[536]

The new law and corresponding regulation is a salutary development. It is time-consuming, costly, and difficult for interested parties to reconcile their differences in a formal rulemaking docket. Negotiations between such parties and the FMC staff may result in a rule, or a decision that no rule is required, that would best serve the interests of all concerned. In addition, costly appeals before busy appellate judges faced with highly technical facts difficult to absorb within a limited time will be avoided. Hopefully, Reg-Neg will substantially alleviate the cumbersome and expensive procedure that has burdened the regulated segments of our ocean transportation, the agency, and the courts.

Section 18—Agency Reports and Advisory Commission [537]

Section 18(a) provided that for a period of five years after passage of the 1984 Act, the FMC shall collect and analyze information concerning the impact of the Act upon the international ocean shipping industry, including data on the level of tariffs; changes in the type of common carrier services available; the number and strength of independent carriers in various trades; and the length of time, frequency, and cost of major types of regulatory proceedings. Under section 18(b), the Commission shall consult with the Department of Transportation (DOT), the Department of Justice (DOJ), and the Federal Trade Commission (FTC) annually concerning the FMC's data collection.

Section 18(c) required the FMC within six months after the five-year period to report the information to the Advisory Commission on Conferences in Ocean Shipping (ACCOS) and to the DOT, DOJ, and FTC. Within sixty days thereafter, these agencies shall furnish their analysis of the impact of the Act to Congress and ACCOS. The reports required by this section would specifically address the advisability of adopting a system of tariffs based on volume and mass of shipment, the need for antitrust immunity for ports and marine terminals, and the continuing need for the requirement of tariff filing and enforcement by the FMC.

Section 18(d) establishes ACCOS consisting of seventeen members: a cabinet member official appointed by the President, four members of the U.S. Senate equally divided between the Senate Commerce and Judiciary Committees, four members from the House of Representatives equally divided between the House Merchant Marine and Judiciary Committees, and eight members from the private sector appointed by the President. Section 18(f) requires ACCOS to conduct a comprehensive study of, and make recommendations concerning conferences in ocean shipping, the study being specifically directed to address whether the nation would best be served by prohibiting conferences or by closed or open conferences. Section 18(h) directs ACCOS to submit its report within one year after its establishment to the President and to the Congress, containing a statement of the findings and conclusions by majority vote, including recommendations for such administrative, judicial, and legislative actions as it deems advisable.

The conferees recognized that their bill, S.47, ultimately enacted as the 1984 Act, was not "an expression of a new policy with respect to agreements among competing carriers in international ocean carriage."[538]

Reliable empirical data about trends and practices in the industry would be valuable in weighing the effectiveness of the reforms that the Act would implement. It was felt that a period of time should elapse before further consideration of the Shipping Act in order to collect information on the effects of the new law. ACCOS was to focus on the single largest question underlying the Shipping Act—whether the nation will best be served by closed conferences, open conferences, or prohibiting conferences. In addition, the conferees expected ACCOS to address other important issues raised during the consideration of S.47, including but not limited to (1) whether tariff filing, and its accompanying enforcement by the FMC, should be continued, and (2) whether independent action should be authorized on service contracts.[539]

ACCOS was established on April 10, 1991, and submitted its report one year later. Over one hundred witnesses were heard during hearings around the country and there were in-depth interviews with approximately 120 industry representatives supplemental to the information provided to ACCOS by the government agencies.

The chairman of ACCOS, the Secretary of Transportation, noted in his letter of transmittal to the President that the report contained an analysis of the major issues that have arisen in connection with ocean shipping conferences, and that the views of interested parties who appeared before ACCOS were set forth. The report also noted that under section 18(f), its mission was to conduct a comprehensive study of and make recommendations concerning conferences in ocean shipping, and that ACCOS should specifically address whether the nation would best be served by prohibiting conferences, or by closed or open conferences. In its performance of this duty, ACCOS stated that it identified the following four issues for review:

1. Antitrust Immunity. It explored the probable consequences of continuing, revising, or eliminating the grant of antitrust immunity to conferences.
2. Open or closed conferences. ACCOS addressed whether conferences served the national interest by being open or closed.
3. Tariffs and service contracts. These areas were "reviewed" to determine their benefits and costs to carriers, shippers, and intermediaries.
4. Relations of conferences with shippers and transportation intermediaries. ACCOS noted that any assessment of the conference system would need also to examine the relationship of conferences to shippers, NVOCCS, freight forwarders, and others who are an integral part of the international ocean liner shipping industry.[540]

After summarizing in detail the views of the interested parties, ACCOS concluded:

> After a considerable amount of discussion, debate and deliberation, the Commissioners recognized that no meaningful consensus on the major issues would be reached. Therefore, the Report does not include conclusions or recommendations. The Report does, however, provide a comprehensive review of the issues considered by the Commission based upon the views and recommendations of shipper, carrier, conference, and intermediary representatives who testified before or were interviewed by the Commission. In addition, individual Commissioners have provided separate statements highlighting certain significant issues in international ocean liner shipping and changes, if any, they would recommend to the current regulatory structure.[541]

It appears regrettable that after a tremendous investment of time, effort, and money by the ACCOS members, its staff, and the government agencies involved (FMC, DOT, DOJ, and FTC), together with the extensive input from interested persons, ACCOS failed to comply with the statutory mandate that it "make recommendations concerning conferences in ocean shipping."[542]

In retrospect, however, it appears likely that the entire project was doomed to failure. It could hardly be reasonably anticipated that the chairman of ACCOS, the Secretary of Transportation, would agree to precise recommendations on far-reaching legislative changes in the 1984 Act without seeking a consensus from other executive departments involved and White House clearance. Similarly, the House and Senate members of ACCOS from the Merchant Marine and Judiciary Committees should not have been expected to lock themselves into fixed positions on controversial issues without consultation with members of their respective committees and approval of House and Senate leadership. With respect to the industry members of ACCOS, it was doubtful whether they could make a significant contribution on the many issues before ACCOS not involving their own particular interests. This being so, it is not surprising that ACCOS could not reach a "meaningful consensus" or make recommendations, as mandated.

The conferees' idea of a review of the effectiveness of the 1984 Act after the expiration of a reasonable period of time had merit, but it was too much to expect concrete recommendations by ACCOS as established. Perhaps a better approach would have been for a study of this sort to have been conducted by nonpartisan, competent people from the private sector with no interest in the outcome.

Section 19—Ocean Freight Forwarders[543]

This section deals with (1) the licensing of ocean freight forwarders, (2) the authority of the Commission to suspend or revoke a license, (3) the exception to the requirement of licensing, and (4) compensation of forwarders by carriers. These subjects, as well as an in-depth treatment of the statutory and regulatory aspects of a forwarder's activities, including relationships with shippers, carriers, and others, will be treated in Chapter VI.

Section 20—Contracts, Agreements, and Licenses Under Prior
Shipping Legislation[544]

The basic purpose of this section is to preserve various rights that had been enjoyed by regulated persons under the 1916 Act. Section 20(d) provides that all agreements and exemptions previously approved or licenses previously issued by the FMC would continue in force and effect as if approved or issued under the 1984 Act. All new agreements, etc., are to be considered under that Act.

Section 20(e), Savings Provisions, preserves other rights. In section 20(e)(1) a service contract between a shipper and carrier entered into before March 20, 1984, the effective date of the 1984 Act, will remain in full force and effect and need not comply for fifteen months after the effective date with the detailed requirements of section 8 of the Act.

Section 20(e)(2)(A) states that the Act and the amendments made by it shall not affect any suit filed before March 20, 1984. Soon after the 1984 Act became effective, the FMC announced that section 20(e)(2)(A) applied to suits with respect to claims arising out of conduct engaged in prior to the Act, but had no application to cases pending before the Commission.[545] The U.S. Court of Appeals has held that the Commission interpretation of section 20(e)(2)(A) was intended only to preserve antitrust actions and not to cases pending before the Commission. The court further stated that since the Commission is charged with the administration of the 1984 Act, its interpretation of the Act is entitled to considerable deference.[546] This section has been held "to share characteristics of both the jurisdictional savings provision and the traditional statute of limitations."[547]

In connection with section 20(e)(2)(A) dealing with proceedings filed before March 20, 1984, a question arose as to whether the 1916 or the 1984 Act would apply. In its May 15, 1984 Notice, the FMC advised that proceedings pending at the time the 1984 Act went into effect would be decided under the 1984 Act rather than the 1916 Act. Exceptions to this policy would be considered under the general rule established by the U.S. Supreme Court, known as the "Bradley Doctrine."[548] Under this doctrine cases are to be determined according to the law as it exists at the time a final decision is issued unless doing so would result in a manifest injustice or there is a statutory directive or legislative history to the contrary.

The application of the Bradley Doctrine was considered by the U.S. Court of Appeals in a 1990 antitrust case.[549] This appeal involved an antitrust suit by ocean freight forwarders against certain steamship lines, asserting, inter alia, that the denial of compensation (brokerage) by the lines to forwarders on surcharge revenue violated the provisions of section 10(c)(5) of the 1984 Act. That section provides that no conference or group of two or more carriers may deny in the export foreign commerce of the United States compensation to an ocean freight forwarder or limit the compensation to less than a reasonable amount. The forwarders urged that this provision of the 1984 Act be applied by the court in its consideration as to whether the lines concertedly denied brokerage on surcharges received by the lines as additional freight revenue.

In rejecting the application of section 10(c)(5) of the 1984 Act, the court cited section 20(e)(2)(A) providing that the Act would not "affect any suit filed before" its effective date. According to the court, this language precluded the application of the Bradley Doctrine.[550] The suit having been filed before the enactment of the 1984 Act, its terms would not apply. The court appears to have plainly erred. Section 20(e)(2)(A) was intended only to allow the continuance of lawsuits filed before the 1984 Act became law. "The intent of this savings provision is to permit such suits to continue to conclusion as if the legislation were never enacted."[551] The provision "precludes interference with suits" filed prior to the enactment of the 1984 Act.[552] This legislative history makes it clear beyond doubt that the provision's purpose was in no way related to the question as to the applicability of the Bradley Doctrine, as the court held, but only to preserve lawsuits begun before the Act was passed.

Section 23—Bonding of Non-Vessel-Operating Common Carriers[553]

This section deals with the bonding of NVOCCs and covers the nature of the bond, claims against it, the designation of a resident agent in the United States by an NVOCC not U.S. domiciled, and the suspension or cancellation of an NVOCC tariff for failure to maintain the required bond. These provisions, as well as an overall treatment of an NVOCC's statutory responsibilities, are covered in Chapter V.

CHAPTER III

SHIPPERS

Introduction

Section 3(23) of the 1984 Act defines a shipper as "an owner or person for whose account the ocean transportation of cargo was provided or other person for whom delivery is to be made."[1] Defined somewhat differently, a shipper is a person for whom the owner of a ship agrees to carry goods to a specified destination at a specified price and is also known as a "consignor."[2] The FMC considers a container shipper to be "small" if the firm annually ships 100 TEUs or less, a medium shipper is one who ships between 101 TEUs and 2000 TEUs yearly, and a large shipper is one whose total shipments are over 2000 TEUs annually.[3]

The 1984 Act had as its basic purpose, as did the 1916 Act, the protection of shippers moving cargo by ocean common carrier transportation. Almost every section of the 1984 Act in some form materially assists shippers in the U.S. foreign commerce. For example, a new rate or a change in an existing rate resulting in an increased cost to the shipper cannot become effective earlier than thirty days after filing with the FMC (§8(d)); section 10(b) prohibitions directed at common carriers are for the benefit of shippers; concerted action by carriers against shippers is significantly limited (§10(c)); ocean freight forwarders must be competent and financially responsible (§19); and NVOCCs must be bonded (§23).

Freight Charges

A rate is a carrier's compensation for the performance of a transportation service.[4] A charge is the segregated item of expense demanded by the carrier for any service in connection with transportation.[5] Wharfage, dockage, and wharf demurrage are transportation rates within the meaning of the Act.[6] The division of the total ocean freight charge into a basic tariff and a surcharge does not remove either part of the total from the general category of freight charges where both parts must necessarily be paid for the transportation of the items of cargo in question.[7] The "regular rate" for the transportation of a commodity is the rate appearing in the carrier's tariff, and none other. Any discounts from that rate or absorptions by the carrier of any charges which would normally be borne by the shipper must appear in the carrier's filed tariff.[8]

There are a number of factors that are considered in the making of a rate. One is the value of the goods shipped, but it is not the only element; the cost of the services rendered is also a factor.[9] Competition is an important element and in the usual sense involves three areas: price, quality, and service. However, since the 1916 and 1984 Acts contemplated the continued existence of price regulation by steamship conferences, the word "competition" as applied in these acts must be given a broad meaning. Competition in this sense is an elastic term not readily categorized or restricted in application.[10] Distance is another factor in formulating a rate which is reasonable for a shipper and yet profitable to a carrier. Other considerations in rating a commodity are density, fragility, stowage characteristics, similarity to other commodities, volume of movement, and possible problems in connection with stevedoring.[11]

In our domestic, offshore trades (e.g., Philippines, Guam), regulated under the 1916 Act, a common carrier is obligated to establish reasonable rates and regulations, and whenever the FMC finds that a rate or regulation is unjust and unreasonable, it may prescribe a just and reasonable maximum rate and regulation.[12] But no such authority exists with respect to the regulation of the U.S. foreign commerce under the 1984 Act.[13] Under the 1916 Act, the FMC held that it could disapprove any conference rate deemed to be unreasonably high or low.[14] Later, this authority was statutorily conferred,[15] but then repealed in the 1984 Act.[16]

Carrier Services

It is the duty of a carrier to issue an original bill of lading for each shipment.[17] The bill of lading provisions affecting transportation rates or the value of transportation service are not governing unless incorporated into the carrier's tariff.[18] A bill of lading is both a receipt and a contract, and under certain circumstances it is also documentary evidence of title to the goods.[19] A bill of lading, being a contract of adhesion, is to be strictly construed against the carrier.[20] The provisions in the bill of lading do not have the force of law merely because the document is filed with the FMC; only the required tariff has this effect. A clause in a bill of lading that is violative of public policy or an existing statute may be held unenforceable.[21]

In marine contracts the word "freight" is generally used to denote the remuneration to a carrier for the carriage of goods by ship, rather than the goods themselves.[22] A carrier has the fundamental right to demand and receive payment of freight charges as a condition precedent to transportation.[23] The courts usually look to the bill of lading provisions to determine whether a consignee has a contractual liability for freight charges. Whatever the exporter's obligations are under a contract of affreightment, a consignee becomes liable for the freight in accepting and exercising control over the goods.[24]

A shipper may ship any quantity it chooses and a carrier is obligated to accept the quantity tendered, due regard being had for the proper loading of the vessel and the available tonnage.[25] A shipper must make diligent inquiry where there is a question as to the classification of a commodity. Indifference by the shipper is tantamount to an outright and active violation of the Act.[26]

The rates of a carrier generally apply at ship's tackle, and the shipper has the duty, not the carrier, to bring its cargo alongside the vessel ready for shipment.[27] A carrier has a duty to mail an arrival notice to the consignee shown in the bill of lading and there may not be an extra charge for this service.[28] A carrier must also give a receipt for cargo received by it.[29] Under tackle-to-tackle rates, the carrier's duty to receive cargo does not arise until it is delivered to a point within reach of the ship's tackle.[30] A carrier must establish a reasonable plan to cope with periods of congestion and should exercise some care in avoiding continual overselling resulting in a refusal to honor a commitment.[31]

A carrier undertakes not only to transport but also to deliver the cargo to the consignee. A carrier should not leave goods exposed on the wharf and should store them in a place of safety and so notify the consignee at that period. At that point the carrier is no longer liable on its contract of affreightment.[32] A carrier is not obligated to make delivery to a consignee's place of business. It must "tender for delivery," and this obligation is met when it places the cargo on the dock reasonably accessible, properly segregated and marked, and leaves it there for a reasonable period to allow the consignee, after notice, to pick it up.[33] A tender is not proper if the goods are in a transit shed to which the consignee has no access.[34]

A carrier is required to allow free time to a shipper or consignee for the assembling of cargo or its removal from a pier.[35] The proper duration of free time is to be determined by applying the appropriate principles of maritime regulatory law to the circumstances pertaining to ocean transportation and ocean terminal facilities.[36] The allowance of free time is a "regulation or practice" under section 10(d) of the 1984 Act requiring just and reasonable practices by carriers.[37]

The weighing of cargo is not a carrier concern, but rather a transaction between the importer and customs. This being so, the delay involved not being attributable to the carrier, its failure to make allowance for the time consumed in weighing is not unjust or unreasonable.[38] So too, the need for cargo inspections or an assembly period is not a transportation condition sufficient to support extended free time for an ordinary shipper.[39] When a consignee has failed to pick up its cargo during free time and the cargo is in demurrage when a strike begins, strike storage may not be assessed against the vessel.[40] Whatever the justification for requiring a showing of a competitive relationship between shippers when determining the existence of a preference or prejudice in ocean freight rates, such a requirement cannot be justified when determining whether there is such preference or prejudice resulting from free time or free storage practices. The equality required in this situation is absolute and not conditioned on such things as competition, appropriate cause, and the like.[41]

Wharf demurrage is the charge accruing on cargo left in possession of the terminal beyond the free time period.[42] It is a rental charge made for the occupation of facilities until performance can be completed.[43] To be entitled to collect demurrage, the right to do so must clearly appear in the tariff regulations.[44] A consignee is not responsible for more than first-period demurrage when third-party action prevents the removal of the consignee's cargo.[45] During a longshoremen's strike, the penalty element of demurrage affords no incentive to remove cargo from the pier, because the consignee cannot do so for reasons entirely beyond its control. Accordingly, it would be an unreasonable practice to assess penal demurrage in this situation.[46] The demurrage rule promulgated by a carrier must in all instances be construed most favorably to the shipper. No demurrage is due by a carrier unless the delay in loading or unloading is clearly attributable to the fault of the shipper or consignee.[47]

A carrier has the right to declare an embargo when circumstances warranting such action are established. The necessity for placing an embargo is a matter to be determined in the first instance by the carrier. On the other hand, an embargo is an emergency measure to be resorted to only where there is congestion of traffic, or when it is impossible to transport the cargo because of the physical limitations of the carrier. During the existence of the embargo, a common carrier's obligations are suspended.[48] Our shipping laws confer no authority on the regulatory body to compel a carrier to continue a service.[49]

Refunds

Even though a tariff rule may provide that a claim for overcharges must be filed within one year from the payment of the freight, since section 11(g) provides that a complaint seeking reparations may be filed within three years after the cause of action accrued, it follows that a recovery is not barred by reason of the tariff's one year provision.[50] The fact that a rate charged is not shown to be unjust, unreasonable, or otherwise unlawful is not determinative of an application for a refund for an overcharge.[51] A complainant seeking reparations for overcharges must show either that it paid the freight or that it has succeeded to the claim by an assignment or other legitimate means.[52] The claimant has the burden of establishing by a preponderance of evidence that the carrier exacted charges for transportation in excess of those lawfully applicable.[53] Undercharges and overcharges arising under separate bills of lading are not permitted to be lumped together and netted out, for each bill of lading constitutes a separate transaction and must be treated as such.[54]

A settlement of an overcharge claim may only be approved on a finding that the settlement reflects a reasonable interpretation of the carrier's tariff, unless circumstances make such a finding unfeasible. Proponents of a settlement of a claim involving overcharges in violation of a carrier's tariff must:

1. submit a signed settlement statement;
2. file an affidavit setting forth the reasons for the settlement and stating that the settlement is a bona fide attempt to terminate the controversy;
3. establish that the complaint on its face presents a genuine dispute.[55]

Upon a petition of a complainant seeking reimbursement for an overcharge, the FMC shall direct reparations to the complainant for "actual injury" and also award the loss of interest at commercial rates compounded from the date of injury together with reasonable attorney's fees.[56] The rate of interest shall be computed on the basis of the average monthly rates on a six-month U.S. Treasury bill.[57] Upon petition, reasonable attorney's fees shall be awarded based upon the number of hours claimed and supported by evidence of the reasonableness of the hours claimed and the customary fees charged by attorneys in the community where the petitioner practices.[58]

Section 8(e) provides for a refund by a carrier to a shipper under specified circumstances.[59] The forerunner section was contained in section 18(b)(3) of the 1916 Act.[60] The FMC may, under the 1984 Act, permit a carrier to refund or waive a portion of the freight charges if (1) there is an error in a tariff of a clerical or administrative nature or due to an inadvertent failure to file a new tariff; (2) prior to filing an application for authority to make a refund, the carrier has filed a new tariff with the FMC setting the rate on which a refund or waiver would be based; (3) permission being granted by the agency, an appropriate notice will be published in the carrier's tariff and additional refunds or waivers shall be made with respect to other shipments; (4) the application for a refund or waiver is filed with the FMC within 180 days of the date of shipment.

To comply with section 8(e)(1), the critical element necessary to show that a carrier has made a mistake in tariff filing is a preshipment intent to change the tariff or to preserve a rate in the tariff. A carrier cannot decide *after* a shipment has begun that it wishes to reduce the applicable tariff rate for the shipment.[61] The fact that a carrier may be willing to accept a lower rate is not controlling.[62] To meet the requirement of section 8(e)(2), the carrier must, prior to filing an application for relief, file a new tariff setting forth the rate upon which the waiver or refund would be based.[63] This is true even though the carrier's failure to file a new rate falls on the shipper.

Section 8(e)(4) is unambiguous. The expression of an intent to file is irrelevant. Accordingly, after the expiration of the statutory period, 180 days from the date of shipment, the FMC no longer has any authority to grant the statutory relief provided.[64]

The refund provisions in section 8(e) do not confer authority to award reparations on "equity" grounds independent of any findings of a violation of the Act.[65] Section 8(e) allows for the filing of a rate which, because of a change in the method of compensation, varies slightly from the intended rate and is accepted by both parties.[66]

Shippers' Associations

As noted above in dealing with section 10(b)(13), *supra,* a shippers' association is defined in section 3(24) of the 1984 Act "as a group of shippers that consolidates or distributes freight on a non-profit basis for the members of the group in order to secure carload, truckload, or other volume rates or service contracts." In its 1992 Report ACCOS summarized the testimony concerning the current status of shippers' associations.

Two types of such associations are operating in the U.S. foreign liner trades. The first type only negotiates rates. While it may also negotiate service contracts with conferences and carriers in the name of the association on behalf of its participating members, the association's minimum volume commitment to the conference or carrier reflects the aggregate commitments made by the members of the association. They own the cargo and pay the ocean transportation costs directly to the carrier. The second type is a full-service shippers' association. It purchases transportation services for its members and arranges for the transportation of goods under service contracts or tariff rates. It is responsible for the payment of freight charges to the carrier and is reimbursed by the association members. The full-service shippers' association acts as a shipper in its relation with a common carrier and is named as such in the transportation documents.

Shippers' associations were intended to be a mechanism for allowing small or medium-sized shippers to use their joint buying power to obtain price discounts from ocean carriers and thereby place them in parity with larger shippers. As previously noted, the record of ACCOS reveals that although there are not as many shippers' associations operating in the marketplace today as had been anticipated, most of them have indicated great concern that conferences are not negotiating in good faith with them and are thereby undermining the role that associations could play. This is disputed by a managing director of one conference who advised ACCOS that the reason his group does not enter into service contracts is that the shippers' associations refuse to commit anything but a token amount of freight to a service contract.[67]

Carrier-Shipper Agreements

Section 8(c), for the first time, statutorily recognizes a service contract.[68] In section 3(21) a service contract "means a contract between the shipper and an ocean common carrier or conference in which the shipper makes a commitment to provide a certain minimum quantity of cargo over a fixed time period, and the ocean common carrier or conference commits to a certain rate or rate schedule as well as a defined service level—such as, assured space, transit time, port rotation, or similar service features." The contract may also specify provisions in the event of nonperformance on the part of either party.

Under section 8(c) an ocean common carrier (vessel operator) or conference may enter into a service contract with a shipper or shippers' association. Except for cargo excluded from tariff filing, each contract shall be filed confidentially with the FMC, and at the same time a concise statement of its essential terms shall also be filed and made available to the general public in tariff format. The essential terms shall be available to all shippers "similarly situated" and shall include (1) the origin and destination of port ranges in the case of port-to-port movements and the origin and destination geographic areas on through intermodal movements; (2) the commodities involved; (3) the minimum volume; (4) the line haul rate; (5) the duration; (6) service commitments; and (7) the liquidated damages for nonperformance, if any.

The legislative history of the 1984 Act indicates that the authority to use service contracts is not limited to those conferences that have loyalty contracts in effect; any common carrier or conference may use a service contract. It is expected that when a shipper desires to enter into such a contract with a conference, the proposal will be submitted to the entire conference membership for disposition.[69] A loyalty contract or a time-volume rate arrangement, each separately authorized in the 1984 Act, are not service contracts within the intended meaning of that term unless accompanied by a bona fide special service commitment by the contracting carrier that deviates from its general tariff obligation.[70]

The disclosure requirement in each "essential term" of a service contract must at the minimum inform other shippers of the rates and services available to them. Nor does the list of "essential terms" imply that a contract must contain each such term to be considered a service contract; it merely means that to the extent that such terms are included in the contract, they must be made public.[71]

Service contracts are specifically exempt from the prohibitions in sections 10(b)(6) dealing with unjust discrimination on rates, cargo classification, etc., and section 10(b)(11) prohibiting the giving of any unreasonable preference. This "except for service contracts" provision was explained in the conference report:

> Because service contracts will selectively favor some shippers, several of the proscribed acts (sections 10(b)(6) and (11)) were amended to assure that service contracts may discriminate as to rates and cargo classification and provide distinct advantages or preferences that might otherwise be in violation of the Act. Such differentials are the very nature of contract service.[72]

In Docket No. 84-21, the FMC concluded that it would not attempt to define what constitutes a similarly situated shipper "because it was a matter more appropriately resolved on a case-by-case basis."[73] The agency stated, however, that in the context of an access request to a service contract, the words "similarly situated shipper" mean a shipper "willing and able to meet all the essential terms of a particular contract." There need not be proof of a competitive relationship between the original contract shipper and an accessing shipper.

An NVOCC may not be precluded from attempting to access a service contract originally entered into with a proprietary interest shipper. There exists no basis to distinguish between NVOCCs and other shippers for the purpose of the section 8(c) access provision on the basis of cargo ownership. However, like any other accessing shipper, the NVOCC must establish its ability to fulfill the essential terms of a particular contract.[74]

A party seeking affirmative relief from the FMC has the initial burden of establishing a violation of the Act. Thus, a shipper claiming it was unlawfully denied access to a service contract has the burden of proving that it was indeed a similarly situated shipper. A shipper seeking to access a service contract is the party with the most relevant and reliable information as to its ability to meet the essential terms of the contract. Carriers may address access requests on an ad hoc basis and require relevant information only when they entertain doubts about an accessing shipper's abilities.[75]

There is nothing in the 1984 Act or its legislative history indicating that a nonparty to a service contract can receive the benefits of such a contract. The cargo of one NVOCC taking advantage of another NVOCC's service contract does not qualify as the cargo of the contracting NVOCC.[76] All persons or entities entitled to receive the service contract's non-tariff rates must be expressly named in the contract of carriage. Non-parties may take advantage of a service contract only if named as an "affiliate."[77]

A carrier offering service contracts under the 1984 Act should have the ability to protect its interest by agreeing to accept a performance bond from such a shipper. Thus, if a carrier entertains doubts about an accessing shipper's ability to meet all the essential terms of a service contract, the carrier could accept a performance bond in lieu of denying the access request. A carrier electing such a course of action must do so on a nondiscriminatory basis.[78]

Because of the common carriage aspects of service contracts, carriers lacking sufficient space must prorate their available space among con-tract shippers as an alternative to possibly acquiring additional capacity. If carriers offer service contracts, they should have reasonably available adequate space to meet the needs of all shippers similarly situated who attempt to access the contract. A carrier may have to charter other space or prorate its capacity among all its service contract shippers.[79]

The mutual termination of a service contract does not extinguish the rights of a shipper who has requested access prior to the termination of the contract. This is consistent with the intent of Congress to subject service contracts to some common carriage principles by making them available to all shippers similarly situated.[80]

Section 8(c) also provides that the exclusive remedy for breach of contract entered into under this section shall be an action in an appro-priate court, unless the parties otherwise agree. In Docket No. 92-38 a group of steamship lines filed a complaint with the FMC alleging that the service contract signatory had failed to ship the minimum cargoes required and, as a result, the lines were seeking damages calculated under the liquidated damages provisions on the ground that the signa-tories had violated section 10(a) of the Act in obtaining transportation at less than the tariff rates as a result of an unfair and unjust device. The complaints of the lines were dismissed by the FMC on the grounds that section 8(c) prevents parties to a service contract from raising issues under the 1984 Act in order to give the Commission jurisdiction to adjudicate what, in essence, is a private contractual dispute to be decided, as the statute requires, by a court, or as the parties agree.[81]

In Docket No. 91-17, a trade conference in the Pacific trade offered a new shippers' association a service contract with a $150 per container surcharge and refused to include a most-favored-shipper (MFS) clause after a detailed analysis of the facts. The FMC concluded that the failure of the conference to offer a service contract with MFS terms excluded was not a violation of sections 10(b)(12), undue prejudice, or 10(c)(1), unreasonable refusal to deal, of the 1984 Act. In so doing the agency set forth various principals that may serve as a guide. It noted that an MFS clause permits the rates in the service contract to be adjusted to or match the rates offered by the carrier in its tariffs or other service contracts, or rates offered by other carriers in the trade. An MFS clause is an advantage given to a shipper with whom the carrier has previously dealt on a mutually satisfactory basis. When viewed this way, there is nothing necessarily inappropriate about not extending an MFS clause to someone with whom one has not done business.

The FMC saw no reason why a carrier or conference should not be permitted to evaluate a shippers' association's ability to fulfill a service contract by examining certain factors relevant to the association. A prospective shipper or shippers' association's ability to fulfill the volume commitment and pay deadfreight damages is a legitimate concern for a carrier or conference in deciding whether to offer a contract in the first instance or impose certain contractual conditions to protect it from default. Service contracts are for the most part "private commercial arrangements" between two business entities. As such, the Commission does not and should not dictate their terms. The FMC found that any disadvantage incurred by the association in this docket as a result of its service contract negotiations with the conference was not "undue or unreasonable" in violation of section 10(b)(12) nor an "unreasonable" refusal to deal in violation of section 10(c)(1).[82]

In Docket No. 92-06 the agency dealt with the question of its jurisdiction to determine whether a service contract is subject to the provision in section 8(c) which provides that the exclusive remedy for a breach of the service contract shall be an action in an appropriate court unless the parties otherwise agree. This proceeding involved complaints filed by a number of shippers against a major conference in the Pacific trade. The shippers had agreed to ship a certain minimum quantity of cargo and the conference had agreed to supply sufficient space and equipment to carry the cargo at certain fixed rates. Upon the failure of the shippers to meet their minimum quantity commitments, the conference sought arbitration pursuant to the service contract. The shippers contended that the agreements were not service contracts as defined by section 3(21) of the 1984 Act because they did not contain a meaningful service commitment by the conference lines.

The shippers also defended on the ground that during the course of the contracts some of the member lines had filed independent action (IA) rates that were lower than the rates contained in the service contracts, and were thus in violation of various provisions of section 10 of the 1984 Act. The attempt by the conference to collect liquidated damages, the shippers further claimed, violated section 10(b)(1) of the Act. Article 9(ii) of the contract provided that if the service commitment of the lines was not met, the shipper's sole remedy shall be a reduction in the minimum quantity commitment of the contract.

The Commission held that a circular letter, discussed below, issued after the execution of the contracts, was prospective only.[83] In so holding the FMC indicated that chaos would have resulted if the Commission declared void ab initio any existing contract containing a clause purporting to limit the remedies of a shipper in the event of the carrier's failure to meet its service commitment. This did not mean, the FMC opined, that the shipper signatories were left without remedy. If the carrier failed to meet its service commitments, the shipper could sue for a breach of contract and a court or arbitrator could refuse to enforce a clause such as Article 9(ii).

The FMC concluded that it had jurisdiction to determine if the contracts were service contracts entered into under section 8(c) of the 1984 Act, and they so found despite the presence of the remedy clause. Nevertheless, the agency concluded, based on its prior decisions, that it was barred by section 8(c) of the 1984 Act from hearing the defense of the shippers since their remedy would be available in a breach of contract action if the matter were brought before a court.

The agency also held that the IA provisions of the Act, section 5(b)(8), granted to the member lines the absolute right to take IA on tariff matters on commodities that may be moved under the service contracts. The statutory right of IA on any rate or service item published in the tariff may not be infringed upon. The fact that the tariff rate for a given commodity differs from the rates shown in a service contract for the same commodity does not establish unjust discrimination under the 1984 Act. Service contracts are fundamentally different from tariff rates. A shipper signatory to such a contract receives a given level of service at a rate which is guaranteed for a fixed period of time. A tariff rate does not assure a given level of service and generally the rate may be increased at any time on thirty days' notice. Shippers are not entitled to the lowest rate possible because they are committing a fixed volume of cargo. They would only be entitled to such rate if the service contracts contained a "most favored shipper" provision.[84]

As previously noted, the essential terms of a service contract filed with the Commission shall be made available to all shippers similarly situated. To the extent that a service contract meets all the essential terms format requirements and is appropriately stated in terms of geographic areas or port ranges, it could be submitted, minus the shipper's name, in lieu of a statement of essential terms. Essential terms may be amended by mutual agreement of the parties to the contract.

In Circular Letter No. 1-89 (CL 1-89),[85] the FMC announced that it had been receiving service contracts which did not appear to contain mutually binding commitments by the contract parties sufficient to meet the definition of "service contract" contained in the 1984 Act.[86] In the letter the FMC stated that a provision for "regular" or "frequent" service is not a commitment to a defined service level, but only a mere recitation of a common carrier's obligation under common law. Similarly, the FMC rejected a provision where a carrier agrees to a specific service commitment (such as assured space) but under another provision vitiates that commitment by stating that a shipper's exclusive remedy in the event of a breach of the carrier's commitment, is a reduction in the shipper's minimum cargo commitment. Under such an arrangement the FMC concluded that the carrier "is in effect committing to nothing."

The FMC further stated that other provisions are similarly not in compliance. A provision that a line's vessel capacity is "adequate" for the shipper's needs while at the same time reciting that the shipper's cargo will be "subject to space availability" is illusory. Similarly, when a carrier agrees to carry a specific number of a shipper's containers per vessel but then states that acceptance of such containers is in the sole discretion of the line, this would not appear to constitute a defined service level.

So, too, would be a provision stating that if a carrier is unable to provide the number of containers or space per sailing as set forth in the contract, the maximum containers per sailing on a succeeding sailing should be adjusted by a corresponding amount of the shortfall. Where a contract recites that if the line is unable to provide the specified space for a stipulated number of containers, the contract minimum shall be reduced by the difference between the number of containers tendered and the number loaded by the line, such a clause would not appear to provide "assured space" as required.[86]

The FMC also noted that while it lacks the authority directly to regulate the use of liquidated damage provisions, nevertheless, the agency maintains that a service contract that allows a shipper to default on its cargo commitment while only paying de minimus damage to the carrier may not be a bona fida contract. The damage provision must bear a reasonable relationship to the cargo commitment and a de minimus liquidated damage provision may render the shipper's cargo commitment meaningless.

It is well recognized that parties to a contract may, under certain conditions, agree in advance what damages will be assessed in the event of a breach. But such liquidated damages provisions must be a reasonable estimate of the probable loss. Liquidated damages are distinguished from a penalty which is designed to deter a party from breaching its contract and punish it in the event the deterrent is ineffective. If the amount stipulated for payment of a breach is out of proportion to the probable damage, there is authority that this is a penalty and not liquidated damages, and such clauses will not ordinarily be enforced by the courts.

Instances have occurred where a liquidated damage clause in a service contract may be a penalty rather than a reasonable estimate of the probable loss to the carrier when a shipper defaults. As an example, one line provided that in the event of a breach by a shipper, the recovery may be equal to the gross freight charges. Such a clause would appear not to be a reasonable estimate of its probable loss, but rather a penalty, since this measure of damages fails to take into account the carrier's various costs in the processing, handling, and transportation of the container, such as loading and unloading charges, port costs, overhead, agent's commission, chassis and container costs, and rental or depreciation thereon. Inasmuch as these costs to a carrier are incurred only when a container is received and transported, allowing a carrier to recover based upon the gross rate charges without deducting operating costs would appear to be an unenforceable penalty rather than a reasonable estimate of the line's loss on a shortfall.

Rule 581.7(c) provides for the termination of a service contract resulting from a mutual agreement of the parties or because the shipper has failed to tender the minimum quantity required by the contract.[87] The rule further provides in Rule 581.7(c)(2) that the cargo previously carried under the contract shall be rerated according to the otherwise applicable tariff provisions of the carrier or conference in effect at the time of each shipment. Attached as Appendix C hereto is an example of a Mutual Termination, Settlement and Release Agreement.

Conceivably, the rule may work a hardship upon a shipper who is not in breach of its contract; for example, where a carrier's service commitment may be illusory. As noted in the discussion above on CL 1-89, some carrier provisions fail to meet the statutory requirement for a valid service contract. Should a shipper be unable to move its containers in a timely fashion because of a carrier's default, the shipper should have the right to demand a mutual termination. Under these circumstances, if the carrier agrees, it would appear unfair, as the rule requires, that the prior movements of the shipper be rerated at tariff rates. On the other hand, where a shipper defaults and there is a mutual agreement to terminate, a rerating seems fair since such shipper should not be entitled to benefit by its default by the lower service contract rate.

As noted above, there have been occasions where a contract shipper finds that a conference has lowered its tariff rate to an amount less than the contract rate, or where one or more member lines have taken independent action resulting in a lower rate, or a nonconference line may offer a lower rate not available before. To protect itself in such a situation, a shipper should insist upon a MFS clause providing that in the event that the service contract carrier or any other carrier, conference member or independent with a comparable service, publishes for the same commodity and the same destination points a rate or volume commitment lower than that specified in the service contract, then the shipper shall be entitled to such lower rate.

The granting of a reduced freight rate based upon volume was recognized in the 1916 Act. Section 14 Fourth provided that no common carrier by water could make any unfair or unjustly discriminatory contract with any shipper based upon the volume of freight offered.[88] Under this provision the FMC has held that a volume discount is not objectionable per se.[89] The 1916 Act provision and decisions thereunder are carried over in section 8(b) of the 1984 Act which provides that "[r]ates shown in tariffs filed under subsection (a) of this section may vary with the volume of cargo offered over a specified period of time."[90]

While the term "time-volume rate" is not defined in the 1984 Act, the FMC has defined it as "a rate published in a tariff which is conditional upon receipt of a specified aggregate volume of cargo or aggregate freight revenue over a specified period of time."[91] The rate shall remain effective for the time specified without amendment. Prior to tendering any shipment the shipper must give notice of its intention to use such a rate. The quantity is variously measured in terms of weight tons, revenue tons, or TEUs. The reduction in freight charges is based upon a negotiated rate, but only if the volume commitment is met. A tariff may provide that the shipper may have the time-volume rate at the outset of its shipments, or it may pay the regular rate with an adjustment in its favor at the expiration of the time period. A loyalty contract, treated under section 10(b)(9), *infra,* and a time-volume rate arrangement are not service contracts with the intended meaning of that term unless accompanied by a bona fida special service commitment by the contracting carrier or conference that deviates from its general tariff obligation.[92]

Similar to the time-volume rate program is the volume incentive program. It provides for a refund to a shipper on a stipulated percentage basis increment of freight dollars received within a stipulated period of time, provided that the total freight dollars paid by an enrollee exceeds certain stated levels of revenue. Such a program need not be specifically authorized in a conference agreement and, when reflected in an appropriate tariff, it is interstitial to the basic agreement itself.[93]

In some cases, a volume incentive program provides that it will be administered by an independent accounting firm which collects the funds from each carrier to pay out the refunds. The accountant invoices each carrier monthly and places the funds received in separate accounts for each member, which funds are kept separate from conference revenues. The accountant directly pays refunds to the qualified enrollee. Such an arrangement does not result in a pooling agreement.[94]

Shipper's Credit Agreements

As will be noted in Chapter VI, Ocean Freight Forwarders, *infra*, considerable litigation has ensued concerning the liability of a shipper for the freight when a carrier has accepted a due bill from a forwarder providing that the forwarder, either individually or jointly with the shipper, has agreed to pay the freight within a stipulated period of time. The usual issue is whether a shipper is liable for the freight, even when it has paid it to the forwarder, or whether the forwarder alone is liable for the freight.

In an effort to make certain that the shipper remains liable for freight regardless of whether the forwarder may have also assumed liability under a due bill, some steamship conferences have adopted a Shipper's Credit Agreement executed between individual shippers and the members of a conference.[95] Under such an agreement, a shipper commits itself to pay the freight directly or through an authorized forwarder named in the agreement to the carrier within a specified number of calendar days of the release of the bill of lading or sailing of the vessel. Payment is to be for the full freight and charges due on the bill of lading received by the forwarder. The agreement further states that the shipper will be absolutely and unconditionally responsible to see that all freight and charges due will be paid, and it guarantees that the freight will be paid irrespective of whether or not funds for payment have been advanced to the forwarder. Credit privileges under the agreement may immediately be suspended for any failure to comply with the provisions of the agreement.

The authorities are divided in construing a shipper's liability under a Shipper's Credit Agreement. A New York federal district court has held that the parties were only bargaining for credit privileges and that the shipper is not ultimately responsible for the payment of the freight already given to the forwarder. According to this court, the guarantee in the agreement meant only that the payment of freight would be made within the agreed upon credit period.[96]

A contrary position has been taken by the 5th Circuit, where the shipper had paid the forwarder who thereafter went bankrupt.[97] Initially, the carrier had sought payment from the forwarder under a freight due bill signed by it. The court did not agree that the carrier's remedies were limited only to the suspension of credit, emphasizing that the agreement specifically imposed liability upon the shipper regardless of whether or not funds for such payment had been advanced to the forwarder.[98]

It would appear that the reasoning of the 5th Circuit is more persuasive even though it requires the shipper to pay twice. The specific and clearly obvious purpose of the agreement is to hold a shipper liable for the transportation service it was furnished regardless of whether the freight was remitted to the forwarder. If a shipper chooses to pay a carrier through its agent, the forwarder, the better view would seem to be that the shipper should bear the risk of a default by its agent, rather than the carrier, which has no voice in the selection of the forwarder as the middleman for the transmittal of the freight.

50-Mile Rule

For a twenty-year period, extensive litigation ensued concerning the efforts of the International Longshoremen's Association (ILA) from East and Gulf ports to restrict the use of containers in our export-import trade. The ILA's stated purpose was to preserve work for its members at the piers by limiting the ability of shippers to process outbound and inbound cargo containerized or received within a 50-mile area of ports from Maine through Texas. In lengthy litigation before the National Labor Relations Board (NLRB), the U.S. Court of Appeals, and the U.S. Supreme Court, it was determined that the agreement between the shipping associations and the ILA on the handling of containers at the piers, known as the "50-Mile Rule," was a legitimate, work-preservation provision under our national labor relations laws.[99]

During the period the issue was before the NLRB and the courts, the FMC had before it the question as to whether the 50-Mile Rule was lawful under the 1916 Act, the 1984 Act, and the Intercoastal Act, 1933. After eight years of proceedings, the agency held that the 50-Mile Rule violated these statutes. The principles of law enunciated therein by the FMC and the U.S. Court of Appeals with certiorari denied by the U.S. Supreme Court should serve as a useful guide that may be applied in the future in weighing how far a labor union may go in protecting the interests of its membership without violating the Congressional objective in the 1984 Act of assuring shippers, consignees, and carriers of the right to move containerized cargo in our foreign commerce without undue restriction.

The basic thrust of the rule was to require that a container be loaded or unloaded by ILA labor at the pier if the container's origin or destination was within 50 miles of an East or Gulf coast port. Only "qualified" shippers (persons whose containers were loaded or unloaded by their own employees at their own facilities) were exempt from the rule. A nonexempted container arriving at the pier was unloaded (stripped) and reloaded (stuffed) by ILA longshoremen, and monetary penalties were assessed against the nonqualified shipper or consolidator.

The rule had a severe impact upon all segments of our foreign, offshore ocean commerce. As one example, if an exporter efficiently loaded a container at a public warehouse near the Port of Boston, filling more than 90 percent of its capacity, when that container was sent to the Port of New York for overseas transportation, some 220 miles away from Boston, the container would be stripped by ILA labor at the pier and the packages therein were restuffed into the same container at a cost that varied from $200 to $325 per container. On occasion, the exporter would need a second container because of the substantially lower load factor of the pier workers, resulting in more freight charges, risk of damage and delay, as well as problems of tracing the shipments, coordinating delivery to another pier, and missing sailings. The initial consolidation having taken place within 50 miles of an ILA port, Boston, the rule permitted such consequences. However, if another exporter loaded a container at a public warehouse 220 miles due west of New York, the box was loaded aboard the vessel at New York without incident, since the consolidation was not accomplished within a 50-mile radius of an ILA port.

Similarly, smaller importers were significantly burdened by the rule. If an importer was large enough to have its own port warehouse to receive its containers within an ILA port area, the container was released from the pier and the merchandise could be distributed immediately from the importer's warehouse. However, if the importer was not large enough to have its own port warehouse, it had only the option of having the container stripped at the pier, exposing the goods to loss, pilferage, damage, and delay, or alternatively, the container would be taken to a public warehouse with its contents not removed (or even sold) for thirty days.

While the NVOCC has long been recognized as a legitimate common carrier by water in our foreign commerce, as will be noted *infra*, this type of ocean carrier was particularly impacted by the rule. By consolidating the packages of smaller exporters, the NVOCC offered lower rates, shorter delivery times, a single through bill of lading with little or no loss, damage, or pilferage problems. The rule flatly prohibited vessel operators from furnishing containers to NVOCCs and other consolidators as had long been the practice. NVOCCs were required to buy containers or lease them (at a cost of $200 to $300 for a one-way voyage), even though they were shippers vis-à-vis the line. As a result, NVOCCs containerizing cargo within the 50-mile zone were subjected to substantial extra costs and shipping delays, necessarily reflected in their rates, not incurred by the "qualified" shippers.

Others involved in the movement of cargo were also substantially restricted in their port activities. Truckers could not load and reload containers off-pier to meet weight, safety, or delivery requirements. Public warehousemen located near port cities were unable to provide the full range of their customary storage services. And containerized traffic was diverted to Canadian and other non-ILA U.S. ports, causing U.S. ports, U.S. flag carriers, local truckers, forwarders, customs brokers, and warehousemen to lose business.

In a 169-page report, reversing the decision of the ALJ, the FMC held the rule unlawful on several grounds.[100] The principal holding was that in determining the lawfulness of the rule, the Commission was not obliged to reach beyond the shipping laws it was enforcing and attempt to take into account evidence of "labor considerations" stemming from the collective bargaining agreement between the carriers and the ILA. The attempted justification for the rule to achieve labor peace on the docks, was not, the agency held, a "traditional transportation factor" in determining legality under our shipping laws. Nor were the opponents of the rule required to prove specific financial harm. Because the denial of containers to the NVOCC was not based on transportation needs or on conditions properly cognizable under our shipping laws, the rule on its face resulted in unfair treatment and unjust discrimination under section 14 Fourth of the 1916 Act and section 10(b)(6)(C) of the 1984 Act.

In a seventy-nine-page decision, the U.S. Court of Appeals unanimously denied the petition for review by the shipping associations and the ILA. Following Supreme Court precedent, the court gave appropriate deference to the FMC interpretation of the shipping statutes it was entrusted to administer, agreeing that the rule could not be upheld, since it was not justified in transportation terms. Furthermore, the FMC's refusal to excuse "obvious" shipping law violations because of a carrier's obligations under a collective bargaining agreement or the threat of labor unrest was neither unreasonable agency action nor inconsistent with its shipper-protective statutory mandate. The Supreme Court denied certiorari.[101]

Misclassification of Goods

There need not be a motive or reason for the finding of a misclassification violation.[102] Where a shipper has doubt as to the proper tariff designation, it has a duty to make a diligent and good faith inquiry of the carrier or conference.[103] The description on the bill of lading is not the single controlling factor; the test is what was actually shipped.[104] This is determined by evidence as to the true nature of the cargo.[105] The shipper cannot ignore a more descriptive classification in the tariff,[106] and must establish by a preponderance of evidence what actually moved.[107] When "use" is a factor in deciding the proper tariff designation of an article, it is the "controlling one" that determines the character of the shipment; the fact that an article may have other subordinate or secondary uses does not alter the nature of the product.[108]

A more extensive discussion dealing with the duty of making a proper classification of goods is set forth in Chapter VI, Ocean Freight Forwarders, Section E(2).

CHAPTER IV

MARINE TERMINAL OPERATORS

Definitions and Interpretations Thereof

In section 3(15) of the 1984 Act a "marine terminal operator" (MTO) is defined as "a person engaged in the United States in the business of furnishing wharfage, dock, warehouse, or other terminal facilities in connection with a common carrier."[1] This definition is a carryover from the 1916 Act which defined "other persons subject" in section 1 as "any person not included in the term 'common carriers by water'," carrying on the business of forwarding or furnishing wharfage, dock, warehouse, or other terminal facilities in connection with a common carrier by water.[2] The MTO is similarly defined by the FMC in its regulations.[3] The decided cases under the 1916 Act do not establish any hard and fast rule as to when a person acts as an MTO; rather, this determination has been based upon the specific facts in each case.

Bethlehem Steel is a leading FMC case on the issue of whether a firm which did not visibly furnish the services of wharfage, dock, etc., could, nevertheless, be held to be an MTO. In that case, a state port commission instituted a harbor service charge levied on all commercial vessels entering the physical limits of the harbor, the assessment being based upon the tonnage of the vessel, but performed no terminal service itself. The FMC held that the purpose of the harbor charge was unrelated to cargo handling, since it was based on the navigational aspect of the harbor, whereas it is the terminal portion of the harbor that truly relates to the receiving, handling, storing, or delivering of property under section 17. The FMC concluding that there was an insufficient relationship between the harbor charge and the receiving, handling, etc., of property under section 17, the agency was, therefore, without jurisdiction to consider the reasonableness of the charge. This decision was affirmed by the D.C. Circuit on appeal.[4]

In *Plaquemines* the same court appears to have reached a conclusion contrary to *Bethlehem*. The port district therein did not own or operate any warehouse or other waterfront facilities, but it did operate fire vessels. After determining that the port district's combination of services and its controlling of access to the private terminal facilities amounted to a furnishing of such facilities, the court held that the port district had the ability to discriminate in the fees it charged by controlling access to the private terminal facilities and that such control was "sufficient" to sustain FMC jurisdiction over the port district as an MTO.[5]

In *Port of Ponce,* the Ports Authority (PRPA) was authorized to levy charges on vessels entering Puerto Rican ports "for general harbor services rendered by the authority and rendered by PRPA for the vigilance, supervision and safety of the harbor and of the vessels within the harbor." Pursuant to such authority, a "port service charge" was levied in the tariff on vessels calling at the port. PRPA justified the charge as one for entering a port and receiving the benefit of general services rendered therein, such as dredging, construction of dykes, radio communications, harbor cleaning, law enforcement, and others. Following the decision in *Plaquemines,* the FMC held that PRPA was acting as an MTO.[6] However, based upon *Bethlehem Steel, supra,* the First Circuit reversed the FMC on the grounds that the charge of PRPA was not for terminal services, since PRPA was not receiving, etc., property under section 17 of the 1916 Act.[7]

Based upon the foregoing, it would appear that the authorities differ as to whether a port agency that does not specifically render terminal services may be regulated as an MTO by the FMC. In *Bethlehem Steel* and *Plaquemines,* the D.C. Circuit seems to have reached contrary results, and in *Port of Ponce* the 1st Circuit disagreed with *Plaquemines.*

The *Port of Ponce* result seems more in accordance with the legislative purpose of conferring jurisdiction upon the FMC to regulate as an MTO a person "furnishing wharfage, dock, warehouse, or other terminal facilities." In *Plaquemines,* no such facilities were actually provided by the port district.

The FMC's rules also provide that the statute includes terminals owned or operated by states and their political subdivisions, railroads performing port terminal services not covered by their line haul rates, common carriers that perform port terminal services, and warehousemen who operate such facilities.[8]

A stevedore who merely furnishes portable labor-saving devices, such as hand tools and lift trucks, for the use of men at the pier is not an MTO; such devices are not considered "terminal facilities."[9] On the other hand, a stevedore who engages in loading and unloading of waterborne traffic is subject to the Act.[10] While terminals servicing interstate carriers are still subject to the 1916 Act, they are excluded under the 1984 Act, which is confined to services performed in our foreign commerce.[11] An off-dock container freight station operator performing terminal services away from the pier is an MTO, since the definition of an MTO does not require that these services be performed at the dock or on the water's edge.[12]

Jurisdiction of MTOs Under the 1984 Act

A principal area of FMC jurisdiction of MTOs is contained in section 10(d)(1) of the 1984 Act which provides, inter alia, that an MTO may not fail to establish, observe, and enforce just and reasonable regulations and practices relating to or connected with receiving, handling, storing, or delivering property.[13] For the FMC to assert jurisdiction under this section, the charges or practices must have an underlying purpose relating to terminal operations and must have more than an incidental relationship to the handling of cargo or the movement of vessels into a harbor.[14] The statutory scheme contemplates regulation of any entity if it exercises sufficient control over terminal facilities to have a discernible effect on the commercial relationship between shippers and carriers involved in that link in transportation.[15]

A person entering an ocean terminal for the sole purpose of picking up or delivering cargo is not furnishing a terminal facility within the Act.[16] Where an MTO usurps the normal function of a carrier and has designated a tugboat operator for tug services under the terms of an exclusive-right contract, the furnishing of tugboat services has, in effect, been transformed into a terminal function under the Act.[17] A finding that a terminal serves common carriers by water is sufficient to support the Commission's jurisdiction.[18]

The Port of Seattle furnished a free consolidation service for certain shipments bound to inland destinations, but it did not indicate the availability of the consolidation service in its terminal tariff. A service charge of 1½ percent of the inland shipment invoice was charged. Port personnel performed the actual physical loading and unloading of the cargo. The issue was whether the FMC had jurisdiction over the port's consolidation services. The FMC held that the service relates to the receiving, handling, etc., of property, and that the consolidation service is part of a broader marine terminal process, in that the port is furnishing terminal facilities in connection with a common carrier by water. The service is, therefore, part of a general ocean terminal operation rather than a separate inland operation, and the port must publish in its tariff a description of the consolidation service and the applicable service charge.[19]

In the above case the FMC noted that the legislative history of the 1916 Act indicates that the term "other person" has been broadly construed. It appears likely that a similar position will be taken under the 1984 Act. For example, the FMC has ruled that a person undertaking to provide services making imported frozen meat available to the importer for official inspection after which the meat is returned to the importer's warehouse, renders a service related to the receiving, etc., of property.[20] The term "other terminal facilities" in the section 3(15) definition of an MTO contemplates not only physical assets, such as docks, wharfs, and warehouses, but also encompasses services rendered in connection with the terminal link in transportation modes. Thus, the practice of a port in assessing a fee for providing vessels and cargo essential health, safety, and security services constitutes the furnishing of "other terminal facilities" within the 1916 Act.[21]

Port authorities strongly support the conference system and the maintenance of antitrust immunity for the vessel operator and the ports. ACCOS has noted that the determination of sailing schedules and the selection of ports to be served by conferences and carriers have a significant impact on the health and prosperity of the different ports and regions they represent.[22]

In addition to section 10(d)(1), the 1984 Act contains a number of other provisions dealing with MTOs. Section 4(b) allows MTOs handling cargo in the U.S. foreign commerce to agree among themselves to (1) discuss, fix, or regulate rates or other conditions of service; and (2) engage in exclusive, preferential, or cooperative working arrangements. According to the Senate Commerce Committee, a predecessor bill, S.504, had authorized MTOs, inter alia, to "pool or portion earnings, losses, or traffic," all of which were permitted under section 15 of the 1916 Act.[23] However, unlike S.504, section 4(b) does not specifically allow the pooling or apportioning of earnings by MTOs. In the past, as noted by the House Judiciary Committee in its consideration of another predecessor bill, H.R.1878, MTOs in the United States had, under section 15 of the 1916 Act, filed agreements with the FMC and obtained antitrust immunity for their joint activities. Port authorities also filed agreements with the Commission contemplating discussion of rates and terms of service among port authorities operating in different cities.[24] Despite the rather broad authority previously enjoyed by MTOs under the 1916 Act, the failure to specifically authorize pooling agreements by MTOs in the 1984 Act, together with the specific granting of such authority to vessel operators under section 4(a)(2), raises a question as to whether pooling by MTOs is allowed.

When MTOs reach agreement among themselves on the subject areas covered by section 4(b), they are required under section 5(a) of the 1984 Act to file a true copy with the FMC. The agreement is reviewed under section 6(g) to determine if, by a reduction in competition, the agreement will produce an unreasonable reduction in transportation service or an unreasonable increase in transportation cost; if not, the agreement

will become "effective" under section 6(c)(1) and is exempt from antitrust laws under section 7(a).[25] The FMC has by rule exempted from
filing a "marine terminal facilities agreement" among MTOs and between MTOs and common carriers by water. In such an agreement one
party conveys to another rights to operate a marine terminal facility.[26]

Under section 10(d)(2), no MTO may agree with another MTO or a
common carrier to boycott or unreasonably discriminate in providing
terminal services to any common carrier (which includes an NVOCC) or
ocean tramp.

Section 10(d)(3) provides that the prohibitions in sections 10(b)(11),
(12), and (16) governing common carriers shall also apply to MTOs.
Accordingly, under section 10(b)(11), an MTO may not make or give
any undue or unreasonable preference or advantage to any particular
person, locality, or description of traffic in any respect whatsoever. The
elements of port discrimination conceptually resemble those of "undue
preference" rather than "unjust discrimination" prohibited in section
10(b)(10).[27] The practice by an MTO of furnishing one service below
cost has the tendency to prevent any downward revisions of rates for
other services however justified they may be. Such a practice is unreasonable.[28] Unless an MTO controls both terminals at which the different
charges are assessed, such MTO cannot be held to have illegally discrimi-
nated against or preferred a carrier.[29] It is unreasonable for an MTO,
charged with the duty to treat all persons alike within the bounds of
reasonableness, to grant preferential treatment to one common carrier
over another on the basis that the preferred carrier is a regular customer.
This is not to say that a failure to serve vessels in order of arrival, standing
alone, is a violation.[30] But an MTO offering a service to common carriers
and to the shipping public is required to serve them on equal terms.[31]

Section 10(b)(12) prohibits an MTO from subjecting any particular
person, locality, or description of traffic to an unreasonable refusal to
deal or any undue or unreasonable prejudice or disadvantage in any
respect whatsoever. As noted in the discussion under section 10(b)(11)
above, this section is not breached when an MTO does not control both
terminals at which different charges are assessed.[32] While the assessment
by a terminal of a charge against the vessel for services rendered to the
cargo for the benefit of the consignee raises issues under section 10(d)(1)
as to the justness and reasonableness of the allocation, it does not
constitute an undue or unreasonable prejudice under section 10(b)(12),
since the cargo and vessel are not users of the same service.[33]

Under section 10(d)(3) no MTO may under section 10(b)(16) knowingly disclose confidential information concerning the nature or routing

of property that may be detrimental to a shipper, improperly disclose its business transactions to a competitor, or be used to the detriment of any common carrier.

MTO Tariffs

Neither the 1916 nor 1984 Acts specifically requires an MTO to file tariffs of its charges or rules. The FMC, however, has by rule traditionally required such a filing.[34] The conferees on the 1984 Act were aware of this FMC rule and stated that if the Commission continued this requirement, the conferees intend that the exempted commodities referred to in sections 8(a)(1) and 8(c) of the Act be exempted.[35]

The FMC regulation provides that except for the exempted commodities referred to in section 8(a) of the 1984 Act, every person, other than the Department of Defense, providing a terminal service, shall file in duplicate a schedule or tariff showing all its rates, charges, rules, and regulations related to the receiving, handling, storing and/or delivering of property at its terminal facilities. Included in the rule are terminals owned or operated by states or their subdivisions, railroads performing port terminal services not covered by their line haul rates, common carriers who perform port terminal services, and warehousemen who operate port terminal facilities. Excepted are rates and charges for terminal services pursuant to negotiated contracts, and rates and charges for storage of cargo and incidental services thereto by public warehousemen pursuant to storage agreements covered by a warehouse receipt.[36] Every tariff or tariff change must be filed on or before the effective date and shall be kept open for public inspection.[37]

In considering the scope of its jurisdiction and the lawfulness of a terminal tariff, the FMC is not required to reach a constitutional issue. Such matters are more appropriately the province of the courts.[38] A terminal tariff requiring a port to be reimbursed if it succeeds in litigation, but which does not require a port to pay expenses if unsuccessful, imposes a unilateral obligation which is an unreasonable practice.[39] So too, a tariff allowing the application of a port user's payments of port charges to the account of another user is unreasonable.[40] A terminal tariff providing that vessel agents were liable for the tariff debts of their principals is a reasonable means of collecting tariff fees due. A vessel agent may protect itself by a contractual arrangement.[41]

A terminal tariff does not operate to put a shipper on constructive notice of any limitation of liability in the tariff. The filing of the tariff gives constructive notice only of those terms which are required to be filed and nothing in the Act or in the applicable regulations requires a terminal to file provisions limiting its liability.[42] The failure of a terminal operator to publish and post a tariff is an unjust and unreasonable practice.[43] The test of reasonableness as applied to terminal practices is that the practice must be otherwise lawful, not excessive, and reasonably related, fit, and appropriate to the ends in view.[44] A provision in a tariff stating that a port is the sole interpreter of the tariffs is unjust and unreasonable.[45]

Service Charges

The collection of a service charge by a terminal for which no service is performed is an unreasonable practice.[46] Arranging for the berth of a vessel is clearly an administrative expense and should be eliminated from a terminal's service charge.[47] In the interest of uniform and clear definitions, the services included in a terminal service charge should be limited to those concerned with or incidental to the receiving and checking of cargo, the principal item going into the service charge. A charge against a vessel for ordering railroad cars alongside should be set up as a special charge and not be included in a service charge.[48] The level of charges must be reasonably related to an actual service performed or a benefit conferred on the person charged.[49]

Services

The FMC has defined various services rendered by MTOs.[50] "Dockage" means the charge assessed against the vessel for berthing on a wharf, pier, bulkhead structure, or bank, or for mooring to a vessel so berthed. It is a charge made for the furnishing of facilities for berthing the vessel.[51] Berthing should be established as a separate item since it is purely a use charge for space occupied by the vessel and has no direct relation to a "service" as such.[52]

"Wharfage" means the charge assessed against the cargo or vessel on all cargo passing or conveyed over a wharf or between vessels. It is solely a charge for use of the wharf; it does not include charges for any other service. A competitive or "triangular" relationship need not be proven to establish an undue preference or advantage.[53]

"Free time" means the specified period during which cargo may occupy space assigned to it on terminal property free of wharf demurrage or terminal storage charges immediately prior to the loading or subsequent to the discharge of cargo on or off the vessel.[54] Free time means that the cargo, once lawfully on the pier, may remain on or during the period established at no extra expense.[55] The allowance of free time is a "regulation or a practice" under the 1984 Act.[56] When a terminal undertakes the ocean carrier's obligation to provide reasonable free time, the terminal has assumed the carrier's responsibility for the allowance of reasonable free time.[57] When the U.S. government is a shipper, it is not necessary to make a strict showing of transportation necessity to establish the lawfulness of an extended free time.[58] Free time is not to be extended for the purpose of consolidating shipments at the pier, since the use of the pier for that purpose is a commercial convenience.[59]

There is a distinction between vessel cancellation and delay insofar as there is an obligation to extend time on the dock free of demurrage. Where there is a vessel cancellation, no demurrage may be exacted for any time the cargo has been on the pier. But in the case of a vessel delay, the assumption is that the vessel will eventually call, so that the prior use of the facility by the cargo without payment of demurrage is proper until the time when the vessel missed its sailing.[60]

Whatever the justification may be for requiring the showing of a competitive relationship between shippers when determining the existence of preference or prejudice in ocean freight rates, such a requirement is not justified when determining whether there is a preference or prejudice resulting from a free time or free storage practice. In the latter case, unequal treatment has no place in a regulated industry. The equality required in such a situation is absolute.[61]

"Wharf Demurrage" means a charge assessed against cargo remaining in or on terminal facilities after the expiration of free time unless arrangements have been made for storage. [62] Demurrage charges have a dual composition, consisting of an element of compensation for the storage of property and an element of penalty to induce its removal.[63] Demurrage rules must in all instances be construed most favorably to the shipper. No demurrage can be exacted unless the delay in loading or unloading is clearly attributable to the fault of the shipper or consignee.[64] On the question as to whether the carrier, the shipper, or the consignee must pay the charge during a strike, the burden is upon the person who at the time of the strike owes an undischarged obligation to the cargo. Thus, where the cargo is in free time and a strike occurs, it is the vessel which has yet to discharge to a consignee its full obligation to tender for delivery and it is, therefore, to the vessel that the terminal looks to pay for the facilities and services used. In such a case it is just and reasonable to require the vessel to pay the cost of the supervening strike which renders the discharge of that responsibility impossible.[65] Any extension of free time or first period demurrage granted after a longshoremen's strike should not be given to cargo that was already on penal demurrage when the strike began.[66]

"Terminal Storage," as defined by the FMC, means the service of providing warehouse or other terminal facilities for the storage of inbound or outbound cargo after the expiration of free time.[67] In effect, storage charges are penalty charges assessed for the purpose of clearing the piers.[68] The failure of a terminal to abide by its tariff in the provisions for free time is unduly prejudicial and preferential and an unjust and unreasonable practice.[69] Furnishing free storage facilities to shippers and consignees beyond a reasonable period results in substantial inequality of service between different shippers.[70] Where cargo is in demurrage at the beginning of a strike, it is an unjust and unreasonable practice to assess strike storage against a vessel.[71] It is the consignee whose free time has expired who should pay such charges. In determining whether a storage practice is an unjust or unreasonable regulation, the question of reasonableness does not depend upon unlawful or discriminatory intent, but rather upon whether the offense is committed by the mere doing of it.[72]

A stevedore is a person employed in loading and unloading vessels. In return for a fixed rate of remuneration, generally so much per ton, a stevedore provides the men, gear, and all other adjuncts for working the cargo in or out of a vessel.[73] The FMC has no authority to regulate stevedoring.[74] This being so, their practices are not forbidden under section 10(b)(11) of the 1984 Act governing common carriers as to the making or giving of any undue or unreasonable preference or advantage.[75] The failure of a stevedore to apportion its available workforce more equitably due to a shortage of shore labor is not a violation.[76] It is the custom in ocean commerce that the vessel be permitted to select the stevedore inasmuch as stevedoring is a responsibility of the vessel.[77]

The FMC defines "handling" as the service of physically moving cargo between the point of rest on any place on the terminal facility, other than the end of ship's tackle.[78] Handling is a separate and distinct service from loading or unloading and a separate charge may be made for handling.[79] The duty of moving freight from the place of delivery on the dock to the ship's tackle and thence to a place on the dock at the port of delivery is a part of the duty of the carrier transporting the freight from port to port.[80]

As defined by the FMC, "loading and unloading" means the service of loading or unloading cargo between any place on the terminal and railroad cars, trucks, lighters, or barges, or any other means of conveyance to or from the terminal facility.[81] Terminal facilities have been defined as all of the arrangements, mechanical and engineering, which make an easy transfer of goods at either end of a stage of transportation service.[82] On imports, a water carrier is required by its transportation obligation, absent a special contract, to unload the cargo onto a dock, segregated by bill of lading and count, put it in a place of rest on the pier so it is accessible to the consignee, and afford the consignee reasonable opportunity to come and get it.[83]

Members of a conference of terminal operators providing loading and unloading services obtain the status of a public utility. It is the terminal operator, holding itself out by tariff to perform truckloading and unloading, that is responsible for completing the service within a reasonable time. Failure to do so is not excused by an inability to obtain labor.[84]

The FMC has also defined other charges involving MTOs. "Usage" means the use of a terminal facility by any rail carrier, lighter operator, trucker, shipper, or consignee, when it performs its own car, lighter or truck loading or unloading, or the use of the facility for any other gainful purpose for which a charge is not otherwise specified. "Checking" means the service of counting and checking cargo against appropriate documents for the account of the cargo or the vessel, or other person requesting same. "Heavy lift" means the service of providing heavy lift cranes and equipment for lifting cargo.[85]

"Lighterage" is a charge for the conveyance of goods by lighters or barges in a harbor or between ship and shore. This charge usually includes the loading into and discharging of the lighters.[86] The FMC has no jurisdiction over those performing the separate and distinct service of lighterage for or on behalf of common carriers or in connection with common carriers; but if a common carrier or other person subject to the 1984 Act offers to render a lighterage service, the FMC has the authority to review such activity.[87]

The assumption by a terminal operator of the carrier's traditional obligation of loading and unloading of necessity carries with it the responsibility for ensuring that just and reasonable rules govern the performance of the obligation. Accordingly, a conference of carriers and terminal operators must adopt a just and reasonable lighter detention rule and regulation in their lighterage tariff.[88] A published tariff is required to inform potential recipients of such services of the exact charges to be expected. Negotiated rates are unsatisfactory.[89]

As earlier noted, under section 15 of the 1916 Act, operators of marine terminals in the United States filed agreements with the FMC and upon their approval obtained antitrust immunity for their joint activities.[90] The 1984 Act confers similar immunity.[91] Using its exemption authority in section 16 of the 1984 Act, the FMC has by rule exempted certain, but not all, marine terminal agreements from the waiting period requirement of section 6 of the 1984 Act.[92]

Terminal Leasing and Rental

The FMC has jurisdiction over the relationship between a port and terminal operators as tenants thereof and has addressed the requirements for establishing a prima facie case of unreasonably discriminatory practices. In reviewing the decisionmaking practices of a port in leasing its terminal facilities, the Commission does not substitute its own business judgment for that of the port, but rather exercises its responsibility to consider whether the port violated the 1984 Act. Accordingly, although monopolistic conditions at a port may be highly relevant to the Commission's ultimate determination of the reasonableness of a port's conduct, and may determine which party has the burden of going forward, such conditions are not a prerequisite for the Commission to exercise jurisdiction to review alleged violations of the prohibited acts provisions of the 1984 Act.[93]

As a marine terminal operator, the port has a statutory obligation to observe the provisions of sections 10(d)(1) and (3) as well as 10(b)(11), (12), and (16).[94] The Commission has jurisdiction, therefore, over a port's leasing activities, which are said to have constituted unlawful exclusion and a refusal to deal in violation of these sections of the Act.[95] Where there are no monopoly or anticompetitive conditions created at the port, no prima facie case is established. Accordingly, the complainant carries the burden of showing that the port's practices were unlawful under the 1984 Act.[96]

The Commission has recognized that it is proper to give deference to a port's discretionary business decisions.[97] The duly authorized port authority is the proper body to weigh and evaluate business risks related to the port's efficiency in the first instance.[98] Nor is the Commission required to tally and compare exactly what benefits are received by the relevant parties. The Act clearly contemplates the existence of permissible preferences and prejudices. Only *undue* or *unreasonable* preferences and prejudices violate the prohibited acts provisions of the 1984 Act.[99]

In determining whether a lease is noncompensatory, resulting in prejudice to any particular port or terminal, the term "compensatory" is given the connotation of fair and reasonable return on an investment.[100] A public terminal is in essence a public utility and as such it is only required to set its rentals at a level which would provide revenues to cover the economic costs of doing business. As a general principle, a public terminal lease is compensatory if the annual minimum rentals cover all fully distributed costs.[101]

Liability of MTOs

A terminal tariff requirement that steamship agencies and stevedoring companies obtain general liability and property damage insurance is reasonable, particularly where there has been a recent history of accidents in a port.[102] An indemnification requirement in a terminal tariff which would relieve a port from liability for its own negligence is an unreasonable practice in violation of the 1984 Act.[103] Similarly, where a provision in a terminal tariff serves to exculpate the port from liability arising from furnishing its cranes, to the extent that the provision exculpates the port for its own negligence, it is unreasonable.[104]

CHAPTER V

NON-VESSEL-OPERATING COMMON CARRIERS BY WATER

NVOCC Defined

The non-vessel-operating common carrier by water, commonly called an NVOCC or NVO, is, as previously noted herein, defined in section 3(17) of the 1984 Act as a common carrier that does not operate the vessels by which the ocean transportation is provided, and is a shipper in its relationship with the ocean common carrier.[1]

This definition includes three other entities defined in the Act: a common carrier, a shipper, and an ocean common carrier. A "common carrier" in section 3(6) means a person holding itself out to the general public to provide transportation by water of passengers or cargo between the United States and a foreign country for compensation that (A) assumes responsibility for the transportation from port or point of receipt to the port or point of destination, and (B) utilizes, for all or part of that transportation, a vessel operating between a port in the United States and a port in a foreign country. Under section 3(23), a "shipper" means an owner or person for whose account the ocean transportation of cargo is provided or the person to whom delivery is to be made. An "ocean common carrier," under section 3(18), means a vessel-operating common carrier. In the legislative history of the 1984 Act, the House Merchant Marine Committee noted that a definition of an NVOCC was added "so that distinctions may be made between those carriers that operate vessels and those that do not. Both types are included in the definition of common carrier."[2]

In a decision under the 1916 Act, the FMC has held that "a person or business association may be classified as a common carrier by water who holds itself out by the establishment and maintenance of tariffs, by advertisement and solicitation, and otherwise, to provide transportation for hire by water in interstate or foreign commerce, as defined in the Shipping Act of 1916; assumes responsibility or has liability imposed by law for the safe transportation of shipments; and arranges in its own name with underlying water carriers for the performance of such transportation, whether or not owning or controlling the means by which such transportation is effected."[3] In commenting on its decisional concept of an NVOCC, the FMC has emphasized that the fact that a carrier does not itself own or operate transportation equipment does not vitiate its common carrier status. For purposes of tariff filing and other laws and regulations, the Commission does not generally distinguish between the vessel-operating and non-vessel-operating common carriers.[4]

The statutory and FMC decisional concept take somewhat different approaches in defining an NVOCC. Under the definition in section 3(17) of the 1984 Act Congress concerned itself with the *relationships* of the NVOCC with others, that is, an NVOCC is a common carrier when dealing with its shippers and a shipper when dealing with a vessel operator. Decisionally, however, the FMC has concentrated on the *functional* aspect of the NVOCC: there is a holding out to provide transportation for hire, an assumption of responsibility or liability, and an arranging as a shipper for the underlying water carriage.

ACCOS recognized the NVOCC as one who takes possession of the cargo of smaller shipper customers and consolidates less-than-container loads (LCLs) shipments into full-container loads (FCLs) charging its own tariff rates to its shipper customers. Once an NVOCC has consolidated LCL packages into a full-container load, it tenders the container shipment to an ocean common carrier, the vessel operator, which in turn issues a bill of lading to the NVOCC as the shipper of the container, charging its own tariff rates, usually known as a "freight-all-kinds" (FAK), to the NVOCC.[5] To obtain an FAK rate, the NVOCC must usually load its container with the goods of at least three different shippers and at least three different commodities, none of which may exceed a specified rate or cube.[6]

In the past, questions have been raised by the FMC as to whether a person processing LCL shipments and arranging for their containerized transportation is an NVOCC or an ocean freight forwarder. If the former, a tariff needs to be filed with the agency; if the latter, no filing is required. This issue has become even more important since the enactment of section 23 of the 1984 Act, requiring an NVOCC to establish its "financial responsibility."

In a leading case, the FMC took a strict look at a person claiming to be an ocean freight forwarder or consolidator and not a carrier when arranging for shipments in our foreign commerce.[7] Even though such person may disclaim liability, the FMC holds that when such a person offers to the general public a coordinated transportation service, including consolidation at its terminals, transportation by water, and distribution to a consignee, such a person is not acting "merely as a shippers' agent," but rather as a common carrier. In this regard, the FMC was strongly influenced by the Interstate Commerce Commission (ICC) position that a person was a domestic freight forwarder under Part IV of the Interstate Commerce Act even though it had specifically disclaimed common carrier liability.[8] According to the FMC, an assumption of liability need not be specifically included in any definition of common carriage because once a person holds himself out generally to carry for hire for whomsoever wishes to employ him, he has undertaken the occupation of a common carrier and liability will be imposed as a matter of law.

However, all persons arranging for the dispatch of LCL ocean shipments in our foreign commerce need not necessarily have the status of an NVOCC. The U.S. Supreme Court has recognized that when an ocean freight forwarder arranges for the movement of goods in such commerce as an agent of the shipper, it does not assume transportation responsibility.[9] However, if a person wishes to act strictly as a forwarder, he must take precautions not to engage, or appear to engage, in an activity that could be considered to be an NVOCC function. Thus, the forwarder should not issue a document designated as a bill of lading or with a similar name. Rather, a Forwarder's Receipt or a Shipper's Advice should be used. Instead of common carrier terms on the reverse side of such documents, it should be clearly stated that the person is acting as a forwarding agent only and not as a common carrier. The standard trading conditions used by the forwarding industry should be adopted and reproduced on the reverse side of its forwarder's invoice to the shipper. Generally, such conditions specifically state that the user is acting as a forwarder and is not assuming responsibility or having liability imposed on it as a matter of law for water transportation. A forwarder frequently assists a shipper in the handling of a claim, but when it does so, the forwarder may not itself assume responsibility for loss or damage or pay out in satisfaction of such claim. It would not appear that a firm becomes an NVOCC merely because it makes a profit on the freight. Under FMC regulations, an ocean freight forwarder may include a fee in addition to the freight charge for its service of arranging the ocean transportation.[10]

Suppose an NVOCC performs a break-bulk service for an overseas NVOCC shipping containers to the United States, but the latter has failed to file a bond, a tariff, and a designation of resident agent in violation of section 23 of the 1984 Act. Does the NVOCC in the United States face problems in rendering its service to the overseas NVOCC?

Two areas of exposure are possible. Firstly, in aiding the overseas NVOCC to operate in the United States in violation of the 1984 Act, the U.S. NVOCC may be charged with failing to observe just and reasonable practices related to the receiving, handling, storing, or delivery of property in violation of section 10(d)(1) and be subject to civil penalties.

Secondly, the possibility exists that the U.S. and the foreign-based NVOCC might be charged with a conspiracy to commit an "offense" against the United States and be subject to fine and imprisonment.

Let us assume that an NVOCC operates from an interior point in the United States and arranges for motor carrier transportation from that point to a Canadian port for transportation overseas. The underlying water carrier from Canada does not call at any U.S. port. The FMC held that so long as the NVOCC solicits and receives cargo in the United State and uses ICC-exempt motor carriage to transport the shipment from the United States on a through route to an overseas consignee, the NVOCC "can and should be effectively regulated" by the Commission.[12] The U.S. Court of Appeals reversed, holding that an NVOCC is required in the 1984 Act to file a tariff for transportation by water of cargo moving between the U.S. port and a foreign country and, inasmuch as the NVOCC did not make use of a U.S. port at any point in its service, having shipped the property overland out of the United States, the transportation was exclusively between foreign ports and not subject to FMC jurisdiction.[13]

A common carrier offering only intermodal rail/water or truck/water service from the U.S. mainland to Puerto Rico is within the exclusive jurisdiction of the Interstate Commerce Commission.[14] The FMC has acknowledged that it does not have jurisdiction over NVOCCs participating in this form of through intermodal movement to U.S. territories or possessions.[15]

In the 50-Mile Rule case, treated earlier, the FMC emphasized the unjustly discriminatory effects of the rule on NVOCCs. The agency noted that in requesting a container from a vessel operator, the NVOCC was acting as a shipper and that the denial of the container, a cargo facility, to an NVOCC solely because of the kind of work it did was not based on transportation needs and was, therefore, unjustly discriminatory and in violation of section 10(b)(6)(C). In addition, inasmuch as the NVOCC competes with the vessel operator for LCL cargo, the rule was in violation of section 10(c)(2), prohibiting any predatory practice designed to eliminate a common carrier in the trade.

Other Provisions on NVOCCs in the 1984 Act

The 1984 Act confers certain advantages upon an NVOCC not previously enjoyed and also imposes certain obligations upon it, both in its capacity as shipper and common carrier. Section 4(a)(5) of the Act provides that among the agreements that ocean common carriers, that is, vessel operators, can make is one to engage in "exclusive, preferential or cooperative working arrangements . . . with one or more non-vessel-operating common carriers." Such an agreement is not directly between one or more vessel operators and the NVOCC; rather, the agreement would be among the vessel operators, and it could provide for an exclusive, preferential, or cooperating working arrangement by the lines with an NVOCC. Such an agreement must be filed with the FMC under section 5(a) and be subject to review under section 6(g)'s "substantially anticompetitive" test. Upon becoming effective, the agreement would be exempt from our antitrust laws under section 7(a)(1). It would appear that any "preferential arrangement" between the lines relating to one or more NVOCCs would be an exception to the broad prohibition in section 10(b)(11) against giving any undue or unreasonable preference or advantage to any person "in any respect whatsoever." Such agreements among vessel operators may be used to confer an opportunity for significant advantages to NVOCCs under the 1984 Act.

Under section 8, the NVOCC is required to file a tariff with the FMC. As a common carrier, the NVOCC may offer a time-volume rate to a shipper under section 8(b). As a shipper, an NVOCC may receive a time-volume rate from the underlying carrier. Under section 8(e), the NVOCC as a shipper may obtain from a vessel operator a refund of a freight charge collected or a waiver of the collection of a charge if there is an error in a tariff of a clerical or administrative nature, or due to inadvertent failure to file a new tariff.

Section 10, Prohibited Acts, confers certain advantages and also imposes obligations upon an NVOCC. Section 10(a) provides that no person may knowingly and willfully obtain ocean transportation for less than the tariff rate by means of a misrepresentation or concealment. The NVOCC as a shipper is subject to a civil penalty for a violation of this section. At the same time, however, as a shipper, the NVOCC obtains the benefits of section 10(b)(6), which prohibits unfair or unjustly discriminatory practices in the matter of rates, cargo classifications, cargo space accommodations, the loading and unloading of freight, and the adjustment and settlement of claims.

When an NVOCC acts as a common carrier under section 10(b), it has the same obligations as a vessel operator. Under section 10(b)(14), an NVOCC may not accept cargo from another NVOCC that does not have an appropriate tariff and bond on file. Proof of the NVOCC's compliance may be obtained by (1) consulting a current list provided by the Commission of tariffed and bonded NVOCCs; or (2) reviewing a copy of the tariff rule published by the NVOCC; or (3) any other appropriate procedure provided that such procedure is set forth in the carrier's tariff of general applicability. A common carrier that employs the procedure described above is deemed to have met its obligations, unless the carrier knew that such NVOCC was not in compliance with the tariff and bonding requirements.[16] Under 10(d)(1), an NVOCC as a common carrier must establish and enforce just and reasonable regulations and practices relating to or connected with receiving, handling, storing, or delivering property.

Under section 11a.(b)(1), Foreign Laws and Practices, the FMC is authorized to investigate the laws or rules of a foreign government or any practice of a foreign carrier or other person providing "maritime-related services" in a foreign country that adversely affect the operations of U.S. carriers in the U.S. oceanborne trade. The term "maritime-related services" is defined under section 11a.(4) to include NVOCC operations. Thus, the FMC may act against a foreign government or carriers if a practice adversely affects a U.S.-based NVOCC.

Under section 15(a), Reports and Certificates, the FMC may require an NVOCC or any officer or employee thereof to file a periodical or special report concerning its transactions and business. Section 15(b) includes the NVOCC among those that must file a periodical certification under oath that it has not engaged in any unlawful rebate.

Bonding of Non-Vessel-Operating Common Carriers

In 1990 Congress, at the request of the industry, required the bonding of NVOCCs.[17] This enactment was incorporated in the 1984 Act as section 23 thereof.[18] The basis for the law was set forth by the chairman of the House Merchant Marine Committee upon the introduction of a bonding bill in June 1990. He noted that at that time there were approximately 1450 NVOCCs operating in the U.S. foreign commerce, and that the FMC had been receiving an increasing number of complaints concerning their practices, reflecting a growing pattern of unlawful conduct that had significant adverse impact often exacerbated by the fact that many NVOCCs lacked tangible assets. A recurring problem arose when a shipper prepaid the freight charges to an NVOCC, but when the consignee attempted to obtain the release of the cargo, it discovered that it must first pay the ocean carrier because the NVOCC had failed to do so. In other instances, NVOCCs had gone bankrupt requiring shippers to pay duplicate charges to obtain release of the cargo.[19]

The FMC issued its initial rules in 1991 dealing with NVOCC bonding in Part 583 of its regulations.[20] At the outset of its report, it responded to a request that the agency define an NVOCC more precisely. In denying this request on the ground that the FMC had already, within the context of the docket, provided adequate guidance as to what constitutes an NVOCC, it stated:

As common carriers, NVOCCs hold themselves out to the public to provide transportation by water between the United States and foreign countries, utilizing vessels operating on the high seas. NVOCCs normally enter into affreightment agreements with their underlying shippers, issue bills of lading or equivalent documents, and assume full responsibility for the shipments they handle from point of origin to point of destination.[21]

Initially, section 23(a) required an NVOCC to furnish a bond in a form and amount determined by the Commission "to be satisfactory to ensure the financial responsibility of that carrier but in any event not less than $50,000." Thereafter, section 23(a) was amended by eliminating the provision for a bond of no less than $50,000 and providing instead that each NVOCC furnish to the FMC "a bond, proof of insurance, or such other surety, as the Commission may require, in a form and amount determined by the Commission to be satisfactory to insure the financial responsibility of that carrier."[22] In support of this change, the agency issued amended rules, entitled "Financial Responsibility for Non-Vessel-Operating Common Carriers."[23]

The above amendment permits an NVOCC to establish its financial responsibility by filing a surety bond for $50,000, providing insurance by insurers, Lloyds, or suppliers lines insurers making certain standards, or filing a guarantee.[24] Such coverage can be provided individually by the NVOCCs or by a group or association of which the NVOCC is a member.[25]

Under section 23(b), the above methods of establishing financial responsibility would be "available to pay any judgment for damages" against an NVOCC arising from "transportation-related activities" under the Act or order for reparations or civil penalty assessed against the NVOCC.

Section 23(c) requires an NVOCC not domiciled in the United States to designate a resident agent in this country for the receipt of service of judicial and administrative process, including subpoenas. If the designated legal agent cannot be served because of death, disability, or unavailability, the secretary of the FMC will be deemed to be the legal agent for the service of process.[26] As the name implies, the resident agent is an agent only and not a principal. Thus, it does not assume the liability of the NVOCC for whom it is acting, the primary purpose of the designation requirement being to confer jurisdiction over a foreign NVOCC in an FMC or other proceeding. The designation of a resident agent shall be published in the NVOCC tariff.[27]

Section 23(d) provides that the Commission may suspend or cancel an NVOCC tariff for failure to maintain the required bond or other security or designate a resident agent as required. In order to prevent an inadvertent mistake, the agency has provided for a procedure for the termination of a bond or designation of a resident agent. Under section 583.6(a) of its rules, upon receipt of a notice of termination of a surety bond, the Commission will notify the NVOCC by certified or registered mail that the FMC shall, without hearing or other proceeding, suspend or cancel the tariff of the NVOCC unless it submits a valid replacement surety bond before the termination date. Similarly, where the FMC has received notice of a termination of the designation of a resident agent, the FMC shall so notify the NVOCC by registered mail, and shall without hearing or other proceeding suspend or cancel the tariff of an NVOCC effective thirty days after receipt of the notice of the termination of the designated resident agent, unless the NVOCC publishes a replacement designation of such agent before the date of suspension or cancellation.[28]

The FMC is not deprived of jurisdiction over allegedly unlawful acts by an NVOCC committed while it had no tariff in effect.[29]

Suppose a firm engaged in the ship brokerage business arranges, for the first and only time, for an exportation wherein it shipped the goods in its own name because the vessel would not accept the supplier as the exporter on the bill of lading and the firm assumed transportation responsibility. The FMC held that as a result of such conduct the firm became an untariffed NVOCC. The U.S. Court of Appeals reversed, concluding that the FMC's decision was "unsupported by substantial evidence." According to the court, an "extraordinary single shot undertaking" does not convert an enterprise engaged in any respect of the shipping business into a common carrier accountable for tariff filing.[30]

Co-Loading by NVOCCs

In 1985, the FMC issued "Special Rules" regulating the co-loading activities of NVOCCs.[31] According to the FMC, the fact that an NVOCC has a carrier alter ego is irrelevant to its status as a shipper when tendering cargo to another NVOCC. Thus, co-loaded cargo tendered by one NVOCC to another is not sufficiently distinct in and of itself to warrant a rate based solely upon the fact that the cargo is tendered by an NVOCC.[32]

The Special Rules governing the co-loading activities of NVOCCs are set forth in Appendix I, attached hereto. An NVOCC must describe its co-loading activities and, if it does not co-load, its tariff must so indicate. If two or more NVOCCs establish a carrier-to-carrier relationship for co-loading, such an agreement must be noted in the tariff of each of the NVOCCs.

NVOCCs wishing to engage in a carrier-to-carrier co-loading operation must make the nature of the arrangement as clear as possible. Otherwise, the danger exists that what has been described as a carrier-to-carrier arrangement is in fact a shipper-to-carrier type of co-loading, and substantial penalties may be assessed by the FMC for a violation of the rules. A carrier-to-carrier co-loading agreement must, therefore, provide as definitively as possible what each NVOCC's rights and responsibilities are, so that the arrangement is not construed as a shipper-to-carrier function.

A copy of a form of a carrier-to-carrier co-loading agreement is attached as Appendix J.[33] The rights and responsibilities of the tendering and receiving NVOCCs under a carrier-to carrier agreement should be accompanied by proper documentation to avoid misunderstandings. It is advisable that they use a co-load cargo receipt, with its terms and conditions to be imprinted on the reverse side for the handling of tendered shipments. A suggested draft of such receipt and terms is attached as Appendix K.

If the co-loading arrangement results in a shipper-to-carrier relationship, the tendering NVOCC shall describe in its tariff its co-loading practices, and specify its responsibility to pay any charges for the transportation of the cargo. A shipper-to-carrier relationship is presumed when the receiving NVOCC issues a bill of lading to the tendering NVOCC for the carriage of the co-loaded cargo. No NVOCC shall offer special co-loading rates for the exclusive use of other NVOCCs. Thus, when an NVOCC tenders cargo in the capacity of a shipper, it must be rated and carried by the receiving NVOCC under tariff provisions available to all shippers.[34]

In *Yangming,* the FMC held that a noncontract signatory NVOCC could not directly book cargo with a line to take advantage of another NVOCC's service contract without the latter's approval.[35] This decision, however, may not be fairly construed to mean that the FMC is prohibiting co-loading on a service contract that does not specifically prohibit such practice. So long as the co-loading rules are adhered to and the noncontract signatory NVOCC tenders its cargo to be co-loaded with a service contract NVOCC signatory, the practice would appear to be authorized.

CHAPTER VI

OCEAN FREIGHT FORWARDERS

The Role of the Forwarder, Its Legal Status, and Jurisdiction Over Its Practices

The 1984 Act defines an "ocean freight forwarder" as "a person in the United States that (A) dispatches shipments from the United States via common carriers and books or otherwise arranges space for those shipments on behalf of shippers; and (B) processes the documentation or performs related activities incident to those shipments."[1] He is sometimes known as an international forwarding agent, a foreign freight forwarder, or a forwarding agent.

History of Forwarding Industry

The forwarding industry developed in this country in the latter part of the nineteenth and the early part of the twentieth century. Prior to World War I, the bulk of our export trade was handled from New York with no appreciable service from the Pacific Coast. Service from the Gulf and the South Atlantic was restricted largely to cotton shipments. When business originated on the West Coast, it was shipped by rail either to New York or to New Orleans.

Large parcels of freight or full shiploads were handled by a freight broker, known as a "ship's broker" when acting for the ship and as an "owner's or cargo broker" when acting for the shipper. These brokers usually consisted of partners with limited clerical assistance who served as an intermediary between the shipper and ocean carrier for the placing of cargo, rarely performing any other services. Formalities in connection with an exportation were at a minimum and when it was necessary for a broker to prepare a bill of lading, he did so generally without a fee.

Prior to World War I the railroads played an important part in the movement of ocean shipments. They maintained foreign freight departments at interior points where merchandise was received and generally issued a through bill of lading which covered the rail transportation to seaboard and the ocean voyage.

With the advent of World War I, the United States suddenly changed from an agricultural nation, whose shipments were largely foodstuffs or raw materials, to a manufacturing nation. The war brought about a great expansion of shipping, and ocean carriers established branch offices in the interior and solicited freight through their own canvassers. The use of the through bill of lading by railroads from interior points declined in importance and the technical requirements with respect to documentation, custom regulations, and consular requirements gave rise to a specialist, the ocean freight forwarder, at the port area to handle individual shipments. Many forwarding concerns originally started as freight brokers, but with the continuing increase in manufactured shipments, the forwarding work took precedence over the broker activities. Today, some forwarders handle shiploads of large parcels either on common carrier or tramp vessels as brokers, but for the most part forwarders deal with individual shipments varying in size or containers.

Services Rendered by Forwarder

For a full understanding of the legal relationship between a forwarder, shipper, and carrier it is well to outline the specific services that a forwarder renders on a shipment.[2] Before the goods actually move from an exporter's plant or warehouse, the forwarder advises him on the various aspects of the shipment. The forwarder recommends what it considers the proper port of exit to be. In so deciding, the forwarder gives consideration to the inland freight rate, the availability of carrier service, and possible congestion at the port. If a shipment requires an export license by our government, the forwarder reviews the license obtained by the shipper to see that it is in order. If the shipper has not obtained a license, the forwarder may do so on its behalf. Where a letter of credit is involved, it is reviewed by the forwarder to make sure that the shipper is able to comply with its terms.

Once the shipment leaves an inland supply point, if it moves by rail, the forwarder "traces" the rail cars to make sure that the shipment is passed on from one railroad to another in good time. If a car is in "bad order," that is, delayed for repairs, the forwarder stays in contact with the rail carrier to "expedite" the return of the car so that it reaches seaboard in time to meet the vessel. On a shipment moving by motor carrier the forwarder works closely with such carrier for the timely arrival of the cargo at the port.

The forwarder usually makes the necessary arrangements to reserve space aboard a particular vessel, known as "booking the cargo." Before it is booked, the forwarder must, in the case of a substantial shipment, consider such factors as the loading equipment of the vessel, its sailing date, and the estimated time of arrival at the loading port. In the New

York area, approximately 75 to 80 percent of the freight that the steam-ship lines receive comes through forwarders. In the case of some lines, it may be virtually all of the freight.

In almost all cases the forwarder prepares the necessary shipping papers. One of these is the shipper's export declaration, a document our government requires for statistical purposes. The declaration is cleared through Customs by the forwarder under a power of attorney from the shipper. The carrier may not lawfully load the cargo until it possesses an authenticated copy of the document. A dock receipt, prepared by the forwarder, is signed by the line acknowledging receipt of the cargo. The delivery order is a direction by the forwarder to the rail or motor carrier as to where and when the cargo is to be delivered to shipside. The forwarder prepares the bill of lading, an essential document in exporta-tion; it acts as the contract of carriage, a final receipt, and a document of title. Twenty-five or thirty copies are made and usually three originals are issued by the line.

On shipments, for instance, to South and Central America, the country of importation requires a consular invoice, its purpose being to accomplish compliance with the exchange restrictions and import laws of the country of destination. The form is also used to determine the rate of duty. The forwarder prepares the document in the foreign language and delivers it to a consular office in the United States for authentication. Careful drafting is needed to avoid substantial fines for any error that may be levied on the shipper and forwarder.

Certain cargo, such as heavy lift items, frequently require that special equipment be used by the ocean carrier to accomplish loading. If the cargo does not arrive at shipside when the special equipment is ready to load, an additional expense is incurred. When a forwarder coordinates the movement efficiently from inland origin to the port of exit, so that it arrives at the right time and place, extra charges and expenses are avoided. On smaller lots the forwarder performs a similar coordinating job between the carrier and the steamship line by arranging for the delivery of the goods to the pier when the line wants it.

Generally, a shipment will require so-called "accessorial services," that is, services to be performed in addition to coordinating the physical movement. Insurance on the cargo is ordinarily arranged by the for-warder, either under the exporter's or the forwarder's open marine policy. Local trucking of the goods from the rail or truck terminal to the pier may also be required on smaller lots. Partial shipments may have to be stored to await the arrival of other goods and the forwarder arranges for warehousing. If the crating of the goods is damaged on arrival at the port, the forwarder arranges for recoopering. The forwarder charges the shipper a fee over and above the actual disbursement for arranging these services.

Shipments frequently move under a letter of credit; at other times they move under either draft terms or an open account. Where a letter of credit is used, the forwarder must be sure that its terms are rigidly complied with; otherwise, an amendment from abroad must be obtained. By making certain that all of the technical requirements of the letter of credit are met within the time specified, the forwarder obtains prompt payment for the exporter and thus significantly contributes to the making of a sale of American goods abroad.

The forwarder receives its revenue from two basic sources. The principal, either the U.S. exporter or the overseas consignee, pays a forwarding fee for the various services rendered in accomplishing the exportation. The ocean carrier compensates the forwarder by a commission based upon a percentage of the ocean freight, known historically as "brokerage," but also referred to as "compensation."[3]

Forwarder Distinguished from Others

The ocean freight forwarder is distinguishable from others rendering services in connection with the transportation of goods. The domestic freight forwarder, also known as a "carloader," issues a bill of lading to its customer for a less-than-carload shipment, which is then consolidated with other shipments to form a carload lot for movement to and from U.S. interior points by an underlying rail or motor carrier. The domestic forwarder receives his profit from the difference between the carload rate charged by the carrier and the less-than-carload rate it charges the shipper (the "spread"). The air freight forwarder performs a similar consolidation function on air shipments, assumes carrier responsibility, and receives his gross profit from the spread in the rates.

An ocean freight broker arranges for a full shipload of cargo or a large parcel, usually moving via a tramp vessel. As indicated earlier, this broker performs little or no documentary services and may employ a forwarder, when needed, to handle the details of an exportation. The freight broker may act on behalf of the ship or the owner of the cargo, depending upon who commissioned him to render the service.[4] He is not directly regulated by any federal agency.

An International Air Transport Association (IATA) cargo sales agent is a person who arranges for the transportation of individual shipments via an air carrier. An IATA agent is not a carrier, its services being similar to those of an ocean freight forwarder, and it receives a fee from the shipper and a commission from the airline.

A customs broker attends to the formalities incident to the clearing of imports through U.S. Customs. It receives a fee from the importer, but no compensation from the carrier. Many firms perform the dual service of arranging exports as a forwarder and clearing imports as a customs broker. The broker is licensed by the Treasury Department through the Commissioner of Customs.

The importance of forwarders to our foreign commerce has been recognized by virtually every official agency which has examined their functions. The Commission has described the forwarding industry as "an integral part of the commerce of the United States."[5] The Senate Commerce Committee considers the industry as "a highly important segment of the economy of the United States in that its functioning makes possible participation in the Nation's foreign commerce by many industries and businesses whose lack of familiarity with the complexities and formalities of exporting procedures might hinder, or even preclude, such participation if forwarding services were not freely available."[6] The U.S. Court of Appeals recognizes that "without the industry's services, our vital export trade would be at a serious disadvantage in intense competition with world commerce."[7]

Legal Status of Forwarder

In rendering its services, the Supreme Court has said that the forwarder acts as an agent of the shipper.[8] However, the shipper does not have the right to control the means and manner by which the forwarder performs his tasks. While the shipper may tell the forwarder what it wants done, the shipper does not specify how the services are to be done. Accordingly, the forwarder has been held to be an independent contractor with respect to its relationship with the shipper,[9] one ground being that inasmuch as a forwarder is compensated by both parties to the transaction, it cannot be a fiduciary.[10] The FMC requires an applicant for a license to establish a high standard of moral conduct,[11] and whether considered as an agent or independent contractor, the forwarder is required to meet its regulatory obligations.[12]

Responsibilities of Forwarders to Carriers and Shippers

In arranging for the overseas dispatch of a shipment, the forwarder necessarily deals with the many parties involved in the transportation and processing of the merchandise. As noted, after leaving the inland supply point, the goods are transported to the port area by rail or motor carrier where they may require local trucking, processing, and packing. Thereafter, the shipment is delivered to a marine terminal, for loading aboard a vessel, and transported overseas to a foreign consignee. Acting as the coordinator of the movement from its inception, the forwarder deals directly with all those who render specific services with respect to the shipment and may be exposed to liability for various charges incurred in the process. In this section the extent of the forwarder's liability to third parties will be treated and suggestions made as to how such liability may possibly be minimized.

Inland Freight

At times, a shipment transported by a rail or motor carrier will be consigned to the forwarder at the port of exportation, the purpose being to permit the forwarder as consignee on the inland bill of lading to issue instructions to the carrier at the port to deliver the shipment to a designated vessel at a particular pier.

A description of the forwarder as the consignee on a rail or motor carrier bill of lading may result in liability for the inland freight charges to the port. The contract terms and conditions of a uniform rail bill of lading usually provide that "the owner or consignee shall pay the freight and demurrage, if any, and all other lawful charges accruing on said property. . . ." Thus, a forwarder may find that as the consignee of the freight, the carrier may look to it for payment of the transportation charges and accrued demurrage. Suppose the carrier is unable to collect the freight charges from the consignor or owner of the goods, and under the bill of lading terms the carrier seeks to collect the freight from the forwarder as consignee in the bill of lading. Is the forwarder liable?

The forwarder may resist the carrier's claim for the freight charges on various grounds. It may argue that the carrier may have known that the forwarder was acting only as a forwarding agent for the shipment to effect the interchange between the rail and ocean carrier, and was not, therefore, the actual owner of the shipment, nor did it have a beneficial interest in it. Based upon these known facts, the forwarder may contend that any presumption of ownership by reason of being named as the consignee is rebutted and there is, accordingly, no implied promise to pay the freight charges.[13] The forwarder may also assert that with respect to the carrier, the forwarder's sole function is merely to advise the carrier as to the location of the designated steamer to which the shipment is to be delivered, and that merely informing the carrier of the pier location is not sufficient to impose liability.[14] Finally, the forwarder may argue that its sole function as forwarding agent was to arrange for the rail and ocean carrier interchange, and since the forwarder only receives the shipment constructively, such receipt was not itself sufficient to impose liability.[15]

It is doubtful that the above-cited authorities, early decisions in this area, will necessarily result in a favorable decision for the forwarder. The forwarder is aware, or should be, of the inland carrier's conditions plainly imposing liability on the consignee and, by exercising dominion over the shipment by issuing delivery instructions to the carrier, the forwarder would ordinarily be liable for the freight charges even though not the owner of the goods.

Congress has by statute conferred a limitation on the liability of a consignee under certain circumstances by the addition of the so-called Newton Amendment to section 3, [par. (2)] of the Interstate Commerce Act [49 U.S.C. 3(2)]. This amendment provides:

> Where carriers by railroad are instructed by a shipper or consignor to deliver property transported by such carriers to a consignee other than the shipper or consignor, such consignee shall not be legally liable for transportation charges in respect of the transportation of such property (beyond those billed against him at the time of delivery for which he is otherwise liable) which may be found to be due after the property has been delivered to him, if the consignee (a) is an agent only and has no beneficial title in the property, and (b) prior to delivery of the property has notified the delivering carrier in writing of the fact of such agency and absence of beneficial title.

This amendment limits the liability of a consignee-agent for transportation charges "which may be found to be due after the property has been delivered to him." The purpose of the law was not to relieve a consignee-agent from the original freight charges, which were due and billed at the time of the delivery of the goods, but only those additional charges found by the carrier to be due at a later date, usually after the consignee has settled with its principal. In enacting this amendment, Congress found that frequently the carrier made mistakes by charging less than the legal rate and then, after discovering the undercharge, would seek to collect an additional amount from the consignee, often long after the actual transportation. Since the consignee-agent has in many instances difficulty in collecting these additional charges from its principal, the amendment was designed to relieve the agent of liability for such after-discovered charges, if he notifies the carrier at delivery time that he is an agent only and has no beneficial title in the property.[16]

To take advantage of the provision limiting liability for additional charges discovered after delivery of the goods, a forwarder should place on his delivery instructions to the carrier a notice reading as follows:

Pursuant to the provisions of the Interstate Commerce Act, notice is hereby given that we are agents only, and have no beneficial title in the property contained in the cars or packages listed above.

XYZ Forwarding Co., Inc.

By _____

Because the amendment does not relieve a forwarder from liability for the inland freight charges billed at the time of delivery, how may a forwarder avoid liability for inland freight charges when named as consignee on the bill of lading? The arrival notice from the carrier usually indicates whether a shipment is freight collect and, if a forwarder is unwilling to assume consignee liability, it should upon receipt of the notice so advise the carrier. If the forwarder is on the credit list of the carrier, the names of customers should be limited, if possible, to consignors to whom the forwarder wishes to extend credit for the inland freight charges.

Liability may also be avoided if the forwarder instructs its principal that it should not be named on the inland bill of lading as the consignee of the shipment, but only as a "notify party" to whom the inland carrier may look for information and instruction as to which pier the goods are to be delivered to. While this procedure is not needed where the forwarder deems that there is no credit risk, it would seem an advisable technique where the forwarder has had no prior dealings with the principal or is otherwise unwilling to assume liability for the freight charges.

Ocean Freight Charges

As noted above, a forwarder prepares an ocean bill of lading, delivers it to the carrier's office and, after computation of the freight and other charges by the carrier, the forwarder picks up the ocean bill of lading. Before it may do so, in many port areas carriers require a forwarder to execute a "due bill." The form of due bills varies somewhat from line to line, but it usually provides that the forwarder agrees to pay the total charges set forth therein within a certain time after receipt of the bill of lading, generally seventy-two hours. The due bill will sometimes provide a space for the name of the shipper as well as the forwarder to be inserted. In this situation the due bill will read that "we jointly and severally agree" to pay the freight within the stipulated period and is usually signed by the forwarder's employee, ostensibly on behalf of both parties.

Despite the fact that the forwarder does not have title or a beneficial interest in the shipment and acts as agent only for a disclosed principal, the execution of the due bill has been held by some courts to impose liability upon the forwarder for the ocean freight charges. The reasoning is that the signing of a due bill by the forwarder constitutes a separate contractual undertaking on its part to pay the charges and in entering such a contract the carrier is waiving any right he may have to resort to the shipper for payment.[17] This line of authority holds that the forwarder is liable for the freight charges while the exporter is not. In a typical case, the forwarder who signed a due bill may be shown as the debtor on the carrier's books. After the forwarder was adjudicated a bankrupt, the carrier sought payment from the exporter. In dismissing the carrier's complaint against an exporter on the merits, the court said:

> Plaintiff, of course, knew that it was dealing with an agent for a disclosed principal but it preferred to deal with the agent and to rely upon the credit of the agent. Having sought the advantages of this arrangement, the plaintiff must accept the disadvantages accruing therefrom. The evidence does not permit of any other inference than that the plaintiff relied solely upon the credit of the freight forwarder and that the demand upon the defendant for payment was a mere afterthought.
>
> * * *
>
> Because of the contractual arrangement between plaintiff and the freight forwarder the debt here was the latter's and not the defendant's. The defendant made prompt payment to the freight forwarder and the plaintiff may not, because of the afterthought which it has had, repudiate its credit arrangement with the freight forwarder and impose a double liability on defendant.[18]

To avoid due bill liability a national forwarder organization importuned the FMC to adopt a rule forbidding carriers from collecting freight charges against a forwarder under a due bill on the ground that it was being coerced into executing the due bill if it wished to obtain the ocean bill of lading, a document vital to the exportation. This request was denied by the FMC, and the U.S. Court of Appeals held that the agency acted within its discretion.[19]

Contrary to most decisions, in a Fifth Circuit case involving a due bill where the shipper had paid the forwarder, the court in a dictum indicated that the carrier could collect against a shipper that had paid the freight to its forwarder in order to enforce the policy against discrimination under our shipping laws.[20] This is a rather doubtful basis for shipper liability, since it had already paid the forwarder.

To minimize the risk by a shipper of a double payment in jurisdictions that do not relieve the shipper from liability where its forwarder has signed a due bill, the following precautions are advisable:

1. The shipper should use great care in selecting its forwarder. The firm chosen should be experienced and its credit rating meticulously checked. While the Commission requires a forwarder to file a bond in the face amount of $30,000,[21] this amount may in many instances be wholly inadequate to satisfy all the creditors of an insolvent forwarder.
2. Inquiry should be made as to whether the forwarder is a member of a forwarder association, ordinarily persuasive evidence that the forwarder is considered reliable by its peers.
3. At times, a shipper may not have the right to select its own forwarder. Based upon the terms of sale, an overseas consignee may have the authority to instruct the U.S. supplier which forwarder to use. Nevertheless, if under such terms the U.S. exporter continues to be responsible for the ocean freight charges, it should make the same careful check of the consignee-designated forwarder as it would do if it were selecting its own.

Since the authorities on the issue of due bill liability are rather unclear and contradictory, what should the appropriate law be? Most exporters, particularly on the Atlantic and Gulf Coasts, are located at inland origin points. Carriers do not usually wish the inconvenience and expense of dealing with a not always knowledgeable exporter on a direct basis frequently located at a distance from the port area and have, therefore, found it more practical and efficient to deal with the exporter's agent, the forwarder processing the shipment at the port, on all aspects of the exportation, including the issuance to the forwarder of a prepaid bill of lading.

When a bill of lading marked "prepaid" was required, it appears that lines in the past were faced with the problem of issuing such a document without having actually received payment of the freight from the shipper or consignee. When a bill of lading states that the freight was "prepaid" if in fact it was not, a question arose as to whether such document contained a false statement in violation of the Harter Act.[22] To meet this problem, a forwarder would sign a due bill at the request of a line and, by obtaining the obligation of the forwarder for the freight, the carrier could, if it so chose, conclude it had been paid and the Harter Act problem was thus avoided.

While exact evidence of the origins of the due bill practice is lacking, it appears doubtful that the carriers intended to use the due bill as a device to hold the forwarder liable for the freight and at the same time relieve the shipper from paying for the transportation of its goods. The average forwarder currently employs about fifteen people, while most shippers and exporters are financially more substantial. This being so, it appears unlikely that in using the due bill procedure the carrier intended to look solely for payment from the party with a lesser ability to pay and with no interest in the goods and, at the same time, lose its claim against the shipper whose goods were being transported.

Where a shipper transmits the freight to the forwarder which thereafter defaults, the real question should be: who shall absorb the loss—the shipper or the line? The carrier has no say in the selection of the forwarder; this is done by the shipper, for whom the forwarder is acting as agent. As a matter of basic fairness, it appears that the shipper rather than the carrier should bear the responsibility for selecting an unreliable agent, even though the consequence is that the shipper may have to pay twice. At the very least, the facts should be carefully examined in each case to determine the actual intent of the parties in using the due bill procedure rather than automatically considering the forwarder liable and the shipper not.

Goods Lost or Damaged

When an exporter seeks redress for a shipment lost or damaged, frequently the forwarder is joined with the ocean carrier in the ensuing litigation. The forwarder thereupon has the burden of establishing its nonliability.

In discussing the liability of the domestic forwarder, the Supreme Court considered the two ways it operates. In the first situation, the domestic forwarder merely arranges for transportation as agent for the shipper by procuring a carrier and handling the details of the shipment until turning it over to the carrier. The domestic forwarder charges a fee for its service, which the shipper pays plus the freight charges. In this case the domestic forwarder is liable "only for its own negligence, including negligence in selecting a carrier." In the second situation, the domestic forwarder acts in its more usual role as a consolidator of LCL shipments into carload lots, issuing its own bill of lading to the shippers. Here the liability of the domestic forwarder is that of a common carrier for loss or damage, regardless of whether it or the underlying carrier is at fault.[23]

The liability of an ocean freight forwarder is similar to that of the domestic forwarder in the first case, that is, where it merely arranges for the transportation. In such a situation it is not a carrier, since it does not assume a transportation liability.[24] The ocean freight forwarder is liable only for its own negligence.

It seems clear that Express Company held itself out merely to handle the details of the shipment to arrange with common carriers for the transportation of the goods. It did not undertake to deliver the shipment safely at its destination. It did not assume any responsibility for the goods but was responsible merely for its own negligence.[25]

While it has no common carrier liability, a forwarder must use due care in the manner in which it processes a shipment for exportation. If, for example, it loses the papers in connection with the shipment, misdirects the cargo to the wrong port, fails to follow a shipper's instructions, or otherwise acts negligently resulting in damage, the forwarder is liable.[26]

The forwarder is also liable if it negligently selects a party to render services with respect to a shipment and damage occurs. What is the measure of care a forwarder must employ in selecting these third parties? The question arises, for example, when a trucker or ocean carrier loses or damages a shipment, or when a forwarder in another port to whom a shipment is referred by a forwarder for processing acts negligently, causing loss to the shipper. The forwarder must select these third parties prudently. In so doing, it should determine whether the party selected is experienced and well established in the trade. If so, and the forwarder has no information that the selected party has mishandled prior shipments, the duty and care required would ordinarily be met, and the forwarder is not liable if the merchandise is lost or damaged by reason of the negligence of such third party.

As in the case of other transportation entities, such as truckers, vessel operators, and warehouseman, it is advisable for a forwarder to limit its liability in writing. The standard limitation of liability used by the industry is contained in the Terms and Conditions of Service (the Terms) approved by the National Customs Brokers and Forwarders Association of America, Inc. (NCBFAA).[27] The salient provisions of the Terms are:

1. The forwarder assumes no liability as a carrier and undertakes only to use reasonable care in the selection of third parties to whom the goods are entrusted for transportation or handling and is not responsible for the negligence of such parties.
2. The forwarder is relieved of liability except where the shipment was in its actual custody or control and the loss or damage was caused by the negligence of the forwarder.
3. The forwarder has complete freedom in choosing the means, route, and procedure to be followed in the handling and transportation of the goods.
4. The forwarder's liability shall not exceed the lesser of $50 per shipment or the fee charged for services, unless a higher value is

declared under a written arrangement with the forwarder to pay an additional fee.

5. A claim against the forwarder for any act, omission, or default must be presented by the exporter to the forwarder within ninety days from the date of exportation.

6. The forwarder is indemnified for any claim made by a carrier or other person for ocean freight or other charges arising out of a shipment.

7. The forwarder has a general lien on all property of the exporter for charges, expenses, or advances incurred by the forwarder in processing the shipment and a public sale of such property is permitted thirty days after a demand for a payment has not been complied with.

Because the authorities require that reasonable notice be given of trading conditions, it is advisable that a new customer be informed in writing that the services of the forwarder are being performed pursuant to the enclosed Terms, and the customer should be requested to acknowledge receipt by returning a signed copy of the terms. If a signed copy is not returned at the inception of business, the forwarder should write the exporter again, R.R.R. (return receipt requested), stating that its shipments are being handled pursuant to the enclosed Terms. In all cases the Terms should be reproduced on the reverse side of the forwarder's invoice and other documents sent to a customer. At the bottom of the front page of each document a legend should be imprinted in bold print reading "ALL SHIPMENTS ARE HANDLED PURSUANT TO THE TERMS AND CONDITIONS ON THE REVERSE SIDE HEREOF."

With the above precautions taken, it may be persuasively argued that the forwarder has given reasonable notice of the Terms so that they constitute a binding contract and not a contract of adhesion.[28] There are decisions sustaining the Terms when proper notice has been given.[29] Without such notice, however, unless it can be established that there were prior dealings between parties involving the limitations of liability or that the limitations were in use with such frequency as to justify a finding that they were a custom in the trade, a court may be reluctant to impose such limitations upon a shipper. When Terms are adopted, care should be taken that they are legible.

Accessorial Services

As indicated above, a forwarder performs various accessorial services in connection with every shipment. It may arrange for insurance under an open marine policy issued by the underwriter to the forwarder, and it also obtains the services, when needed, of third parties prior to the actual ocean transportation for trucking, warehousing, and packing. In connection therewith, the forwarder may become responsible for accrued charges.

Where the forwarder's open marine policy is used to cover a shipment, the forwarder becomes liable to the underwriter for the premium, even though it is known that the shipment insured is that of a third party. The forwarder has sought a policy in its own name for business convenience and, having entered into a contract with the underwriter for the payment of premiums, it may not avoid liability on the ground that it is agent for a disclosed principal.[30]

Liability for warehousing, trucking, and packing charges may likewise be incurred by the forwarder if it deals as a principal with the one rendering the service. It is not uncommon, for example, to place a customer's shipment in a warehouse in the forwarder's name. Under these circumstances the warehouseman may properly claim that the forwarder is liable for the charges. This liability may be avoided if the documents clearly show that the warehouseman or trucker is rendering the services for the account of a named shipper.[31]

Obligations of Ocean Freight Forwarder Under 1984 Act

Regulatory Responsibilities

Regulation under the 1916 Act of forwarders began in 1946 when the Supreme Court held that a forwarder was subject to the Act as an "other person" when "carrying on the business of forwarding" in the foreign commerce of the United States.[32] Thereafter, at the request of forwarders, section 44 was added in 1961 to require the licensing by the FMC of forwarders if found to be "independent" of shipper connections and "fit, willing, and able" properly to carry on the business of forwarding.[33] In 1981, the "independent" requirement was eliminated so that a holding company could have one subsidiary act as a forwarder and another as a shipper, provided that compensation from a carrier was prohibited when the forwarder handled the shipments of the shipper affiliate.

Under the 1984 Act, the holding company mechanism to allow forwarding by a shipper was eliminated. Under section 3(19), an "ocean freight forwarder" is a person in the United States who dispatches shipments from the United States via common carriers, books, or otherwise arranges space, for those shipments on behalf of shippers, and processes the documentation or performs related activities incident to those shipments.[34] This definition does not restrict a shipper from being licensed as an ocean freight forwarder, but it may not under section 19(d)(4) receive compensation from a carrier "with respect to a shipment in which the forwarder has a direct or indirect beneficial interest."[35] According to the Senate Commerce Committee, this restriction prevents the resurgence of the "dummy forwarder,"[36] that is, a shipper acting as a forwarder to receive brokerage, which would result in rebates, but permits forwarders to operate as export trading companies.[37] The FMC has by rule fortified the "no beneficial interest" restriction by requiring a licensee, which is a shipper or seller of goods in international commerce, to identify itself as such or give notice on its stationery or billing forms of the shipper status.[38]

Sections 4, 5, and 6 of the Act confer jurisdiction upon the FMC to review and allow agreements between or among ocean common carriers. Eliminated from the 1984 Act was section 15 of the 1916 Act,[39] requiring a forwarder as an "other person" to file for approval any agreement reached with a carrier or other person subject to the Act. Unlike the NVOCCs, which have strongly complained about losing the opportunity to obtain antitrust immunity under agreements fixing rates and practices, the forwarders have not objected.

In the late 1970s a group of thirty-nine forwarders (CONFICO) entered into an agreement to form a corporation to consolidate and arrange for the movement of cargo in our foreign commerce. Approval of the agreement was strenuously contested by major steamship conferences and, after extensive litigation, the FMC held that although freight consolidation is not itself a function regulated by the Shipping Act, it was sufficiently related to the forwarders' activities for section 15 jurisdiction to attach.[40] Due to the delays and expense involved in lengthy litigation, CONFICO abandoned its effort to obtain approval of its cooperative working arrangement.

In 1986, CONFICO applied to the Antitrust Division, Department of Justice (DOJ) for a Business Review Letter asking DOJ what its current enforcement intentions would be with respect to CONFICO's proposal to form a corporation of forwarder stockholders to consolidate cargo and operate as an NVOCC. The division replied that it had "no present intention" to challenge the CONFICO activities. It believed that collective rate negotiation and purchasing by forwarders had the potential to create efficiencies that result in lower freight rates. In addition, the proposal essentially enables a group of small forwarders to provide consolidation services. As a result, since exporters would be able to take advantage of the benefits of off-pier consolidation and to enjoy volume rates to the extent that they occur, the formation and operation of CONFICO could be pro-competitive.

DOJ added a cautionary note. Competition is harmed, it said, if CONFICO could collectively exert market power to depress transportation rates below competitive levels, but it concluded that the proposal did not appear to raise this risk. DOJ also noted that it would challenge the formation of NVOCC concerted activity "if it would be likely to facilitate collusions or otherwise reduce competition among its members in the sale of their products or services." Here, however, DOJ felt that there did not appear to be a risk of such an effect. Rather, the proposed activities appeared likely to increase the incentives and ability of small freight forwarders to compete for LCL traffic. The plan should reduce costs and enable the participants to service markets that are now, for all practical purposes, unavailable to small-volume freight forwarders.[41]

The 1984 Act deregulated the forwarders in other areas. There is no longer any prohibition against their giving an undue preference, subjecting any person or description of traffic to an unreasonable prejudice or disadvantage, or disclosing confidential information concerning an exportation without a shipper's consent. Despite these areas of deregulation, a question remains as to whether such practices may be considered to affect a forwarder's license on the issue of "character." Also eliminated was the FMC's authority under section 20 of the 1916 Act to require a forwarder to furnish a report to the Commission of its business activities.

Misclassification of Shipments

There is no general rule as to what constitutes the due care standard that a forwarder has failed to meet before it may be said that the forwarder has engaged in a misclassification. Each case depends on its own facts. Particular examples follow.

In a case involving a paper exportation,[42] a shipper caused certain paper to be prepared for export to the Philippine Islands. The forwarder was advised by the supplier of the shipper that the paper was "brown kraft paper." The forwarder accordingly prepared all the preliminary documents referring to the shipment as brown kraft paper. A day later, the forwarder received written shipping instructions from the shipper describing the shipment as "newsprint." On the same day the forwarder was advised by the carrier that the cartons in which the paper was being shipped were marked "napkin tissue." Upon receiving such advice, the forwarder called the shipper and was told that because of the size of the sheets the merchandise could be used only for printing and could, therefore, be shipped as newsprint. The shipper later instructed the forwarder in writing to ship the paper as such. The conference tariff had different rates for napkins, newsprint, and tissue, the newsprint rate being the lowest.

The shipper having conceded that it knowingly and willfully misclassified the paper, the remaining issue in the case was whether the forwarder had also misclassified the shipment. The Commission held that the forwarder's action was not purposeful or lacking in diligence, that it appeared to have used reasonable means to determine the proper classification and, in discontinuing the action against the forwarder, the agency said:

> We agree that a persistent failure to inform or even to attempt to inform himself by means of normal business resources might mean that a shipper or forwarder was acting knowingly and willfully in violation of the Act. Diligent inquiry must be exercised by shippers and by forwarders in order to measure up to the standards set by the Act. Indifference on the part of such persons is tantamount to outright and active violation.[43]

In another docket involving a shipment of paper the forwarder did not do as well. The exporter shipped composition books, writing books, and paper for school or business. In previous shipments handled by the forwarder, the shipper had described the goods in ocean bills of lading as "stationery," the proper classification. However, to meet competition, the exporter instructed the forwarder to change the classification to "printing paper," despite the fact that the commercial invoices described the product in a manner which showed that it was not printing paper. The forwarder had copies of such invoices which also showed the exporter to be engaged in business as "Manufacturing Stationers."

In preparing the export declarations the forwarder selected a Schedule B code number which correctly covered the items shipped by the exporter, but the forwarder wrote on the declarations the words "printing paper" to conform to the description on the bill of lading. The forwarder had a tariff book available, but made no effort to be guided by the book or discover what the many different invoice numbers and prices referred to. Instead, he assumed that all items shipped were "printing paper."

The Commission held that both the shipper and the forwarder misclassified the goods and referred the case to the Department of Justice for prosecution.[44] The forwarder "consistently and continually ignored a more descriptive classification than printing paper." The use of the correct Schedule B number prevented the carrier from making comparisons between the export declaration and the bill of lading, which the Commission considered "thought-out deception."

In another case of misclassification by a forwarder, the FMC was confronted with a lack of preciseness in the tariff language. The shipper manufactured a filtering product with the trade name of Dicalite. The raw material for this product was obtained from open-pit mines of diatomaceous silica. The forwarder described the product in the ocean bill of lading as "silica" in accordance with written instructions received from the shipper. Documents from the inland rail carriers described the product as "diatomaceous or infusorial earth." The forwarder did not solicit the advice of the ocean carrier as to the proper classification and did not question the variance in the descriptions. The carrier's tariff contained a classification for diatomaceous earth at a higher rate than silica. None of the tariffs had a classification for diatomaceous silica. Both diatomaceous silica and earth are distinguishable from silica by the presence of fossil remains.

The tariffs of the conferences involved were not at that time generally available to the public, and requests to examine the tariffs at the conference's offices were refused. The carrier's employees verbally advised the shipper as to the rates on silica and on infusorial earth.

The FMC held that the forwarder was not guilty of assisting in a misclassification of the product, laying special emphasis on the fact that the tariffs were unavailable. Moreover, the Commission concluded that the tariff was ambiguous, particularly since the shipper and forwarder had to rely upon verbal statements from the carrier's employees. Two interpretations were possible—the first based on the diatomaceous characteristics of the product and the second based on its dominantly siliceous composition. This created an ambiguity, which the shipper and forwarder could resolve in favor of the lower rate.[45]

While a forwarder is deemed to be expert in tariff construction and is frequently relied upon by the shipper to advise him as to the proper classification of a shipment, the task of the forwarder in properly applying the tariff based upon the facts available is not always easy. A slight variation in the facts may require a different classification based upon the language of the tariff.

Ordinarily, a tariff is to be construed in a manner consistent with general understanding and accepted commercial usage.[46] The construction should be the meaning which the words used might reasonably carry to the shipper.[47] However, if a tariff reasonably permits two meanings, the shipper and his forwarder may construe it in the most favorable way which the term permits.[48] Thus, where more than one description is equally appropriate, the shipper is entitled to have applied the one specifying the lower rate.[49] It is not the Commission's function to change the plain meaning of a tariff to secure an interpretation in accordance with the unexpressed intention of the carrier.[50]

The difficulties facing a shipper and forwarder in construing a tariff may be shown in two cases decided by two different U.S. Courts of Appeal on shipments involving glassware. In the first case,[51] the Second Circuit had before it the construction of a tariff that had two classifications, one of which was "Bottles or Jars, Empty, Glass," and the other was "Tumblers." The exporter shipped glass containers, called packer's tumblers, as "jars," which had a lower rate than "tumblers." The packer's tumblers were primarily empty glass jars used as glass containers for packaging. They were ordered as containers by the consignee, which was in the business of manufacturing and packaging food, although they had another use as a drinking glass by the ultimate purchaser.

The initial decision of the ALJ held that the packer's tumblers were jars rather than tumblers and that there was, therefore, no misclassification. The Commission, in a 4 to 1 decision, disagreed, holding that the shipper had knowingly and willfully misclassified the goods. The Commission found that the forwarder "has a duty to take reasonable steps to inform itself as to the nature of the cargo it is handling and to act lawfully with respect thereto," but since the record failed to set forth what the precise conduct of the forwarder was, the proceeding was remanded.[52]

On appeal to the Second Circuit, the order of the Commission was reversed by a three-judge panel, each of whom rendered a separate opinion. The prevailing view held that the shipper was wholly justified in considering the containers as glass jars. They were not sold by the shipper's customer as drinking glasses, and the primary purpose of a packer's tumbler, i.e., to contain food, was certain. The court stated that the controlling use determined the classification and that any ambiguity should be resolved against the carrier, noting that there was no proof that the controlling use was intended to be a drinking glass or tumbler.[53]

A similar issue before the D.C. Circuit involved the charge of misclassification by a forwarder in connection with the exportation of glassware. The customer was a manufacturer and exporter of glassware products. In preparing a shipment for its foreign customer, the shipper's loading department at the plant described the various articles on a loading tally and from it prepared an inland bill of lading for shipment by truck to the port of departure. These two documents were sent to the forwarder, who prepared an ocean bill of lading and export declaration based upon the loading tally and inland bill of lading or upon oral advice received from the shipper.

The applicable tariffs contained rates for three kinds of glassware: "Tumblers," "Bottles or Jars," and "Glassware N.O.S." (not otherwise specified). The rate for jars was a stated sum per ton. Tumblers (table glassware) took a higher rate based on cubic contents; Glassware N.O.S. a still higher rate. The exporter shipped a quantity of drinking glasses, which it argued were correctly classified as jars instead of tumblers, because it was informed that its customers intended to use them as packaging containers for food products and other articles.

In rejecting this argument the court said:

> The present case is distinguishable. [The shipper] did not list the articles as "packer's tumblers" in its catalogue, and did not identify any Venezuelan consignee as a packer. Its contention was that the mere possibility that tumblers might be capped and used as jars or packer's tumblers should control the tariff classification. Moreover, the catalogue and loading tally descriptions were not followed in preparing the ocean bills of lading. These facts seem to us to justify the Board's inference that [the shipper] and [the forwarder] had falsely classified the shipments in order to obtain a more favorable ocean freight rate.[54]

Based upon the foregoing, the court concluded that the Commission properly held that the shipper and forwarder had violated section 16 (Second) of the 1916 Act by knowingly and willfully obtaining transportation at less than the applicable charges by means of a false classification. In so doing, the court was undoubtedly influenced to resolve any doubt against the forwarder because it had also classified as empty glass jars certain items of glassware that clearly did not fall within that category. The court also pointed out that the words "knowingly and willfully" did not involve turpitude, a mean or evil purpose, criminal intent, or the like; rather, these words are employed to characterize "conduct marked by careless disregard whether or not one has the right so to act."

From these two glassware cases it is evident that the forwarder must tread carefully to avoid a false classification accusation. In the D.C. Circuit case the forwarder was found guilty of participating in a violation based upon two facts which ordinarily may not be at the forwarder's disposal, namely, that the shipper did not list the articles as packer's tumblers in its catalogue and did not identify the overseas consignee as a packer. In the course of handling a large number of shipments a week, it is difficult, if not virtually impossible, for a forwarder, no matter how meticulous it may be, to have always at its disposal such extraneous facts as the contents of its shipper's catalogues or the nature of the business of the consignee. Nevertheless, there is authority that appears to impose a substantial burden upon the forwarder to inform itself of the nature of the shipment not only from the documents submitted to it and any oral advice received, but also on the basis of whatever extraneous facts it may be able to gather by "diligent inquiry."

With the advent of containerization in our export commerce, of interest is an FMC case involving the charge against a forwarder of misclassifying the contents of a trailer van. The forwarder tendered to the underlying carrier a number of containers a year. These containers held numerous individual shipments which had been consolidated for ocean carriage by one other than the forwarder. The particular container involved arrived at the vessel's pier in a sealed condition and the record does not show that the forwarder ever saw the contents of the van. Acting on behalf of the exporter, the forwarder presented the carrier with a bill of lading covering the shipment, showing itself as the shipper and describing the contents as containing various items. The carrier subsequently ascertained by inspection that the actual contents of the container were different than as described in the bill of lading and that the correct ocean freight on the shipment was twice the amount paid for the items described in the bill of lading.

The ALJ's initial decision found that the forwarder had violated section 16 (Second) of the 1916 Act, stating the test to be whether the forwarder had knowingly and willfully presented a false bill of lading to the carrier. The ALJ concluded that it was unnecessary to determine whether the forwarder had any actual knowledge of the contents of the container in question or that he had prepared a false bill of lading. On this reasoning the mere presentation of a bill of lading to the carrier by a forwarder carried with it the implied representation that the lading accurately described the contents of the trailer, even when received by the forwarder under seal and regardless of whether the forwarder had any knowledge of the trailer's contents.

The Commission rejected the ALJ's strict basis of culpability. In its view the reasonableness of the decision was "dependent upon a far broader consideration of the day-to-day operations of forwarders handling containerized shipments than was possible from the record in that case." After noting that misclassification cases presented continuing problems, the Commission stated that:

> While it may eventually prove true that the forwarder must be held to an implied representation as to the correctness of the description of the shipments on the bill of lading, such a decision should be made only upon thorough investigation of the terms and conditions surrounding the handling of containerized shipments. Moreover, the investigation should include the question of the nature and scope of

the duties and responsibilities of the exporter and the carrier under section 16.

For the foregoing reasons we find the record in this proceeding insufficient to conclude that Hasbaxt violated section 16 with respect to the shipment of bathtubs in question.[55]

As noted above, no hard and fast rules may readily be gleaned from the above cases. However, the following general principles may serve as a guide for forwarders:

1. A forwarder is not justified in relying entirely upon the shipper's instructions as to the classification of a shipment. A forwarder must reasonably be satisfied in its own mind that the shipper's classification is proper and when in doubt, the forwarder must make diligent inquiry and in good faith of both the shipper and the carrier.

2. A variance in the description between shipper's invoice, bill of lading, other shipping documents or publications, and the shipper's instructions to the forwarder puts the latter on guard and requires further inquiry.

3. Section 8(a)(2) of the 1984 Act requires that a carrier's tariff be made available to any person and the charge for a copy be reasonable.[56] Having ready access now to a carrier's tariff, a forwarder may not ignore a classification which is more descriptive of the goods than the shipper's instructions. It may be imprudent for a forwarder to maintain that it relied only on verbal information supplied by a carrier's employees in determining a proper classification for a shipment.

4. The selection of a proper Schedule B number by the forwarder for the export declaration at variance with the shipper's instructions or description of the goods may indicate, prima facie, an intent by the forwarder to assist the shipper in a false classification.

5. While a forwarder is not required to be an expert on every product being shipped, when the controlling use of the goods is readily apparent, the forwarder cannot ignore that obvious fact and use an improper classification in order to comply with a shipper's instructions.

The Forwarder, Shipper, and Rebating

The 1916 Act did not initially ban rebating. Subsequent amendments to that Act and section 10(b)(2) of the 1984 Act prohibits a common carrier from giving a rebate.[57] Somewhat strangely, the term "rebate" is not itself defined in the Act. The FMC has stated that a rebate, as well as the words "refund" or "remit," also in section 10(b)(2), involves a return to a ship-per of a portion of the rate or charge received by the carrier.[58]

Suppose a forwarder aids and abets a shipper in obtaining a rebate from a common carrier. Since a rebate is a violation of section 10(b)(2) only when made by a carrier and there is no prohibition against the receipt of a rebate by a shipper or forwarder, may either of them be held accountable?

Our federal conspiracy laws provide that if two or more persons conspire to commit any "offense" against the United States, they are subject to a criminal penalty.[59] The Supreme Court has held that the conspiracy statute covers any "offense" which by act of Congress is prohibited in the interest of the public policy of the United States, although not of itself punishable by a criminal prosecution, but only by a suit for a penalty.[60] Thus, even though neither the forwarder nor the shipper committed an offense under section 10(b)(2), may it be said that they "conspired" with the carrier to engage in rebating, a carrier "of-fense" under the 1984 Act, and if so, are the forwarder and shipper thus subject to prosecution for conspiracy?

Section 13(f)(1) provides that no penalty may be imposed on any person for conspiracy to violate section 10(a)(1), obtaining transporta-tion at less than the tariff rates by fraud or concealment; section 10(b)(1), charging rates different than those in the tariff; or section 10(b)(4), allowing a person to obtain transportation at less than the tariff rates by fraud or concealment. It appears, therefore, that the limited exemption in section 13(f)(1) from a conspiracy prosecution is unavailing to a shipper, forwarder, and carrier, since the offense of rebating, prohibited by section 10(b)(2), is not specifically included in the immunity provision of section 13(f)(1).

May a forwarder be individually liable for a civil penalty for being a party to a rebate under section 10(a)(1) of the 1984 Act?[61] In summary, this section provides that "no person" may knowingly and willfully di-rectly or indirectly "obtain or attempt to obtain" ocean transportation at less than the rates or charges otherwise applicable by means of a false billing, classification, weighing or measurement, or by any other unjust or unfair device or means. The term "no person" is broad enough to include a forwarder.[62] However, may it plausibly be argued that a for-warder "obtains" transportation when it receives no benefit of the rebate to the shipper? It would seem that ordinarily it is the shipper who "obtains" the lower rate since it pays the freight charges. On the other hand, when a forwarder requests a carrier to grant a rebate to a shipper, it may be argued that the forwarder is making an "attempt to obtain transportation" at less than the tariff rate and would thus be violating section 10(a)(1) regardless of whether the carrier complied with the forwarder's request.

Suppose a forwarder accepts brokerage from a common carrier in excess of the amount provided in the carrier's tariff, but no part of the excess is, directly or indirectly, paid over by the forwarder to the shipper. On these facts is the forwarder guilty of a violation of section 10(a)(1) or any other provision of the 1984 Act? It may be argued that the ocean carrier who pays excess brokerage is offering transportation at a net charge less than the applicable tariff rate and that as a consequence the forwarder is obtaining transportation at rates or charges less than would be applicable otherwise.[63]

The argument appears to lack merit. Firstly, the carrier has not provided transportation at less than the applicable tariff rate; in fact, the shipper has paid and the carrier has received the full tariff rate. Secondly, the forwarder has not "obtained" transportation at less than the tariff rate; not being the shipper, the forwarder has obtained no transportation for itself. It is the shipper's goods for which the transportation was obtained, and the proper rate thereon was paid. Thirdly, the receipt of excess brokerage is not relevant to the issue. The 1984 Act does not, directly or impliedly, make either the payment by the carrier or the receipt by the forwarder of brokerage in excess of the tariff amount illegal. Finally, the amount of brokerage received by the forwarder is beyond the scope and purpose of section 10(a)(1). The legislative purpose of that section is to protect carriers against unscrupulous shippers rather than regulate what may be conceived of as excessive brokerage.[64]

Qualifying for a Forwarder License

The provisions for the licensing of forwarders are contained in section 19 of the 1984 Act,[65] replacing section 44 of the 1916 Act.

Experience and Character

Section 19(a) states that no person may act as an ocean freight forwarder unless that person holds a license issued by the Commission. Some persons have in the past performed forwarding services without a license in the mistaken notion they may do so if no brokerage is received from carriers. Such is not the case. It is the rendering of forwarding services that requires a license, not the receipt of brokerage.

A license shall be issued when the Commission determines that the applicant is "qualified by experience and character to render forwarding services."[66] In its consideration of a predecessor bill, S.504, the Senate Commerce Committee noted that "(t)he requirement that one be qualified by experience and character to render forwarding services is a modification of the existing standard and is meant to be liberal so as not to pose an unreasonable restraint on entry to the business."[67] The requirement of experience and character replaces the test of "fit, willing and able" in the 1961 law. The new test would appear to be more precise. Obviously, an applicant for a license is "willing." Also, the distinction between "fit" and "able" was not entirely clear and perhaps somewhat redundant.

In its Rule 11(a)(1), the FMC requires that the applicant demonstrate that it possesses the necessary experience, that is, "its qualifying individual must have a minimum of three years' experience in ocean freight forwarding duties in the United States."[68] However, the FMC has said that an applicant may gain sufficient knowledge of forwarder functions, duties, and activities while working in related areas of the ocean export field.[69] A determination as to the ability of an applicant must be in the sound discretion of the FMC, but it may not be exercised in an arbitrary or capricious manner. In licensing or refusal to license, consideration must be given to constitutional and lawful safeguards of individuals and their right to make a living.[70] It is crucial that the applicant intends to and will in good faith adhere to a high standard of conduct and that it intends to and will obey the Commission's rules and policies for the conduct of licensed forwarders.[71]

In its investigation of an application for a license the FMC may address the accuracy of the information submitted in the application, the integrity and financial responsibility of the applicant, the character of the applicant and its qualifying individual, and the length and nature of the qualifying individual's experience in handling freight forwarder duties.[72]

The FMC may deny a license if it determines after investigation that the applicant does not possess the necessary experience or character to render forwarding services, has failed to respond to any lawful inquiry, or has made any willfully false or misleading statement to the FMC in connection with its application. A letter of intent to deny the application will be sent to the applicant setting forth the FMC's reason for its intent to deny, and the applicant may request a hearing within twenty days after receipt of the notification.[73]

The Forwarder Bond

Section 19(a)(2) requires that an applicant furnish a bond in a form and amount determined by the FMC to insure financial responsibility that is issued by a surety company found acceptable by the secretary of the treasury.[74] The FMC has fixed the amount of the bond at $30,000 with an additional $10,000 for each unincorporated branch office.[75]

Suppose a carrier has a dispute with a forwarder as to whether the latter owes the former a sum of money, but there has been no judgment entered by the carrier against the forwarder. Nevertheless, the carrier files a claim with the surety company under the forwarder's bond. On these facts the attempt by a carrier to use a claim against a surety bond seemingly as leverage to force payment by the forwarder appears improper. The bond underwriter is required to pay a claim if, but only if the forwarder is in actual default and not merely in a dispute with a carrier. A final determination by a judgment of a court in favor of the carrier and an inability to collect on the judgment would appear necessary.[76]

Suspension or Revocation of a License

Section 19(b) provides that after notice and hearing the FMC "shall" suspend or revoke a license if it finds that the ocean freight forwarder is not qualified to render forwarding services or that it willfully failed to comply with a provision of the Act or with a lawful order, rule, or regulation of the agency.[77] The grounds for revocation are set forth in Rule 16.[78] It provides that a license "may" (rather than "shall" as section 19(b) of the Act provides) be revoked or suspended after notice of hearing for:

1. violation of any provision of the Act, or any other statute or commission order or regulation relating to carrying on the business of forwarding;
2. failure to respond to any lawful order or inquiry by the Commission;
3. making a willfully false or misleading statement to the Commission in connection with an application for a license or its continuance in effect;
4. a determination by the Commission that the licensee is not qualified to render freight forwarder services; or
5. failure to honor the licensee's financial obligations to the Commission, such as for civil penalties assessed or agreed to in a settlement agreement.

Even in cases where the violation by a forwarder is clear, the FMC has said that evidence of mitigation will be considered in tailoring the sanctions to the facts of the specific case. The shipping laws are based on an underlying remedial public purpose and the sanctions imposed must serve such a purpose and not be punitive in character.[79]

Section 19(b) of the Act also provides that the FMC may revoke a forwarder's license for failure to maintain a bond. Unlike the provisions for the suspension or revocation of a license which may only be done "after notice and hearing," there is no similar requirement when the revocation is for a failure to maintain the required bond. Rule 14(d) provides that upon receipt of a notice of termination of a surety bond, the Commission shall notify the concerned licensee by certified U.S. mail that the Commission shall, without hearing or other proceeding, revoke the license as of the termination date of the bond unless the licensee shall have submitted a valid replacement surety bond before such termination date.[80]

Exceptions to Licensing Requirement

Section 19(c) of the Act provides that a person whose primary business is the sale of merchandise may forward shipments of the merchandise for its own account without a license.[81] This provision is a carryover from the 1961 law, the purpose being to assure merchants that they may perform the usual forwarding services on their own goods without a license. In conformity with section 19(c), the FMC rule states that any person whose primary business is the sale of merchandise, may, without a license, dispatch and perform freight forwarding services on behalf of its own shipments or those of a parent, subsidiary, affiliate, or associated company.[82]

This exception to licensing applies to the merchandise of a seller shipping "for his own account." Suppose the sale of the merchandise is made on an "ex factory" basis. Under this term the price quoted applies only at the point of origin, and the seller is agreeing to place the goods at the disposal of the buyer at such point on the date or within the period fixed. The seller must render the buyer, at the buyer's request and expense, assistance in obtaining the documents issued in the country of origin which the buyer may require either for purposes of exportation or importation at destination.[83]

Under ex factory terms of sale, title to the goods usually passes to the buyer upon pickup of the goods at the factory platform and thereafter, the seller's only obligation is to assist the buyer in obtaining the documents necessary for exportation. Title being in the buyer, query whether any forwarding service on the merchandise by the seller is "for its own account" as the law and the FMC rule require. It is interesting to note that the phrase "for its own account" was not in the 1916 Act, but the legislative history of the 1984 Act is silent on the reason for this change.

The FMC has added another exception not contained in section 19(c) or elsewhere. A common carrier or agent thereof may perform ocean freight forwarding services without a license with respect to cargo carried under such carrier's own bill of lading. Charges for such forwarding services shall be assessed in conformance with the carrier's published tariffs on file with the Commission.[84]

In actual practice many NVOCCs perform export forwarding services for their customers on shipments moving under their own bills of lading. These services are not limited simply to booking the container to be shipped with the vessel or preparing the bill of lading. Rather, these NVOCCs offer the full gamut of forwarder services, including, but not limited to: the preparing and processing of various shipping documents; commercial paper, such as sight drafts; and certificates of insurance and export declarations, requiring technical knowledge and experience. If the NVOCC performs these same services on shipments not moving under its own bill of lading, it "may" obtain a forwarder license.[85]

As noted above, under the 1984 Act, no person may act as a forwarder on merchandise other than on its own shipments until the FMC finds that an applicant is qualified "by experience and character to render forwarding services." Despite this unambiguous statutory mandate, the NVOCC may, without a license, render the same forwarding services as does a licensee on shipments under its own bill of lading without showing that it has either the experience or character to render such services. Nor does the NVOCC need to comply with all of the other requirements of Part 510 required of a licensee.

The organized forwarding industry petitioned the FMC for the withdrawal of Part 510.4(c) for lack of statutory authority. The petition being denied, an appeal was taken to the District of Columbia U.S. Court of Appeals.[86] It was urged that the purpose of the licensing bill to protect the U.S. shipping public from incompetents or persons lacking moral character and financial responsibility was being thwarted, citing the House Merchant Marine Committee intent in passing the 1961 licensing law:

> The intention of the bill . . . under the licensing provisions is to have every person, firm or corporation who holds himself out as a forwarder to be fully competent and qualified to act in a fiduciary relationship which such business necessitates. Your committee believes that when the licensing requirements become effective this important industry will be able better to serve the commerce of the United States.[87]

The D.C. Circuit affirmed the FMC's refusal to act based primarily upon the court's view that its authority to review the FMC's interpretation of its rules, was "extremely limited," because it was required to be "highly deferential" to the agency's conclusion. Consequently, it may not overrule the FMC except for a compelling cause, such as plain error of law or a fundamental change in the factual premises previously considered by the agency. The decision emphasized that under the instructions of the Supreme Court,[88] to the extent that the intent of the Congress was not clear, the Court must accept an agency's reasonable interpretation of the substantive terms of a statute it is charged to administer. According to the Court, the forwarders' argument established no more than that the phrase "act as an ocean freight forwarder" (section 19[a]) in the licensing provision was "ambiguous" (a questionable conclusion) with respect to a carrier's offering forwarding services only in conjunction with shipments carried under their own bills of lading. This being so, the court believed that it had "no warrant to reject the FMC's reasonable interpretation."

Because the decision permits NVOCCs to forward thousands of shipments a year not for their "own account" with no assurance that the shipping public is being served by an experienced person of good character, it would appear that this conclusion of the D.C. Circuit should be revisited. While the Supreme Court has said that an agency's construction of the statute it administers is entitled to "deference" and that our courts should affirm an agency interpretation if reasonable, the Court has also held that on issues of statutory construction, courts are not obliged to stand aside and "rubber stamp" their affirmations of administrative decisions that they deem inconsistent with a statutory mandate or that frustrate the congressional policy underlying a statute. The deference owed to an expert tribunal, the Supreme Court emphasized, "cannot be allowed to slip into judicial inertia."[89] The requirement that a person rendering forwarding services to our shipping public be competent and of good character being the fundamental purpose of the 1984 Act, no matter how deferential a court believes it should be, it seems obvious that the court should not sanction an activity wholly contrary to the explicit legislative intent.

Compensation by Carriers to Forwarders

Payment by carriers to forwarders for services rendered, historically known as "brokerage," commenced more than one hundred years ago. Nevertheless, in 1961, the FMB, predecessor of the FMC, held brokerage payments to be unlawful.[90] Later in the same year, however, by adding section 44(e) to the 1961 licensing law, Congress overruled the FMB and recognized that payment by carriers to forwarders, called "compensation" in the law, was justified.[91] The earlier law was carried forward in section 19(d) of the 1984 Act, which provides that a common carrier "may" compensate a licensee when it has:

(A) engaged, booked, secured, reserved, or contracted directly with the carrier or its agent for space aboard a vessel or confirmed the availability of that space, and

(B) prepared and processed the ocean bill of lading, dock receipt, or other similar document with respect to the shipment.[92]

The word "secure" was not defined in either the 1916 or 1984 Acts, but was explained in a bill preceding the 1961 licensing law where the House Merchant Marine Committee stated:

> It is not intended in order for the forwarder to qualify under the solicit and secure clause that he be specifically designated as agent of the carrier. Where the forwarder has solicited and obtained export freight from a shipper which is thereafter turned over to a carrier, it is the view of the committee that the forwarder has "solicited and secured" the cargo within the meaning of the bill.[93]

Suppose a carrier provides in its tariff for compensation to forwarders rendering the required services, but in a particular instance the line refuses to compensate a particular forwarder who complied with the statute. Does the forwarder have any redress in view of the fact that section 19(d)(1) provides that a carrier "may" compensate a forwarder but does not mandate payment?

In its consideration of the 1961 licensing law the House Merchant Marine Committee noted that the amount that many conferences traditionally paid, 1¼ percent of the freight charges, was "a fair and equitable charge," and that the forwarder or broker should be compensated in this amount whenever he has performed the requisite services set out in the bill.[94] Moreover, since the carrier held itself out in its tariff to compensate forwarders rendering specified services, it may be plausibly argued that the carrier was impliedly agreeing to pay for such services as per its tariff, and in the absence of notice to the contrary, the forwarder could reasonably expect compensation and should receive it.[95] The FMC supports this view, Rule 23(b) stating that where a common carrier's tariff provides for compensation, it "shall be paid on any shipment forwarded on behalf of others" where the licensee has provided a required certification.[96]

When a person acts as both an NVOCC and a licensee, it may collect compensation only when it certifies that it has not issued a bill of lading or otherwise undertaken common carrier responsibility as an NVOCC on the shipment. However, if an NVOCC/licensee serves as a forwarder and not as an NVOCC on a shipment, the underlying carrier may pay brokerage.[97]

Under Rule 19(d)(2) no carrier may pay compensation for services described in the Act more than once on the same shipment.[98] On occasions, an ocean freight broker—as distinguished from a forwarder—will arrange a contract of affreightment with a vessel for a substantial parcel, but the booking arrangements for shipments to follow and the performance of usual forwarder services are rendered by a licensee. Under section 19(d)(2), may a carrier pay both the broker and the forwarder? The answer appears to be in the affirmative. The restriction in the rule is against paying "compensation" twice. Under Rule 2(f), the FMC defines compensation as a payment to a forwarder for services rendered. An ocean freight broker does not receive "compensation," but rather "brokerage," as defined by the FMC.[99]

Rule 23(d)(3) states that no compensation may be paid to an ocean freight forwarder except in accordance with the carrier's tariff. The rule is based upon section 19(d)(3) of the 1984 Act providing that no licensee or employee thereof shall accept compensation from a common carrier which is different than that specifically provided for in the carrier's effective tariff lawfully on file with the Commission.[100]

Rule 23 relates to the individual relationship between a carrier and a forwarder with respect to brokerage.[101] In the past, serious differences arose between a number of important conferences and forwarders concerning concerted action by the lines to deny compensation entirely or limit it below the traditional level of 1¼ percent of the freight charges. Some forty years ago the U.S. Maritime Commission, predecessor to the FMC, held that prohibiting brokerage by carriers to forwarders or limiting payment to less than 1½ percent resulted in detriment to the commerce of the United States in violation of section 15 of the 1916 Act in that the consequent loss of revenue would have a serious effect upon the forwarding industry.[102] Four years later the FMB had before it the denial by one conference of surcharge revenue on "heavy lift" and "long length" cargo. The agency held that "the special charges named are part of the total freight charges on which brokerage may not be prohibited or reduced below 1¼ percent by the conference tariffs."[103]

Despite these clear rulings, harmony between many conferences, carriers, and forwarders was not achieved. Forwarders complained that the lines concertedly and systematically removed particular services ordinarily included in the base freight rate on which brokerage had been paid, and instead described them as "surcharges" on which compensation was denied. In response to forwarder complaints, Congress in 1986 provided that no conference or group of two or more ocean common carriers in the foreign commerce of the United States authorized to fix the level of forwarder compensation may: (A) deny to any conference member the right to take independent action on the level of compensation paid to a forwarder who is also a customs broker, and (B) agree to limit compensation of the forwarder/customs broker to less than 1¼ percent of all rates and charges on cargo on which forwarding services were provided. [104]

The purpose of this amendment was to make clear that when compensation is paid to a forwarder also licensed as a customs broker, the compensation must be based on all of the freight charges including any and all surcharges, currency adjustment factors, and other charges required to be paid by the shipper or consignee. The protection in the law was confined to forwarders also licensed as customs brokers due to the fact that the House Ways and Means Committee, which processed the bill, had jurisdiction over customs brokers only, and to remain within the Committee's authority the law was drafted to apply only to forwarders who were also customs brokers.

A number of conferences reacted concertedly and strongly. Where a conference had been paying more than 1¼ percent brokerage, the rate was reduced to that level, the minimum allowed for concerted action. The impact upon the "pure" forwarder, that is, the forwarder not licensed as a customs broker, was also substantial. Such a licensee lost the higher brokerage it had received in some trades, sometimes as much as 5 percent. At this writing the forwarding industry is seeking to eliminate legislatively the distinction between forwarders licensed as customs brokers and those who are not.

As above noted, prior to the enactment of the 1984 Act, the statutory protection of forwarders against conferences, prohibitions, or limitation on brokerage of less than 1¼ percent was based upon the FMC's authority under section 15 to disapprove agreements which were "detrimental to the commerce of the United States" or "contrary to public interest." These standards were not included in the 1984 Act. Without such protection, forwarders were concerned that there would be no limit on conference-concerted action on brokerage. To meet this apprehension, Congress provided in section 10(c)(5) that no conference or group of two or more common carriers may "deny in the export foreign commerce of the United States compensation to an ocean freight forwarder or limit that compensation to less than the reasonable amount. [105]

Rather than refer specifically in the law to the traditional limitation of 1¼ percent of the freight charges below which a conference could not go, the conferees agreed, as above noted, to proscribe any denial of compensation at less than a "reasonable amount." The conferees recognized that "unreasonable" had been determined by the FMC to be any limitation of compensation that was less than 1¼ percent, and they agreed that the approach taken by the Commission was "consistent with their continuing regulatory responsibility," and it was assumed that the agency would be "guided by its past actions when determining what a 'reasonable amount' would be."[106]

Beneficial Interest

As earlier noted, in 1981 Congress amended the forwarder provisions of the 1916 Act by eliminating the restriction on the licensing of an applicant having a beneficial interest in an exportation. Nevertheless, under section 19(d)(4) of the 1984 Act, a forwarder may not receive compensation from a common carrier on any shipment in which it had "a direct or indirect beneficial interest."[107]

The scope of section 19(d)(4) was reviewed in the Memphis Forwarding case.[108] The licensee was indirectly owned by a consignee which in turn was owned by the Government of Egypt. The question was whether Memphis as a forwarder could collect compensation from carriers on the shipments of the consignee owned by Egypt. Describing this docket as one of "first impression" because foreign government entities were involved, the Commission concluded that when Memphis collected compensation, the consignee, payor of the ocean freight charges, "indirectly and directly received through Memphis fees and compensation which offset transportation charges," an unlawful arrangement under section 19(d)(4). Rule 23(h) repeats the statutory interdict of section 19(d)(4), but expands the ban on compensation to include shipments of any holding company, subsidiary, affiliate, officer, director, agent, or executive of the licensee.[109]

The Commission has defined "beneficial interest" as follows:

> "Beneficial interest" includes a lien or interest in or right to use, enjoy, profit, benefit, or receive any advantage, either proprietary or financial, from the whole or any part of a shipment of cargo where such interest arises from the financing of the shipment or by operation of law, or by agreement, express or implied.[110]

In *Bolton & Mitchell* (BMI), the ramification of the above definition of beneficial interest was treated at length.[111] At the request of an overseas purchaser, BMI, a licensee, would locate U.S. suppliers, advance the purchase price to them, add an interest charge for its advances, and add a markup to the supplier's invoice price for its services. The FMC concluded that these practices violated Part 510.23(h), in that BMI had a beneficial interest in the shipments as a financier of the merchandise, or as a seller and shipper of shipments to foreign countries, or as one who has exercised proprietary rights over the merchandise. By retaining a "proprietary interest" in the merchandise and collecting compensation from a carrier, BMI was held to be in violation of the 1916 Act.[112]

In an effort to preserve its license, BMI offered to eliminate its markup when it performed its purchasing service, and suggested instead that during the time its money was outstanding, it would impose only an interest charge at usual bank rates. This offer was rejected by the FMC, which noted that the term "beneficial interest" included any financing of a shipment and, so long as interest was being paid, there was no compliance with the rule. The agency insisted that by accepting brokerage when it had a beneficial interest in the goods, BMI was guilty of receiving a rebate under section 16 of the 1916 Act.

It would appear that the definition of beneficial interest in the FMC rule is unclear and the holding in BMI may be error. The rule is harmful to our export foreign commerce by depriving a foreign consignee, particularly smaller ones, of the services of U.S. forwarders who are able to locate and ship goods otherwise difficult to obtain.

It is questionable, too, as to whether the FMC's definition of "beneficial interest" is sound as a matter of law. In 1974 the FMC was unequivocally told by the 8th Circuit that a "beneficial interest" has the "traditional meaning" of being "the right to the use of enjoyment of property" and that this right is normally owned by the legal title holder.[113] It has long been the law that a lien on property is not an ownership or beneficial interest, but only a charge or hold on the property to secure payment.[114] Moreover, a forwarder does not have the right to the use and enjoyment of a shipment. Nor does the advancing of the purchase price of merchandise by a forwarder, even with an interest charge, standing by itself, create a lien on the goods unless the parties specifically so agree. The term "beneficial interest" should be redefined to reflect its true common law meaning.[115]

When this rule was attacked by forwarders on the ground that neither a lien on the goods nor the financing of a shipment constituted a beneficial interest as a matter of law, the Second Circuit held otherwise, accepting the FMC argument that the definition of beneficial interest was "reasonable and necessary" to prevent forwarders from selling goods under the guise of "financing," and then using this subterfuge to receive a discounted freight rate.[116] The reason given by the FMC to the court has no factual substantiation in any of the several proceedings involving forwarders since the inception of federal regulation. Its derivation lay in a single sentence in a Senate Commerce Committee Report in 1961 which noted the Commerce Department position that a lien on a shipment could "give a freight forwarder sufficient beneficial interest in a shipment to cause payments thereon by the carrier to the forwarder to be a form of indirect rebate of the freight."[117]

Not only was the Commerce opinion speculative and unsupported by a scintilla of evidence but wrong as a matter of law. Inasmuch as the customer of BMI paid the full freight charges to the carriers, there is no way that a forwarder could have received, as Commerce asserted, a "discounted freight rate" by the financing of the shipment. Any revenue to BMI from its financing service was no different from income, over cost, for other services rendered by BMI as a forwarder. To deny U.S. suppliers the opportunity of selling goods to overseas consignees by prohibiting a forwarder from rendering valuable purchasing services assuredly does not promote export sales.

The FMC's "Reasonable Practice Authority"

Section 10(d)(1) provides that no common carrier, ocean freight forwarder, or marine terminal operator may fail to establish, observe, and enforce just and reasonable regulations and practices relating to or connected with receiving, handling, storing, or delivering property. As earlier noted, the FMC's authority under section 10 over discriminatory rates and unduly preferential practices does not include the services of forwarders. The only language that may include forwarder acts other than section 10(d)(1) and the licensing provisions is the all-inclusive provision of section 10(a)(1), stating that "no person" may obtain transportation at less than tariff rates by a false practice or unjust device.

Section 10(d)(1) carries forward the second paragraph of section 17 of the 1916 Act with one exception. The earlier Act provided that where the FMC finds any practice by a forwarder to be unjust and unreasonable, it could prescribe a "just and reasonable practice." This additional authority was not included in the 1984 Act, the reason for this deletion not appearing to be explained in the legislative history of the 1984 Act.

Based on past FMC decisions, forwarders have argued that the FMC's authority under section 10(d)(1) was limited to "terminal type services,"[118] and that forwarders do not, as a rule, physically receive, handle, store, or deliver property. Forwarders have, however, acknowledged that some of their activities may be "related to or connected with" terminal type services, e.g., preparation and processing of a dock receipt, but other standard services, forwarders have claimed, are unrelated to such activity and are not, therefore, subject to section 10(d)(1).

Forwarders asserted that one such unrelated service is the forwarder's fee to the exporter and that consequently, the FMC lacked authority to ban free or reduced rate services under Rule 22(i). The D.C. Circuit rejected this attempted distinction, holding that the FMC "in the reasonable exercise of its rulemaking authority may interpret section 10(d)(1) to prohibit forwarder discrimination in the charges billed to customers,"[119] relying on the concern expressed by the Supreme Court in *American Union* that the forwarder interpretation of the scope of the 1916 Act would "in large measure place freight forwarders outside the statute."[120] The forwarders' position was that a single rule of the FMC being without authority may hardly be considered an attempt by the industry to avoid all regulation. At most, were the forwarder view adopted, the FMC's authority over licensees' conduct under section 10(d)(1) would be somewhat reduced but hardly eliminated.

It would seem that the reasoning by the D.C. Circuit in this case graphically illustrates the strong tendency of our courts to interpret the regulatory authority of administrative agencies most broadly even when a statutory basis is lacking. For example, forwarders are no longer subject to the antidiscrimination prohibitions of the 1984 Act, so, for the D.C. Circuit to sustain a FMC regulation, Rule 21(i), by interpreting section 10(d)(1) "to prohibit forwarder discrimination" in their charges, appears to be an unwarranted extension of the agency's authority and directly contrary to specific Congressional intent.[121]

Miscellaneous FMC Regulations

Various FMC rules in Part 510, Licensing of Ocean Freight Forwarders,[122] have been discussed earlier. The FMC has on occasion informally issued an "Alert" by focusing on particular rules with which a licensee should be closely familiar. One such "Alert" concerned:

1. *Part 46 CFR 510.12(e)* —Licensee's continuing obligation to advise of changes in its FMC-18 application.
2. *Part 46 CFR 510.14(c)* —Licensee's obligation to increase its surety bond prior to date licensee commences operation of any branch office.
3. *Part 46 CFR 510.21(c)* —Licensee prohibited from permitting its license or name to be used by one who is not a bona fide individual employee of licensee.
4. *Part 46 CFR 510.21(f)* —Licensee's duty to refrain from imparting false information (see also 510.22(e)).
5. *Part 46 CFR 510.21(g)* —Licensee's duty to respond to any lawful inquiries from any authorized representative of the Commission.
6. *Part 46 CFR 510.21(h)* —Licensee's duty to comply with the Commission's directions concerning rebates.

7. *Part 46 CFR 510.22(a)*—Licensee's obligation not to share, directly or indirectly, any compensation with shipper, consignee, seller, or purchaser, or any agent or employee thereof.
8. *Part 46 CFR 510.22(b)*—Licensee's obligation not to withhold any information concerning a forwarding transaction from its principal.
9. *Part 46 CFR 510.22(d)*—Licensee's duty to withdraw from participating in an unlawful act or process any document containing an error, misrepresentation, or omission.
10. *Part 46 CFR 510.22(h)*—Licensee's obligation not to deny equal terms or special arrangements in contracts to other shippers similarly situated.
11. *Part 46 CFR 510.22(l)*—Licensee's duty not to render, or offer to render, any freight forwarding service free of charge or at a reduced fee in consideration of receiving compensation from a common carrier or for any other reason.
12. *Part 46 CFR 510.24*—Licensee required to maintain books of account, shipping records, and special contracts for a period of five years.

One of the above-mentioned rules merits further consideration. Rule 22(a) provides that no licensee shall share, directly or indirectly, any compensation or freight forwarding fee with a shipper, consignee, seller or purchaser, or any agent, affiliate, or employee thereof.[123] The purpose of this rule is to prevent indirect rebating to a shipper, the theory being that if a forwarder shares any part of its revenue, whether brokerage from a carrier or a forwarding fee from the exporter, the forwarder is in effect lowering the shipper's transportation cost.

The prohibition against a forwarder's sharing of compensation from a carrier with a shipper is understandable, since the result of such a sharing would lower the net freight cost of the shipper to less than the tariff rate. However, it is difficult to apply this same theory to a "sharing" of a freight forwarding fee. How does a forwarder "share" with a shipper a fee paid by the shipper? In effect, the forwarder is merely reducing its charge to the shipper, which is not a rebate since the forwarder's charges are not tariffed and the shipper has not paid less than the carrier's tariffed charge.

The above rule prohibiting the sharing of the brokerage on a shipment applies to an "agent, affiliate, or employee" of a shipper. On occasion a forwarder may share its brokerage with an overseas forwarder/broker handling the importation, e.g., when such broker has obtained patronage for the U.S. forwarder. In a broad sense the overseas broker may be an "agent" of the consignee by performing services for it on the importation. However, if such broker has no corporate connection with the foreign importer, the sharing of revenue by the U.S. forwarder with the overseas broker would not result in a lowering of the consignee's freight charges, and hence, it could not be a rebate. As a measure of protection, however, it is advisable for the forwarder to obtain from the foreign broker a written statement reciting that no part of any revenue from the forwarder will revert, directly or indirectly, to the consignee or any affiliate thereof. The FMC has defined an affiliate as one who is subject to common control or where one dominates the other by effective control through legal affiliation.[124] An overseas broker is, ordinarily, not an affiliate of the foreign consignee.

Part 510.22(g) provides that "[a] licensee may charge its principal for services rendered."[125] This language is somewhat cryptic and not entirely clear. Obviously, it is unnecessary to provide that a forwarder may charge for its services. The rule was intended to replace a former controversial rule requiring a forwarder to state separately in its invoice to the exporter the forwarder's disbursement for a particular service and the markup or fee for arranging such services, e.g., insurance, cartage, and warehousing. The new rule also replaced a requirement that a forwarder show its exact disbursement for ocean freight. In withdrawing these earlier burdensome requirements the FMC advised:

> We have amended . . . the language of the rule so as not to prescribe a specific format that forwarders must follow. The rule will allow a forwarder to bill its principal for services rendered by the forwarder in any manner the forwarder so chooses.[126]

Thus, as a result of the above change the rule permits a forwarder to show a total charge for a particular service. For example, if the ocean freight was $3,000, and the forwarder's service charge for making a booking was $100, the old rule would require that these figures be separately shown. The current rule allows the ocean freight to be shown as $3,100.

The second sentence of the rule states that upon request of its principal, a licensee shall provide a complete breakout of the components of its charges and a true copy of any underlying document. The rule further requires a forwarder to give notice in its invoice to the shipper of this requirement. With the approval of the FMC staff, this notice requirement is satisfied when included in paragraph 14 of the forwarding industry's Terms and Conditions.[127]

Part 510.22(i) provides that no licensee shall render, or offer to render, any freight forwarding service free of charge or at a reduced rate in consideration of receiving compensation from a common carrier or for any other reason.[128] Rule 510.2(p) defines "reduced forwarding fees" to mean charges to a principal for forwarding services that are below the licensee's "usual charges for such services,"[129] but the phrase "usual charges" is not defined. As noted above, the D.C. Circuit has upheld the Commission's authority to promulgate this rule under section 10(d)(1) of the 1984 Act.[130]

This rule has presented substantial and still unresolved difficulties on government shipments. The rule had its origin in a 1957 case where a forwarder performed forwarding services for a consignee without charging a forwarding fee, relying upon the brokerage anticipated from the carriers as its full compensation for handling the exportation. The FMC held, and the D.C. Circuit affirmed, that the waiving of the forwarding fee from the consignee and the collection thereof from the carrier "under the guise of brokerage" would be an indirect rebate to the consignee to the extent that the brokerage payment included the cost of the freight forwarding services, and therefore was an "unjust or unfair device or means" under section 16 (Second) of the 1916 Act.[131]

Despite this ruling, the General Services Administration (GSA) and other government departments have continued through the years to obtain forwarding services free or at reduced rates. The validity of this practice was tested in Docket No. 74-10, where four forwarders had successful bids of 4½ ¢, 5¢, $1.25, and $4.00, each much below their usual forwarding charges to commercial shippers. The FMC held that such practices violated section 16 (First) of the 1916 Act.[132]

In so holding the agency agreed with a statement in the Initial Decision to the effect that the "average" commercial fee for a given port reflects the forwarder's "usual fee" for that port. However, the FMC advised that it was reluctant to establish a binding rule of universal application governing the level of freight forwarding fees on the basis of the "limited record" in the docket. Instead, the FMC told forwarders that it would "expect that whatever GSA fee established, it should be "compensatory, equitable and nondiscriminatory vis-à-vis commercial accounts" and that the rates and charges assessed the government should be "reasonable and nondiscriminatory and otherwise comply fully with the substantive provisions of the Shipping Act, 1916."

Soon thereafter two forwarder groups petitioned for a reconsideration, requesting the FMC to adopt a specific rule providing that with respect to shipments handled for a government agency, the forwarding fee should not be less than the average freight forwarding fee received by a licensee on commercial accounts in the preceding fiscal year. The petition was denied, the FMC stating that the problem was not a "major" one, and that it preferred to deal with the issue on an ad hoc process of investigation and adjudication.

In 1978, an apparently concerned GSA petitioned the FMC for a declaratory order confirming the lawfulness of rates it had accepted for forwarding services. The petition was denied, the Commission saying that it would "take steps to institute an appropriate investigation into the probable violations revealed by the instant petition," but no further action has been taken on this issue. As a result, despite the fact that a very large number of exportations are made by forwarders on government exports, currently there are no specific guidelines for the GSA or forwarders as to what charges may be unlawful.

As a guide in dealings with the FMC, the various divisions under which the FMC operates are shown in Appendix O.[133]

APPENDICES

SHIPPING ACT OF 1984
AN ACT

To improve the international ocean commerce transportation system
of the United States.

*Be it enacted by the Senate and House of Representatives of the United States
of America in Congress assembled,* That this Act may be cited as the
"Shipping Act of 1984."

TABLE OF CONTENTS

SEC. 2. DECLARATION OF POLICY.

The purposes of this Act are—

(1) to establish a nondiscriminatory regulatory process for the
common carriage of goods by water in the foreign commerce of the
United States with a minimum of government intervention and regulatory costs;

(2) to provide an efficient and economic transportation system in the ocean commerce of the United States that is, insofar as possible, in harmony with, and responsive to, international shipping practices; and

(3) to encourage the development of an economically sound and efficient United States-flag liner fleet capable of meeting national security needs.

SEC. 3. DEFINITIONS.

As used in this Act—

(1) "agreement" means an understanding, arrangement, or association (written or oral) and any modification or cancellation thereof; but the term does not include a maritime labor agreement.

(2) "antitrust laws" means the Act of July 2, 1890 (ch. 647, 26 Stat. 209), as amended; the Act of October 15, 1914 (ch. 323, 38 Stat. 730), as amended; the Federal Trade Commission Act (38 Stat. 717), as amended; sections 73 and 74 of the Act of August 27, 1894 (28 Stat. 570), as amended; the Act of June 19, 1936 (ch. 592, 49 Stat. 1526), as amended; the Antitrust Civil Process Act (76 Stat. 548), as amended; and amendments and Acts supplementary thereto.

(3) "assessment agreement" means an agreement, whether part of a collective-bargaining agreement or negotiated separately, to the extent that it provides for the funding of collectively bargained fringe benefit obligations on other than a uniform man-hour basis, regardless of the cargo handled or type of vessel or equipment utilized.

(4) "bulk cargo" means cargo that is loaded and carried in bulk without mark or count.

(5) "Commission" means the Federal Maritime Commission.

(6) "common carrier" means a person holding itself out to the general public to provide transportation by water of passengers or cargo between the United States and a foreign country for compensation that—

(A) assumes responsibility for the transportation from the port or point of receipt to the port or point of destination, and

(B) utilizes, for all or part of that transportation, a vessel operating on the high seas or the Great Lakes between a port in the United States and a port in a foreign country, except that the term does not include a common carrier engaged in ocean transportation by ferry boat, ocean tramp, or chemical parcel-tanker. As used in this paragraph, "chemical parcel-tanker" means a vessel whose cargo-carrying capability consists of individual cargo tanks for bulk chemicals that are a permanent part of the vessel, that have segregation capability with piping systems to permit simultaneous carriage of several bulk chemical cargoes with minimum risk of cross-contamination, and that has a valid certificate of fitness under the International Maritime Organization Code for the Construction and Equipment of Ships Carrying Dangerous Chemicals in Bulk.

(7) "conference" means an association of ocean common carriers permitted, pursuant to an approved or effective agreement, to engage in concerted activity and to utilize a common tariff; but the term does not include a joint service, consortium, pooling, sailing, or transshipment arrangement.

(8) "controlled carrier" means an ocean common carrier that is, or whose operating assets are, directly or indirectly, owned or controlled by the government under whose registry the vessels of the carrier operate; ownership or control by a government shall be deemed to exist with respect to any carrier if—

(A) a majority portion of the interest in the carrier is owned or controlled in any manner by that government, by any agency thereof, or by any public or private person controlled by that government; or

(B) that government has the right to appoint or disapprove the appointment of a majority of the directors, the chief operating officer, or the chief executive officer of the carrier.

(9) "deferred rebate" means a return by a common carrier of any portion of the freight money to a shipper as a consideration for that shipper giving all, or any portion, of its shipments to that or any other common carrier, or for any other purpose, the payment of which is deferred beyond the completion of the service for which it is paid, and is made only if, during both the period for which computed and the period of deferment, the shipper has complied with the terms of the rebate agreement or arrangement.

(10) "fighting ship" means a vessel used in a particular trade by an ocean common carrier or group of such carriers for the purpose of excluding, preventing, or reducing competition by driving another ocean common carrier out of that trade.

(11) "forest products" means forest products in an unfinished or semifinished state that require special handling, moving in lot sizes too large for a container, including, but not limited to, lumber in bundles, rough timber, ties, poles, piling, laminated beams, bundled siding, bundled plywood, bundled core stock or veneers, bundled particle or fiber boards, bundled hardwood, wood pulp in rolls, wood pulp in unitized bales, paper board in rolls, and paper in rolls.

(12) "inland division" means the amount paid by a common carrier to an inland carrier for the inland portion of through transportation offered to the public by the common carrier.

(13) "inland portion" means the charge to the public by a common carrier for the nonocean portion of through transportation.

(14) "loyalty contract" means a contract with an ocean common carrier or conference, other than a service contract or contract based upon time-volume rates, by which a shipper obtains lower rates by committing all or a fixed portion of its cargo to that carrier or conference.

(15) "marine terminal operator" means a person engaged in the United States in the business of furnishing wharfage, dock, warehouse, or other terminal facilities in connection with a common carrier.

(16) "maritime labor agreement" means a collective-bargaining agreement between an employer subject to this Act, or group of such employers, and a labor organization representing employees in the maritime or stevedoring industry, or an agreement preparatory to such a collective-bargaining agreement among members of a multiemployer bargaining group, or an agreement specifically implementing provisions of such a collective-bargaining agreement or providing for the formation, financing, or administration of a multiemployer bargaining group; but the term does not include an assessment agreement.

(17) "non-vessel-operating common carrier" means a common carrier that does not operate the vessels by which the ocean transportation is provided, and is a shipper in its relationship with an ocean common carrier.

(18) "ocean common carrier" means a vessel-operating common carrier.

(19) "ocean freight forwarder" means a person in the United States that —

(A) dispatches shipments from the United States via common carriers and books or otherwise arranges space for those shipments on behalf of shippers; and

(B) processes the documentation or performs related activities incident to those shipments.

(20) "person" includes individuals, corporations, partnerships, and associations existing under or authorized by the laws of the United States or of a foreign country.

(21) "service contract" means a contract between a shipper and an ocean common carrier or conference in which the shipper makes a commitment to provide a certain minimum quantity of cargo over a fixed time period, and the ocean common carrier or conference commits to a certain rate or rate schedule as well as a defined service level — such as, assured space, transit time, port rotation, or similar service features; the contract may also specify provisions in the event of nonperformance on the part of either party.

(22) "shipment" means all of the cargo carried under the terms of a single bill of lading.

(23) "shipper" means an owner or person for whose account the ocean transportation of cargo is provided or the person to whom delivery is to be made.

(24) "shippers' association" means a group of shippers that consolidates or distributes freight on a nonprofit basis for the members of the group in order to secure carload, truckload, or other volume rates or service contracts.

(25) "through rate" means a single amount charged by a common carrier in connection with through transportation.

(26) "through transportation" means continuous transportation between origin and destination for which a through rate is assessed and which is offered or performed by one or more carriers, at least one of which is a common carrier, between a United States point or port and a foreign point or port.

(27) "United States" includes the several States, the District of Columbia, the Commonwealth of Puerto Rico, the Commonwealth of the Northern Marianas, and all other United States territories and possessions.

SEC. 4. AGREEMENTS WITHIN SCOPE OF ACT.

(a) OCEAN COMMON CARRIERS.—This Act applies to agreements by or among ocean common carriers to—

(1) discuss, fix, or regulate transportation rates, including through rates, cargo space accommodations, and other conditions of service;

(2) pool or apportion traffic, revenue, earnings, or losses;

(3) allot ports or restrict or otherwise regulate the number and character of sailings between ports;

(4) limit or regulate the volume or character of cargo or passenger traffic to be carried;

(5) engage in exclusive, preferential, or cooperative working arrangements among themselves or with one or more marine terminal operators or non-vessel-operating common carriers;

(6) control, regulate, or prevent competition in international ocean transportation; and

(7) regulate or prohibit their use of service contracts.

(b) MARINE TERMINAL OPERATORS.—This Act applies to agreements (to the extent the agreements involve ocean transportation in the foreign commerce of the United States) among marine terminal operators and among one or more marine terminal operators and one or more ocean common carriers to —

(1) discuss, fix, or regulate rates or other conditions of service; and

(2) engage in exclusive, preferential, or cooperative working arrangements.

(c) ACQUISITIONS.—This Act does not apply to an acquisition by any person, directly or indirectly, of any voting security or assets of any other person.

SEC. 5. AGREEMENTS.

(a) FILING REQUIREMENTS.—A true copy of every agreement entered into with respect to an activity described in section 4(a) or (b) of this Act shall be filed with the Commission, except agreements related to transportation to be performed within or between foreign countries and agreements among common carriers to establish, operate, or maintain a marine terminal in the United States. In the case of an oral agreement, a complete memorandum specifying in detail the substance of the agreement shall be filed. The Commission may by regulation prescribe the form and manner in which an agreement shall be filed and the additional information and documents necessary to evaluate the agreement.

(b) CONFERENCE AGREEMENTS.—Each conference agreement must —

(1) state its purpose;

(2) provide reasonable and equal terms and conditions for admission and readmission to conference membership for any ocean common carrier willing to serve the particular trade or route;

(3) permit any member to withdraw from conference membership upon reasonable notice without penalty;

(4) at the request of any member, require an independent neutral body to police fully the obligations of the conference and its members;

(5) prohibit the conference from engaging in conduct prohibited by section 10(c) (1) or (3) of this Act;

(6) provide for a consultation process designed to promote —

(A) commercial resolution of disputes, and

(B) cooperation with shippers in preventing and eliminating malpractices;

(7) establish procedures for promptly and fairly considering shippers' requests and complaints; and

(8) provide that any member of the conference may take independent action on any rate or service item required to be filed in a tariff under section 8(a) of this Act upon not more than 10 calendar days' notice to the conference and that the conference will include the new rate or service item in its tariff for use by that member, effective no later than 10 calendar days after receipt of the notice, and by any other member that notifies the conference that it elects to adopt the independent rate or service item on or after its effective date, in lieu of the existing conference tariff provision for that rate or service item.

(c) INTERCONFERENCE AGREEMENTS.—Each agreement between carriers not members of the same conference must provide the right of independent action for each carrier. Each agreement between conferences must provide the right of independent action for each conference.

(d) ASSESSMENT AGREEMENTS.—Assessment agreements shall be filed with the Commission and become effective on filing. The Commission shall thereafter, upon complaint filed within 2 years of the date of the agreement, disapprove, cancel, or modify any such agreement, or charge or assessment pursuant thereto, that it finds, after notice and hearing, to be unjustly discriminatory or unfair as between carriers, shippers or ports. The Commission shall issue its final decision in any such proceeding within 1 year of the date of filing of the complaint. To the extent that an assessment or charge is found in the proceeding to be unjustly discriminatory or unfair as between carriers, shippers, or ports, the Commission shall remedy the unjust discrimination or unfairness for the period of time between the filing of the complaint and the final decision by means of assessment adjustments. These adjustments shall be implemented by prospective credits or debits to future assessments or charges, except in the case of a complainant who has ceased activities subject to the assessment or charge, in which case reparation may be awarded. Except for this subsection and section 7(a) of this Act, this Act, the Shipping Act, 1916, and the Intercoastal Shipping Act, 1933, do not apply to assessment agreements.

(e) MARITIME LABOR AGREEMENTS.—This Act, the Shipping Act, 1916, and the Intercoastal Shipping Act, 1933, do not apply to maritime labor agreements. This subsection does not exempt from this Act, the Shipping Act, 1916, or the Intercoastal Shipping Act, 1933, any rates, charges, regulations, or practices of a common carrier that are required to be set forth in a tariff, whether or not those rates, charges, regulations, or practices arise out of, or are otherwise related to, a maritime labor agreement.

SEC. 6. ACTION ON AGREEMENTS.

(a) NOTICE.—Within 7 days after an agreement is filed, the Commission shall transmit a notice of its filing to the Federal Register for publication.

(b) REVIEW STANDARD.—The Commission shall reject any agreement filed under section 5(a) of this Act that, after preliminary review, it finds does not meet the requirements of section 5. The Commission shall notify in writing the person filing the agreement of the reason for rejection of the agreement.

(c) REVIEW AND EFFECTIVE DATE.—Unless rejected by the Commission under subsection (b), agreements, other than assessment agreements, shall become effective—

(1) on the 45th day after filing, or on the 30th day after notice of the filing is published in the Federal Register, whichever day is later; or

(2) if additional information or documentary material is requested under subsection (d), on the 45th day after the Commission receives—

(A) all the additional information and documentary material requested; or

(B) if the request is not fully complied with, the information and documentary material submitted and a statement of the reasons for noncompliance with the request. The period specified in paragraph (2) may be extended only by the United States District Court for the District of Columbia upon an application of the Commission under subsection (i).

(d) ADDITIONAL INFORMATION.—Before the expiration of the period specified in subsection (c)(1), the Commission may request from the person filing the agreement any additional information and documentary material it deems necessary to make the determinations required by this section.

(e) REQUEST FOR EXPEDITED APPROVAL.—The Commission may, upon request of the filing party, shorten the review period specified in subsection (c), but in no event to a date less than 14 days after notice of the filing of the agreement is published in the Federal Register.

(f) TERM OF AGREEMENTS.—The Commission may not limit the effectiveness of an agreement to a fixed term.

(g) SUBSTANTIALLY ANTICOMPETITIVE AGREEMENTS.—If, at any time after the filing or effective date of an agreement, the Commission determines that the agreement is likely, by a reduction in competition, to produce an unreasonable reduction in transportation service or an unreasonable increase in transportation cost, it may, after notice to the person filing the agreement, seek appropriate injunctive relief under subsection (h).

(h) INJUNCTIVE RELIEF.—The Commission may, upon making the determination specified in subsection (g), bring suit in the United States District Court for the District of Columbia to enjoin operation of the agreement. The court may issue a temporary restraining order or preliminary injunction and, upon a showing that the agreement is likely, by a reduction in competition, to produce an unreasonable reduction in transportation service or an unreasonable increase in transportation cost, may enter a permanent injunction. In a suit under this subsection, the burden of proof is on the Commission. The court may not allow a third party to intervene with respect to a claim under this subsection.

(i) COMPLIANCE WITH INFORMATIONAL NEEDS.—If a person filing an agreement, or an officer, director, partner, agent, or employee thereof, fails substantially to comply with a request for the submission of additional information or documentary material with the period specified in subsection (c), the United States District Court for the District of Columbia, at the request of the Commission—

(1) may order compliance,

(2) shall extend the period specified in subsection (c)(2) until there has been substantial compliance; and

(3) may grant such other equitable relief as the court in its discretion determines necessary or appropriate.

(j) NONDISCLOSURE OF SUBMITTED MATERIAL.—Except for an agreement filed under section 5 of this Act, information and documentary material filed with the Commission under section 5 or 6 is exempt from disclosure under section 552 of title 5, United States Code and may not be made public except as may be relevant to an administrative or judicial action or proceeding. This section does not prevent disclosure to either body of Congress or to a duly authorized committee or subcommittee of Congress.

(k) REPRESENTATION.—Upon notice to the Attorney General, the Commission may represent itself in district court proceedings under subsections (h) and (i) of this section and section 11(h) of this Act. With the approval of the Attorney General, the Commission may represent itself in proceedings in the United States Courts of Appeal under subsections (h) and (i) of this section and section 11(h) of this Act.

SEC. 7. EXEMPTION FROM ANTITRUST LAWS.

(a) IN GENERAL.—The antitrust laws do not apply to—

(1) any agreement that has been filed under section 5 of this Act and is effective under section 5(d) or section 6, or is exempt under section 16 of this Act from any requirement of this Act;

(2) any activity or agreement within the scope of this Act, whether permitted under or prohibited by this Act, undertaken or entered into with a reasonable basis to conclude that (A) it is pursuant to an agreement on file with the Commission and in effect when the activity took place, or (B) it is exempt under section 16 of this Act from any filing requirement of this Act;

(3) any agreement or activity that relates to transportation services within or between foreign countries, whether or not via the United States, unless that agreement or activity has a direct, substantial, and reasonably foreseeable effect on the commerce of the United States;

(4) any agreement or activity concerning the foreign inland segment of through transportation that is part of transportation provided in a United States import or export trade;

(5) any agreement or activity to provide or furnish wharfage, dock, warehouse, or other terminal facilities outside the United States; or

(6) subject to section 20 (e)(2) of this Act, any agreement, modification, or cancellation approved by the Commission before the effective date of this Act under section 15 of Shipping Act, 1916, or permitted under section 14b thereof, and any properly published tariff, rate, fare, or charge, classification, rule, or regulation explanatory thereof implementing that agreement, modification, or cancellation.

(b) EXCEPTIONS.—This Act does not extend antitrust immunity—

(1) to any agreement with or among air carriers, rail carriers, motor carriers, or common carriers by water not subject to this Act with respect to transportation within the United States;

(2) to any discussion or agreement among common carriers that are subject to this Act regarding the inland divisions (as opposed to the inland portions) of through rates within the United States; or

(3) to any agreement among common carriers subject to this Act to establish, operate, or maintain a marine terminal in the United States.

(c) LIMITATIONS.—

(1) Any determination by an agency or court that results in the denial or removal of the immunity to the antitrust laws set forth in subsection (a) shall not remove or alter the antitrust immunity for the period before the determination.

(2) No person may recover damages under section 4 of the Clayton Act (15 U.S.C. 15), or obtain injunctive relief under section 16 of that Act (15 U.S.C. 26), for conduct prohibited by this Act.

SEC. 8. TARIFFS.[1]

(a) IN GENERAL.—

(1) Except with regard to bulk cargo, forest products, recycled metal scrap, waste paper, and paper waste, each common carrier and conference shall file with the Commission, and keep open to public inspection, tariffs showing all its rates, charges, classifications, rules, and practices between all points or ports on its own route and on any through transportation route that has been established. However, common carriers shall not be required to state separately or otherwise reveal in tariff filings the inland divisions of a through rate. Tariffs shall —

(A) state the places between which cargo will be carried;

(B) list each classification of cargo in use;

(C) state the level of ocean freight forwarder compensation, if any, by a carrier or conference;

(D) state separately each terminal or other charge, privilege, or facility under the control of the carrier or conference and any rules or regulations that in any way change, affect, or determine any part or the aggregate of the rates or charges; and

---

[1] Section 2 of Public Law 101-92 (103 Stat. 601) provides:

SEC. 2. (a) The Federal Maritime Commission shall require that complete and updated electronic copies of the Automated Tariff Filing and Information data base are made available (in bulk) in a timely and nondiscriminatory fashion, and the Commission shall assess reasonable fees for this service consistent with section 552 of title 5, United States Code.

(b) The Commission shall impose reasonable controls on the system to limit remote access usage by any one person.

(c) The Commission shall provide that any information from the Automated Tariff Filing and Information System that is made available to the public may be used, resold, or disseminated by any person without restriction and without payment of additional fees or royalties.

(E) include sample copies of any loyalty contract, bill of lading, contract of affreightment, or other document evidencing the transportation agreement.

(2) Copies of tariffs shall be made available to any person, and a reasonable charge may be assessed for them.

(b) TIME-VOLUME RATES.—Rates shown in tariffs filed under subsection (a) may vary with the volume of cargo offered over a specified period of time.

(c) SERVICE CONTRACTS.—An ocean common carrier or conference may enter into a service contract with a shipper or shippers' association subject to the requirements of this Act. Except for service contracts dealing with bulk cargo, forest products, recycled metal scrap, waste paper, or paper waste, each contract entered into under this subsection shall be filed confidentially with the Commission, and at the same time, a concise statement of its essential terms shall be filed with the Commission and made available to the general public in tariff format, and those essential terms shall be available to all shippers similarly situated. The essential terms shall include —

(1) the origin and destination port ranges in the case of port-to-port movements, and the origin and destination geographic areas in the case of through intermodal movements;

(2) the commodity or commodities involved;

(3) the minimum volume;

(4) the line-haul rate:

(5) the duration;

(6) service commitments; and

(7) the liquidated damages for nonperformance, if any.

The exclusive remedy for a breach of a contract entered into under this subsection shall be an action in an appropriate court, unless the parties otherwise agree.

(d) RATES.—No new or initial rate or change in an existing rate that results in an increased cost to the shipper may become effective earlier than 30 days after filing with the Commission. The Commission, for good cause, may allow such a new or initial rate or change to become effective in less than 30 days. A change in an existing rate that results in a decreased cost to the shipper may become effective upon publication and filing with the Commission.

(e) REFUNDS.—The Commission may, upon application of a carrier or shipper, permit a common carrier or conference to refund a portion of freight charges collected from a shipper or to waive the collection of a portion of the charges from a shipper if —

(1) there is an error in a tariff of a clerical or administrative nature or an error due to inadvertence in failing to file a new tariff and the refund will not result in discrimination among shippers, ports, or carriers;

(2) the common carrier or conference has, prior to filing an application for authority to make a refund, filed a new tariff with the

Commission that sets forth the rate on which the refund or waiver would be based:

(3) the common carrier or conference agrees that if permission is granted by the Commission, an appropriate notice will be published in the tariff, or such other steps taken as the Commission may require that give notice of the rate on which the refund or waiver would be based, and additional refunds or waivers as appropriate shall be made with respect to other shipments in the manner prescribed by the Commission in its order approving the application; and

(4) the application for refund or waiver is filed with the Commission within 180 days from the date of shipment.

(f) FORM.—The Commission may by regulation prescribe the form and manner in which the tariffs required by this section shall be published and filed. The Commission may reject a tariff that is not filed in conformity with this section and its regulations. Upon rejection by the Commission, the tariff is void and its use is unlawful.

SEC. 9. CONTROLLED CARRIERS.

(a) CONTROLLED CARRIER RATES.—No controlled carrier subject to this section may maintain rates or charges in its tariffs filed with the Commission that are below a level that is just and reasonable, nor may any such carrier establish or maintain unjust or unreasonable classifications, rules, or regulations in those tariffs. An unjust or unreasonable classification, rule, or regulation means one that results or is likely to result in the carriage or handling of cargo at rates or charges that are below a just and reasonable level. The Commission may, at any time after notice and hearing, disapprove any rates, charges, classifications, rules, or regulations that the controlled carrier has failed to demonstrate to be just and reasonable. In a proceeding under this subsection, the burden of proof is on the controlled carrier to demonstrate rates, charges, classifications, rules, or regulations are just and reasonable. Rates, charges, classifications, rules, or regulations filed by a controlled carrier that have been rejected, suspended, or disapproved by the Commission are void and their use is unlawful.

(b) RATE STANDARDS.—For the purpose of this section, in determining whether rates, charges, classifications, rules, or regulations by a controlled carrier are just and reasonable, the Commission may take into account appropriate factors including, but not limited to, whether —

(1) the rates or charges which have been filed or which would result from the pertinent classifications, rules, or regulations are below a level which is fully compensatory to the controlled carrier based upon that carrier's actual costs or upon its constructive costs, which are hereby defined as the costs of another carrier, other than a controlled carrier, operating similar vessels and equipment in the same or a similar trade;

(2) the rates, charges, classifications, rules, or regulations are the

same as or similar to those filed or assessed by other carriers in the same trade;

    (3) the rates, charges, classifications, rules, or regulations are required to assure movement of particular cargo in the trade; or

    (4) the rates, charges, classifications, rules, or regulations are required to maintain acceptable continuity, level, or quality of common carrier service to or from affected ports.

    (c) EFFECTIVE DATE OF RATES.—Notwithstanding section 8(d) of this Act, the rates, charges, classifications, rules, or regulations of controlled carriers may not, without special permission of the Commission, become effective sooner than the 30th day after the date of filing with the Commission. Each controlled carrier shall, upon the request of the Commission, become effective sooner than the 30th day after the date of filing with the Commission. Each controlled carrier shall, upon the request of the Commission, file, within 20 days of request (with respect to its existing or proposed rates, charges, classifications, rules, or regulations), a statement of justification that sufficiently details the controlled carrier's need and purpose for such rates, charges, classifications, rules, or regulations upon which the Commission may reasonably base its determination of the lawfulness thereof.

    (d) DISAPPROVAL OF RATES.—Whenever the Commission is of the opinion that the rates, charges, classifications, rules, or regulations filed by a controlled carrier may be unjust and unreasonable, the Commission may issue an order to the controlled carrier to show cause why those rates, charges, classifications, rules, or regulations should not be disapproved. Pending a determination as to their lawfulness in such a proceeding, the Commission may suspend the rates, charges, classifications, rules, or regulations at any time before their effective date. In the case of rates, charges, classifications, rules, or regulations that have already become effective, the Commission may, upon the issuance of an order to show cause, suspend those rates, charges, classifications, rules, or regulations on not less than 60 days' notice to the controlled carrier. No period of suspension under this subsection may be greater than 180 days. Whenever the Commission has suspended any rates, charges, classifications, rules, or regulations under this subsection, the affected carrier may file new rates, charges, classifications, rules, or regulations to take effect immediately during the suspension period in lieu of the suspended rates, charges, classifications, rules, or regulations—except that the Commission may reject the new rates, charges, classifications, rules, or regulations if it is of the opinion that they are unjust and unreasonable.

    (e) PRESIDENTIAL REVIEW.—Concurrently with the publication thereof, the Commission shall transmit to the President each order of suspension or final order of disapproval of rates, charges, classifications, rules, or regulations of a controlled carrier subject to this section. Within 10 days after the receipt or the effective date of the Commission order, the President may request the Commission in writing to stay the effect of the Commission's order if the President finds that the stay is required for reasons of national defense or foreign policy, which reasons shall be specified in the report. Notwithstanding any other law, the Commission shall immediately grant the request by the issuance of an order in which the President's request shall be described. During any such stay, the President shall, whenever practicable, attempt to resolve the matter in controversy by negotiation with representatives of the applicable foreign governments.

(f) EXCEPTIONS.—This section does not apply to —

(1) a controlled carrier of a state whose vessels are entitled by a treaty of the United States to receive national or most-favored-nation treatment;

(2) a controlled carrier of a state which, on the effective date of this section, has subscribed to the statement of shipping policy contained in note 1 to annex A of the Code of Liberalization of Current Invisible Operations, adopted by the Council of the Organization for Economic Cooperation and Development;

(3) rates, charges, classifications, rules, or regulations of a controlled carrier in any particular trade that are covered by an agreement effective under section 6 of this Act, other than an agreement in which all of the members are controlled carriers not otherwise excluded from the provisions of this subsection;

(4) rates, charges, classifications, rules, or regulations governing the transportation of cargo by a controlled carrier between the country by whose government it is owned or controlled, as defined herein and the United States; or

(5) a trade served exclusively by controlled carriers.

SEC. 10. PROHIBITED ACTS.

(a) IN GENERAL.—No person may—

(1) knowingly and willfully, directly or indirectly, by means of false billing, false classification, false weighing, false report of weight, false measurement, or by any other unjust or unfair device or means obtain or attempt to obtain ocean transportation for property at less than the rates or charges that would otherwise be applicable;

(2) operate under an agreement required to be filed under section 5 of this Act that has not become effective under section 6, or that has been rejected, disapproved, or canceled; or

(3) operate under an agreement required to be filed under section 5 of this Act except in accordance with the terms of the agreement or any modifications made by the Commission to the agreement.

(b) COMMON CARRIERS.— No common carrier, either alone or in conjunction with any other person, directly or indirectly, may —

(1) charge, demand, collect, or receive greater, less, or different compensation for the transportation of property or for any service in connection therewith than the rates and charges that are shown in its tariffs or service contracts;

(2) rebate, refund, or remit in any manner, or by any device, any portion of its rates except in accordance with its tariffs or service contracts:

(3) extend or deny to any person any privilege, concession, equipment, or facility except in accordance with its tariffs or service contracts;

(4) allow any person to obtain transportation for property at less than the rates or charges established by the carrier in its tariff or service contract by means of false billing, false classification, false weighing, false measurement, or by any other unjust or unfair device or means;

(5) retaliate against any shipper by refusing, or threatening to refuse, cargo space accommodations when available, or resort to other unfair or unjustly discriminatory methods because the shipper has patronized another carrier, or has filed a complaint, or for any other reason;

(6) except for service contracts, engage in any unfair or unjustly discriminatory practice in the matter of —

(A) rates;

(B) cargo classifications;

(C) cargo space accommodations or other facilities, due regard being had for the proper loading of the vessel and the available tonnage;

(D) the loading and landing of freight; or

(E) the adjustment and settlement of claims;

(7) employ any fighting ship;

(8) offer or pay any deferred rebates;

(9) use a loyalty contract, except in conformity with the antitrust laws;

(10) demand, charge, or collect any rate or charge that is unjustly discriminatory between shippers or ports;

(11) except for service contracts, make or give any undue or unreasonable preference or advantage to any particular person, locality, or description of traffic in any respect whatsoever;

(12) subject any particular person, locality, or description of traffic to an unreasonable refusal to deal or any undue or unreasonable prejudice or disadvantage in any respect whatsoever;

(13) refuse to negotiate with a shippers' association;

(14) [2] knowingly and willfully accept cargo from or transport cargo for the account of a non-vessel-operating common carrier that does not have a tariff and a bond as required by sections 8 and 23 of this Act;

(15) [2] knowingly and willfully enter into a service contract with a non-vessel-operating common carrier or in which a non-vessel-operat-

---

[2] Section 710 of Public Law 101-595, approved November 16, 1990 (104 Stat. 2996), added section 23 to the Shipping Act of 1984, and amended section 10(b) of that Act. Section 710 (d) and (e) of Public Law 101-595 provide:

(d) INTERIM RULES. — The Commission may prescribe interim rules and regulations necessary to carry out the amendments made by this section.

(e) EFFECTIVE DATE. — This section shall become effective 90 days after the date of its enactment.

ing common carrier is listed as an affiliate that does not have a tariff and a bond as required by sections 8 and 23 of this Act; or

(16) knowingly disclose, offer, solicit, or receive any information concerning the nature, kind, quantity, destination, consignee, or routing of any property tendered or delivered to a common carrier without the consent of the shipper or consignee if that information—

(A) may be used to the detriment of prejudice of the shipper or consignee;

(B) may improperly disclose its business transaction to a competitor; or

(C) may be used to the detriment or prejudice of any common carrier.

Nothing in paragraph (16) shall be construed to prevent providing such information, in response to legal process, to the United States, or to an independent neutral body operating within the scope of its authority to fulfill the policing obligations of the parties to an agreement effective under this Act. Nor shall it be prohibited for any ocean common carrier that is a party to a conference agreement approved under this Act, or any receiver, trustee, lessee, agent, or employee of that carrier, or any other person authorized by that carrier to receive information, to give information to the conference or any person, firm, corporation, or agency designated by the conference, or to prevent the conference or its designee from soliciting or receiving information for the purpose of determining whether a shipper or consignee has breached an agreement with the conference or its member lines or for the purpose of determining whether a member of the conference has breached the conference agreement, or for the purpose of compiling statistics of cargo movement, but the use of such information for any other purpose prohibited by this Act or any other Act is prohibited.

(c) CONCERTED ACTION.—No conference or group of two or more common carriers may —

(1) boycott or take any other concerted action resulting in an unreasonable refusal to deal;

(2) engage in conduct that unreasonably restricts the use of intermodal services or technological innovations;

(3) engage in any predatory practice designed to eliminate the participation, or deny the entry, in a particular trade of a common carrier not a member of the conference, a group of common carriers, an ocean tramp, or a bulk carrier;

(4) negotiate with a nonocean carrier or group of nonocean carriers (for example, truck, rail, or air operators) on any matter relating to rates or services provided to ocean common carriers within the United States by those nonocean carriers: *Provided*, That this paragraph does not prohibit the setting and publishing of a joint through

rate by a conference, joint venture, or an association of ocean common carriers;

(5) deny in the export foreign commerce of the United States compensation to an ocean freight forwarder or limit that compensation to less than a reasonable amount; or

(6) allocate shippers among specific carriers that are parties to the agreement or prohibit a carrier that is a party to the agreement from soliciting cargo from a particular shipper, except as otherwise required by the law of the United States or the importing or exporting country, or as agreed to by a shipper in a service contract.

(d) COMMON CARRIERS, OCEAN FREIGHT FORWARDERS, AND MARINE TERMINAL OPERATORS. —

(1) No common carrier, ocean freight forwarder, or marine terminal operator may fail to establish, observe, and enforce just and reasonable regulations and practices relating to or connected with receiving, handling, storing, or delivering property.

(2) No marine terminal operator may agree with another marine terminal operator or with a common carrier to boycott, or unreasonably discriminate in the provision of terminal services to, any common carrier or ocean tramp.

(3) The prohibitions in subsection (b) (11), (12), and (16) of this section apply to marine terminal operators.

(e) JOINT VENTURES.—For purposes of this section, a joint venture or consortium of two or more common carriers but operated as a single entity shall be treated as a single common carrier.

SEC. 11. COMPLAINTS, INVESTIGATIONS, REPORTS, AND REPARATIONS.

(a) FILING OF COMPLAINTS.—Any person may file with the Commission a sworn complaint alleging a violation of this Act, other than section 6(g), and may seek reparation for any injury caused to the complainant by that violation.

(b) SATISFACTION OR INVESTIGATION OF COMPLAINTS.—The Commission shall furnish a copy of a complaint file pursuant to subsection (a) of this section to the person named therein who shall, within a reasonable time specified by the Commission, satisfy the complaint or answer it in writing. If the complaint is not satisfied, the Commission shall investigate it in an appropriate manner and make an appropriate order.

(c) COMMISSION INVESTIGATIONS.—The Commission, upon complaint or upon its own motion, may investigate any conduct or agreement that it believes may be in violation of this Act. Except in the case of an injunction granted under subsection (h) of this section, each agreement under investigation under this section remains in effect until the Commission issues an order under this subsection. The Commission may by order disapprove, cancel, or modify any agreement filed under section 5(a) of this Act that operates in violation of this Act. With respect to agreements inconsistent with section 6(g) of this Act, the Commission's sole remedy is under section 6(h).

(d) CONDUCT OF INVESTIGATION.—Within 10 days after the initiation of a proceeding under this section, the Commission shall set a date on or before which its final decision will be issued. This date may be extended for good cause by order of the Commission.

(e) UNDUE DELAYS.—If, within the time period specified in subsection (d), the Commission determines that it is unable to issue a final decision because of undue delays caused by a party to the proceedings, the Commission may impose sanctions, including entering a decision adverse to the delaying party.

(f) REPORTS.—The Commission shall make a written report of every investigation made under this Act in which a hearing was held stating its conclusions, decisions, findings of fact, and order. A copy of this report shall be furnished to all parties. The Commission shall publish each report for public information, and the published report shall be competent evidence in all courts of the United States.

(g) REPARATIONS.—For any complaint filed within 3 years after the cause of action accrued, the Commission shall, upon petition of the complainant and after notice and hearing, direct payment of reparations to the complainant for actual injury (which, for purposes of this subsection, also includes the loss of interest at commercial rates compounded from the date of injury) caused by a violation of this Act plus reasonable attorney's fees. Upon a showing that the injury was caused by activity that is prohibited by section 10(b) (5) or (7) or section 10(c) (1) or (3) of this Act, or that violates section 10(a) (2) or (3), the Commission may direct the payment of additional amounts; but the total recovery of a complainant may not exceed twice the amount of the actual injury. In the case of injury caused by an activity that is prohibited by section 10(b)(6) (A) or (B) of this Act, the amount of the injury shall be the difference between the rate paid by the injured shipper and the most favorable rate paid by another shipper.

(h) INJUNCTION.—

(1) In connection with any investigation conducted under this section, the Commission may bring suit in a district court of the United States to enjoin conduct in violation of this Act. Upon a showing that standards for granting injunctive relief by courts of equity are met and after notice to the defendant, the court may grant a temporary restraining order or preliminary injunction for a period not to exceed 10 days after the Commission has issued an order disposing of the

issues under investigation. Any such suit shall be brought in a district in which the defendant resides or transacts business.

(2) After filing a complaint with the Commission under subsection (a), the complainant may file suit in a district court of the United States to enjoin conduct in violation of this Act. Upon a showing that standards for granting injunctive relief by courts of equity are met and after notice to the defendant, the court may grant a temporary restraining order or preliminary injunction for a period not to exceed 10 days after the Commission under paragraph (1); or, if no suit has been filed, in a district in which the defendant resides or transacts business. A defendant that prevails in a suit under this paragraph shall be allowed reasonable attorney's fees to be assessed and collected as part of the costs of the suit.

SEC. 12. SUBPOENAS AND DISCOVERY.

(a) IN GENERAL.—In investigations and adjudicatory proceedings under this Act —

(1) depositions, written interrogatories, and discovery procedures may be utilized by any party under rules and regulations issued by the Commission that, to the extent practicable, shall be in conformity with the rules applicable in civil proceedings in the district courts of the United States; and

(2) the Commission may by subpoena compel the attendance of witnesses and the production of books, papers, documents, and other evidence.

(b) WITNESS FEES.—Witnesses shall, unless otherwise prohibited by law, be entitled to the same fees and mileage as in the courts of the United States.

SEC. 13. PENALTIES

(a) ASSESSMENT OF PENALTY.—Whoever violates a provision of this Act, a regulation issued thereunder, or a Commission order is liable to the United States for a civil penalty. The amount of the civil penalty, unless otherwise provided in this Act, may not exceed $5,000 for each violation unless the violation was willfully and knowingly committed, in which case the amount of the civil penalty may not exceed $25,000 for each violation. Each day of a continuing violation constitutes a separate offense.

(b) ADDITIONAL PENALTIES.—

(1) For a violation of section 10(b) (1), (2), (3), (4), or (8) of this Act, the Commission may suspend any or all tariffs of the common carrier, or that common carrier's right to use any or all tariffs of conferences of which it is a member, for a period not to exceed 12 months.

(2) For failure to supply information ordered to be produced or compelled by subpoena under section 12 of this Act, the Commission may, after notice and an opportunity for hearing, suspend any or all tariffs of a common carrier, or that common carrier's right to use any or all tariffs of conferences of which it is a member.

(3) A common carrier that accepts or handles cargo for carriage under a tariff that has been suspended or after its right to utilize that tariff has been suspended is subject to a civil penalty of not more than $50,000 for each shipment.

(4) If, in defense of its failure to comply with a subpoena or discovery order, a common carrier alleges that documents or information located in a foreign country cannot be produced because of the laws of that country, the Commission shall immediately notify the Secretary of State of the failure to comply and of the allegation relating to foreign laws. Upon receiving the notification, the Secretary of State shall promptly consult with the government of the nation within which the documents or information are alleged to be located for the purpose of assisting the Commission in obtaining the documents or information sought.

(5) If, after notice and hearing, the Commission finds that the action of a common carrier, acting alone or in concert with any person, or a foreign government has unduly impaired access of a vessel documented under the laws of the United States to ocean trade between foreign ports, the Commission shall take action that it finds appropriate, including the imposition of any of the penalties authorized under paragraphs (1), (2), and (3) of this subsection.[3]

(6) Before an order under this subsection becomes effective, it shall be immediately submitted to the President who may, within 10 days after receiving it, disapprove the order if the President finds that disapproval is required for reasons of the national defense or the foreign policy of the United States.

(c) ASSESSMENT PROCEDURES.—Until a matter is referred to the Attorney General, the Commission may, after notice and an opportunity for hearing, assess each civil penalty provided for in this Act. In determining the amount of the penalty, the Commission shall take into account the nature, circumstances, extent, and gravity of the violation committed and, with respect to the violator, the degree of culpability, history of prior offenses, ability to pay, and such other matters as justice may require. The

---

[3] See also section 10002(h) of Public Law 100-418, that provides: "(h) The actions against foreign carriers authorized in subsections (e) and (f) of this section may be used in the administration and enforcement of section 13(b)(5) of the Shipping Act of 1984 (46 App. U.S.C. 1712(b)(5)) or section 19(1)(b) of the Merchant Marine Act, 1920 (46 App. U.S.C. 876)."

Commission may compromise, modify, or remit, with or without conditions, any civil penalty.

(d) REVIEW OF CIVIL PENALTY.—A person against whom a civil penalty is assessed under this section may obtain review thereof under chapter 158 of title 28, United States Code.

(e) FAILURE TO PAY ASSESSMENT.—If a person fails to pay an assessment of a civil penalty after it has become final or after the appropriate court has entered final judgment in favor of the Commission, the Attorney General at the request of the Commission may seek to recover the amount assessed in an appropriate district court of the United States. In such an action, the court shall enforce the Commission's order unless it finds that the order was not regularly made or duly issued.

(f) LIMITATIONS.—

(1) No penalty may be imposed on any person for conspiracy to violate section 10(a)(1), (b)(1), or (b)(4) of this Act, or to defraud the Commission by concealment of such a violation.

(2) Each proceeding to assess a civil penalty under this section shall be commenced with 5 years from the date the violation occurred.

SEC. 14. COMMISSION ORDERS.

(a) IN GENERAL.—Orders of the Commission relating to a violation of this Act or a regulation issued thereunder shall be made, upon sworn complaint or on its own motion, only after opportunity for hearing. Each order of the Commission shall continue in force for the period of time specified in the order or until suspended, modified, or set aside by the Commission or a court of competent jurisdiction.

(b) REVERSAL OR SUSPENSION OF ORDERS.—The Commission may reverse, suspend, or modify any order made by it, and upon application of any party to a proceeding may grant a rehearing of the same or any matter determined therein. No rehearing may, except by special order of the Commission, operate as a stay of that order.

(c) ENFORCEMENT OF NONREPARATION ORDERS.—In case of violation of an order of the Commission, or for failure to comply with a Commission subpoena, the Attorney General, at the request of the Commission, or any party injured by the violation, may seek enforcement by a United States district court having jurisdiction over the parties. If, after hearing, the court determines that the order was properly made and duly issued, it shall enforce the order by an appropriate injunction or other process, mandatory or otherwise.

(d) ENFORCEMENT OF REPARATION ORDERS.—

(1) In case of violation of an order of the Commission for the payment of reparation, the person to whom the award was made may

seek enforcement of the order in a United States district court having jurisdiction of the parties.

(2) In a United States district court the findings and order of the Commission shall be prima facie evidence of the facts therein stated, and the petitioner shall not be liable for costs, nor for the costs of any subsequent stage of the proceedings, unless they accrue upon his appeal. A petitioner in a United States district court who prevails shall be allowed reasonable attorney's fees to be assessed and collected as part of the costs of the suit.

(3) All parties in whose favor the Commission has made an award of reparation by a single order may be joined as plaintiffs, and all other parties in the order may be joined as defendants, in a single suit in a district in which any one plaintiff could maintain a suit against any one defendant. Service of process against a defendant not found in that district may be made in a district in which is located any office of, or point of call on a regular route operated by, that defendant. Judgment may be entered in favor of any plaintiff against the defendant liable to that plaintiff.

(e) STATUTE OF LIMITATIONS.—An action seeking enforcement of a Commission order must be filed within 3 years after the date of the violation of the order.

SEC. 15. REPORTS AND CERTIFICATES.

(a) REPORTS.—The Commission may require any common carrier, or any officer, receiver, trustee, lessee, agent, or employee thereof, to file with it any periodical or special report or any account, record, rate, or charge, or memorandum of any facts and transactions appertaining to the business of that common carrier. The report, account, record, rate, charge, or memorandum shall be made under oath whenever the Commission so requires, and shall be furnished in the form and within the time prescribed by the Commission. Conference minutes required to be filed with the Commission under this section shall not be released to third parties or published by the Commission.

(b) CERTIFICATION.—The Commission shall require the chief executive officer of each common carrier and, to the extent it deems feasible, may require any shipper, shippers' association, marine terminal operator, ocean freight forwarder, or broker to file a periodic written certification made under oath with the Commission attesting to —

(1) a policy prohibiting the payment, solicitation, or receipt of any rebate that is unlawful under the provisions of this Act;

(2) the fact that this policy has been promulgated recently to each owner, officer, employee, and agent thereof;

(3) the details of the efforts made within the company or otherwise to prevent or correct illegal rebating; and

(4) a policy of full cooperation with the Commission in it efforts to end those illegal practices.

Whoever fails to file a certificate required by the Commission under this subsection is liable to the United States for a civil penalty of not more than $5,000 for each day the violation continues.

SEC. 16. EXEMPTIONS.

The Commission, upon application or on its own motion, may by order or rule exempt for the future any class of agreements between persons subject to this Act or any specified activity of those persons from any requirement of this Act if it finds that the exemption will not substantially impair effective regulation by the Commission, be unjustly discriminatory, result in a substantial reduction in competition, or be detrimental to commerce. The Commission may attach conditions to any exemption and may, by order, revoke any exemption. No order or rule of exemption or revocation of exemption may be issued unless opportunity for hearing has been afforded interested persons and departments and agencies of the United States.

SEC. 17. REGULATIONS.

(a) The Commission may prescribe rules and regulations as necessary to carry out this Act.

(b) The Commission may prescribe interim rules and regulations necessary to carry out this Act. For this purpose, the Commission is excepted from compliance with the notice and comment requirements of section 553 of title 5, United States Code. All rules and regulations prescribed under the authority of this subsection that are not earlier superseded by final rules shall expire no later than 270 days after the date of enactment of this Act.

SEC. 18. AGENCY REPORTS AND ADVISORY COMMISSION.

(a) COLLECTION OF DATA.—For a period of 5 years following the enactment of this Act, the Commission shall collect and analyze information concerning the impact of this Act upon the international ocean shipping industry, including data on:

(1) increases and decreases in the level of tariffs;

(2) changes in the frequency or type of common carrier services available to specific ports or geographic regions;

(3) the number and strength of independent carriers in various trades; and

(4) the length of time, frequency, and cost of major types of regulatory proceedings before the Commission.

(b) CONSULTATION WITH OTHER DEPARTMENTS AND AGENCIES.—The Commission shall consult with the Department of Transportation, the Department of Justice, and the Federal Trade Commission annually concerning data collection. The Department of Transportation, the Department of Justice, and the Federal Trade Commission shall at all times have access to the data collected under this section to enable them to provide comments concerning data collection.

(c) AGENCY REPORTS.—

(1) Within 6 months after expiration of the 5-year period specified in subsection (a), the Commission shall report the information, with an analysis of the impact of this Act, to Congress, to the Advisory Commission on Conferences in Ocean Shipping established in subsection (d), and to the Department of Transportation, the Department of Justice, and the Federal Trade Commission.

(2) Within 60 days after the Commission submits its report, the Department of Transportation, the Department of Justice, and the Federal Trade Commission shall furnish an analysis of the impact of this Act to Congress and to the Advisory Commission on Conferences in Ocean Shipping.

(3) The reports required by this subsection shall specifically address the following topics:

(A) the advisability of adopting a system of tariffs based on volume and mass of shipment;

(B) the need for antitrust immunity for ports and marine terminals; and

(C) the continuing need for the statutory requirement that tariffs be filed with and enforced by the Commission.

(d) ESTABLISHMENT AND COMPOSITION OF ADVISORY COMMISSION.—

(1) Effective 5½ years after the date of enactment of this Act, there is established the Advisory Commission on Conferences in Ocean Shipping (hereinafter referred to as the "Advisory Commission").

(2) The Advisory Commission shall be composed of 17 members as follows:

(A) a cabinet level official appointed by the President;

(B) 4 members from the United States Senate appointed by the President pro tempore of the Senate, 2 from the membership of the Committee on Commerce, Science, and Transportation and 2 from the membership of the Committee on the Judiciary;

(C) 4 members from the United States House of Representatives appointed by the Speaker of the House, 2 from the membership of the Committee on Merchant Marine and Fisheries, and 2 from the membership of the Committee on the Judiciary; and

(D) 8 members from the private sector appointed by the President.

(3) The President shall designate the chairman of the Advisory Commission.

(4) The term of office for members shall be for the term of the Advisory Commission.

(5) A vacancy in the Advisory Commission shall not affect its powers, and shall be filled in the same manner in which the original appointment was made.

(6) Nine members of the Advisory Commission shall constitute a quorum, but the Advisory Commission may permit as few as 2 members to hold hearings.

(e) COMPENSATION OF MEMBERS OF THE ADVISORY COMMISSION.—

(1) Officials of the United States Government and Members of Congress who are members of the Advisory Commission shall serve without compensation in addition to that received for their services as officials and Members, but they shall be reimbursed for reasonable travel, subsistence, and other necessary expenses incurred by them in the performance of the duties vested in the Advisory Commission.

(2) Members of the Advisory Commission appointed from the private sector shall each receive compensation not exceeding the maximum per diem rate of pay for grade 18 of the General Schedule under section 5332 of title 5, United States Code, when engaged in the performance of the duties vested in the Advisory Commission, plus reimbursement for reasonable travel, subsistence, and other necessary expenses incurred by them in the performance of those duties, notwithstanding the limitations in section 5701 through 5733 of title 5, United States Code.

(3) Members of the Advisory Commission appointed from the private sector are not subject to section 208 of title 18, United States Code. Before commencing service, these members shall file with the Advisory Commission a statement disclosing their financial interests and business and former relationships involving or relating to ocean transportation. These statements shall be available for public inspection at the Advisory Commission's offices.

(f) ADVISORY COMMISSION FUNCTIONS.—The Advisory Commission shall conduct a comprehensive study of, and make recommendations concerning, conferences in ocean shipping. The study shall specifically address whether the Nation would be best served by prohibiting conferences, or by closed or open conferences.

(g) POWERS OF THE ADVISORY COMMISSION.—

(1) The Advisory Commission may, for the purpose of carrying out its functions, hold such hearings and sit and act at such times and places, administer such oaths, and require, by subpoena or otherwise, the attendance and testimony of such witnesses, and the production of such books, records, correspondence, memorandums, papers, and

documents as the Advisory Commission may deem advisable. Subpoenas may be issued to any person within the jurisdiction of the United States courts, under the signature of the chairman, or any duly designated member, and may be served by any person designated by the chairman, or that member. In case of contumacy by, or refusal to obey a subpoena to, any person, the Advisory Commission may advise the Attorney General who shall invoke the aid of any court of the United States within the jurisdiction of which the Advisory Commission's proceedings are carried on, or where that person resides or carries on business, in requiring the attendance and testimony of witnesses and the production of books, papers, and documents; and the court may issue an order requiring that person to appear before the Advisory Commission, there to produce records, if so ordered, or to give testimony. A failure to obey such an order of the court may be punished by the court as a contempt thereof. All process in any such case may be served in the judicial district whereof the person is an inhabitant or may be found.

(2) Each department, agency, and instrumentality of the executive branch of the Government, including independent agencies, shall furnish to the Advisory Commission, upon request made by the chairman, such information as the Advisory Commission deems necessary to carry out its functions.

(3) Upon request of the chairman, the Department of Justice, the Department of Transportation, the Federal Maritime Commission, and the Federal Trade Commission shall detail staff personnel as necessary to assist the Advisory Commission.

(4) The chairman may rent office space for the Advisory Commission, may utilize the services and facilities of other Federal agencies with or without reimbursement, may accept voluntary services notwithstanding section 1342 of title 31, United States Code, may accept, hold, and administer gifts from other Federal agencies, and may enter into contracts with any public or private person or entity for reports, research, or surveys in furtherance of the work of the Advisory Commission.

(h) FINAL REPORT.—The Advisory Committee shall, within 1 year after all of its members have been duly appointed, submit to the President and to the Congress a final report containing a statement of the findings and conclusions of the Advisory Commission resulting from the study undertaken under subsection (f), including recommendations for such administrative, judicial, and legislative action as it deems advisable. Each recommendation made by the Advisory commission to the President and to the Congress must have the majority vote of the Advisory Commission present and voting.

(i) EXPIRATION OF THE COMMISSION.—The Advisory Commission shall cease to exist 30 days after the submission of its final report.

(j) AUTHORIZATION OF APPROPRIATION.—There is authorized to be appropriated $500,000 to carry out the activities of the Advisory Commission.

SEC. 19. OCEAN FREIGHT FORWARDERS.

(a) LICENSE.—No person may act as an ocean freight forwarder unless that person holds a license issued by the Commission. The Commission shall issue a forwarder's license to any person that —

(1) the Commission determines to be qualified by experience and character to render forwarding services; and

(2) furnishes a bond in a form and amount determined by the Commission to insure financial responsibility that is issued by a surety company found acceptable by the Secretary of the Treasury.

(b) SUSPENSION OR REVOCATION.—The Commission shall, after notice and hearing, suspend or revoke a license if it finds that the ocean freight forwarder is not qualified to render forwarding services or that it willfully failed to comply with a provision of this Act or with a lawful order, rule, or regulation of the Commission. The Commission may also revoke a forwarder's license for failure to maintain a bond in accordance with subsection (a)(2).

(c) EXCEPTION.—A person whose primary business is the sale of merchandise may forward shipments of the merchandise for its own account without a license.

(d) COMPENSATION OF FORWARDERS BY CARRIERS.[4]—

(1) A common carrier may compensate an ocean freight forwarder in connection with a shipment dispatched on behalf of others only

---

[4] Section 1888(8) of Public Law 99-514, the Tax Reform Act of 1986 (100 Stat. 2085, 2925, approved October 22, 1986) amended section 641 of the Tariff Act of 1930, as amended (19 U.S.C. 1641) by adding at the end thereof the following new subsection:

(i) COMPENSATION OF OCEAN FREIGHT FORWARDERS.—

(1) IN GENERAL.—Notwithstanding any other provision of law, no conference or group of two or more ocean common carriers in the foreign commerce of the United States that is authorized to agree upon the level of compensation paid to ocean freight forwarders may—

(A) deny to any member of such conference or group the right, upon notice of not more than 10 calendar days, to take independent action on any level compensation paid to an ocean freight forwarder who is also a customs broker, and

(B) agree to limit the payment of compensation to an ocean freight forwarder who is also a customs broker to less than 1.25 percent of the aggregate of all rates and charges applicable under the tariff assessed against the cargo on which the forwarding services are provided.

(2) ADMINISTRATION.—The provisions of this subsection shall be enforced by the agency responsible for administration of the Shipping Act of 1984 (46 U.S.C. 1701, et seq.).

(3) REMEDIES.—Any person injured by reason of a violation of paragraph (1) may, in addition to any other remedy, file a complaint for reparation as provided in section 11 of the Shipping Act of 1984 (46 U.S.C. 1710), which may be enforced pursuant to section 14 of such Act (46 U.S.C. 1713).

(4) DEFINITIONS.—For purposes of this subsection, the term "conference," "ocean common carrier," and "ocean freight forwarder" have the respective meaning given to such terms by section 3 of the Shipping Act of 1984 (46 U.S.C. 1702).

when the ocean freight forwarder has certified in writing that it holds a valid license and has performed the following services:

(A) Engaged, booked, secured, reserved, or contracted directly with the carrier or its agent for space aboard a vessel or confirmed the availability of that space.

(B) Prepared and processed the ocean bill of lading, dock receipt, or other similar document with respect to the shipment.

(2) No common carrier may pay compensation for services described in paragraph (1) more than once on the same shipment.

(3) No compensation may be paid to an ocean freight forwarder except in accordance with the tariff requirements of this Act.

(4) No ocean freight forwarder may receive compensation from a common carrier with respect to a shipment in which the forwarder has a direct or indirect beneficial interest nor shall a common carrier knowingly pay compensation on that shipment.

SEC. 20. REPEALS AND CONFORMING AMENDMENTS.

(b) CONFORMING AMENDMENTS.—The Shipping Act, 1916 (46 App. U.S.C. 801 et seq.), is amended as follows:

(1) in section 1 by striking the definitions "controlled carrier" and "independent ocean freight forwarder";

(2) in sections 14, 15, 16, 20, 21(a), 22, and 45 by striking "common carrier by water" wherever it appears in those sections and substituting "common carrier by water in interstate commerce";

(3) in section 14, first paragraph, by striking "or a port of a foreign country";

(4) in section 14, first paragraph, by striking all after the words "for each offense" and substituting a period;

(5) in section 15, fourth paragraph, by striking "(including changes in special rates and charges covered by section 14b of this Act which do not involve a change in the spread between such rates and charges and the rates and charges applicable to nonconstruct shippers)" and also "with the publication and filing requirements of section 18(b) hereof and";

(6) in section 15, sixth paragraph, by striking "or permitted under section 14b," and in the seventh paragraph, by striking "or of section 14b";

(7) in section 16, in the paragraph designated "First", by striking all after "disadvantage in any respect" and substituting "whatsoever.";

(8) in section 17 by striking the first paragraph, and in the second paragraph, by striking "such carrier and every";

(9) in section 21(b) by striking "The Commission shall require the chief executive officer of every vessel operating common carrier by

water in foreign commerce and to the extent it deems feasible, may require any shipper, consignor, consignee, forwarder, broker, other carrier or other person subject to this Act," and substituting "The Commission may, to the extent it deems feasible, require any shipper, consignor, consignee, forwarder, broker, or other person subject to this Act.";

(10) in section 22 by striking subsection (c);

(11) in section 25, at the end of the first sentence , by adding "under this Act";

(12) in section 29 by striking "any order of the board, the board," and substituting "any order of the Federal Maritime Commission under this Act, the Commission,";

(13) in sections 30 and 31, after the words "any order of the board", by adding under this Act,";

(14) in section 32(a) by striking "and section 44"; and

(15) in section 32(c), after the words, "or functions," adding "under this Act,".

(c) TECHNICAL AMENDMENTS.—Section 212 of the Merchant Marine Act, 1936 (46 App. U.S.C. 1122) is amended by —

(1) striking after subsection (d) the following undesignated paragraph: "The Federal Maritime Commission is authorized and directed—"; and

(2) striking after subsection (e) the following undesignated paragraph: "The Secretary of Transportation is authorized and directed—".

(d) EFFECTS ON CERTAIN AGREEMENTS AND CONTRACTS.—All agreements, contracts, modifications, and exemptions previously approved or licenses previously issued by the Commission shall continue in force and effect as if approved or issued under this Act; and all new agreements, contracts, and modifications to existing, pending, or new contracts or agreements shall be considered under this Act.

(e) SAVINGS PROVISIONS.—

(1) Each service contract entered into by a shipper and an ocean common carrier or conference before the date of enactment of this Act may remain in full force and effect and need not comply with the requirements of section 8(c) of this Act until 15 months after the date of enactment of this Act.

(2) This Act and the amendments made by it shall not affect any suit —

(A) filed before the date of enactment of this Act; or

(B) with respect to claims arising out of conduct engaged in before the date of enactment of this Act, filed within 1 year after the date of enactment of this Act.

SEC. 23.[5] BONDING OF NON-VESSEL-OPERATING COMMON CARRIERS.

(a) BOND.—Each non-vessel-operating common carrier shall furnish to the commission a bond in a form and an amount determined by the Commission to be satisfactory to insure the financial responsibility of that carrier, but in any event not less than $50,000.

(b) SURETY.—A bond submitted pursuant to this section shall be issued by a surety company found acceptable by the Secretary of the Treasury.

(c) CLAIMS AGAINST BOND.—A bond obtained pursuant to this section shall be available to pay any judgment for damages against a non-vessel-operating common carrier arising from its transportation-related activities or order for reparations issued pursuant to section 11 of this Act or any penalty assessed against a non-vessel-operating carrier pursuant to section 13 of this Act.

(d) RESIDENT AGENT.—A non-vessel-operating common carrier not domiciled in the United States shall designate a resident agent in the United States for receipt of service of judicial and administrative process, including subpoenas.

(e) TARIFFS.—The Commission may suspend or cancel any or all tariffs of a non-vessel-operating common carrier for failure to maintain the bond required by subsection (a) of this section or to designate an agent as required by subsection (d) of this section or for a violation of section 10(a)(1) of this Act.

---

[5] Section 710 of Public Law 101-595 (104 Stat. 2996, approved November 16, 1990), added section 23 to the Shipping Act of 1984, and amended section 10(b) of that Act. Section 710 (d) and (e) of Public Law 101-595 provide:

(d) INTERIM RULES. — The Commission may prescribe interim rules and regulations necessary to carry out the amendments made by this section.

(e) EFFECTIVE DATE. — This section shall become effective 90 days after the date of its enactment.

APPENDIX A — PART II

FOREIGN SHIPPING PRACTICES ACT
TITLE X[1]—OCEAN AND AIR TRANSPORTATION

Subtitle A—Foreign Shipping Practices

SEC. 10001. SHORT TITLE.
This subtitle may be cited as the "Foreign Shipping Practices Act of 1988."

SEC. 10002. FOREIGN LAWS AND PRACTICES.
(a) DEFINITIONS.—For purposes of this section—
(1) "Common carrier," "marine terminal operator," "non-vessel-operating common carrier," "person," "shipper," "shippers' association," and "United States" have the meanings given each such term, respectively, in section 3 of the Shipping Act of 1984 (46 App. U.S.C. 1702);
(2) "foreign carrier" means an ocean common carrier a majority of whose vessels are documented under the laws of a country other than the United States;
(3) "maritime services" means port-to-port carriage of cargo by the vessels operated by ocean common carriers;
(4) "maritime-related services" means intermodal operations, terminal operations, cargo solicitation, forwarding and agency services, non-vessel-operating common carrier operations, and all other activities and services integral to total transportation systems of ocean common carriers and their foreign domiciled affiliates on their own and others' behalf;
(5) "United States carrier" means an ocean common carrier which operates vessels documented under the laws of the United States; and
(6) "United States oceanborne trade" means the carriage of cargo between the United States and a foreign country, whether direct or indirect, by an ocean common carrier.
(b) AUTHORITY TO CONDUCT INVESTIGATIONS.—The Federal Maritime Commission shall investigate whether any laws, rules, regulations, policies, or practices of foreign governments, or any practices of foreign carriers or other persons providing maritime or maritime-related services in a foreign country result in the existence of conditions that—

---

[1] Title X of Public Law 100–418, approved August 23, 1988, the "Omnibus Trade and Competitiveness Act of 1988."

(1) adversely affect the operations of United States carriers in United States oceanborne trade; and

(2) do not exist for foreign carriers of that country in the United States under the laws of the United States or as a result of acts of United States carriers or other persons providing maritime or maritime-related services in the United States.

(c) INVESTIGATIONS.—

(1) Investigations under subsection (b) of this section may be initiated by the Commission on its own motion or on the petition of any persons, including any common carrier, shipper, shippers' association, ocean freight forwarder, or marine terminal operator, or any branch, department, agency, or other component of the Government of the United States.

(2) The Commission shall complete any such investigation and render a decision within 120 days after it is initiated, except that the Commission may extend such 120-day period for an additional 90 days if the Commission is unable to obtain sufficient information to determine whether a condition specified in subsection (b) of this section exists. Any notice providing such an extension shall clearly state the reasons for such extension.

(d) INFORMATION REQUESTS.—

(1) In order to further the purposes of subsection (b) of this section, the Commission may, by order, require any person (including any common carrier, shipper, shippers' association, ocean freight forwarder, or marine terminal operator, or any officer, receiver, trustee, lessee, agent or employee thereof) to file with the Commission any periodic or special report, answers to questions, documentary material, or other information which the Commission considers necessary or appropriate. The Commission may require that the response to any such order shall be made under oath. Such a response shall be fur- nished in the form and within the time prescribed by the Commission.

(2) In an investigation under subsection (b) of this section, the Commission may issue subpoenas to compel the attendance and testimony of witnesses and the production of records or other evidence.

(3) Notwithstanding any other provision of law, the Commission may, in its discretion, determine that any information submitted to it in response to a request under this subsection, or otherwise, shall not be disclosed to the public.

(e) ACTION AGAINST FOREIGN CARRIERS.—

(1) Whenever, after notice and opportunity for comment or hearing, the Commission determines that the conditions specified in subsection (b) of this section exist, the Commission shall take such

action as it considers necessary and appropriate against any foreign carrier that is a contributing cause to, or whose government is a contributing cause to, such conditions, in order to offset such conditions. Such action may include—

(A) limitations on sailings to and from United States ports or on the amount or type of cargo carried;

(B) suspension, in whole or in part, of any or all tariffs filed with the Commission, including the right of an ocean common carrier to use any or all tariffs of conferences in United States trades of which it is a member for such period as the Commission specifies;

(C) suspension, in whole or in part, of the right of an ocean common carrier to operate under any agreement filed with the Commission, including agreements authorizing preferential treatment at terminals, preferential terminal leases, space chartering, or pooling of cargo or revenues with other ocean common carriers; and (D) a fee, not to exceed $1,000,000 per voyage.

(2) The Commission may consult with, seek the cooperation of, or make recommendations to other appropriate Government agencies prior to taking any action under this subsection.

(3) Before a determination under this subsection becomes effective or a request is made under subsection (f) of this section, the determination shall be submitted immediately to the President who may, within 10 days after receiving such determination, disapprove the determination in writing, setting forth the reasons for the disapproval, if the President finds that disapproval is required for reasons of the national defense or the foreign policy of the United States.

(f) ACTIONS UPON REQUEST OF THE COMMISSION.—Whenever the conditions specified in subsection (b) of this section are found by the Commission to exist, upon the request of the Commission—

(1) the collector of customs at any port or place of destination in the United States shall refuse the clearance required by section 4197 of the Revised Statutes (46 App. U.S.C. 91) to any vessel of a foreign carrier that is identified by the Commission under the subsection (e) of this section; and

(2) the Secretary of the department in which the Coast Guard is operating shall deny entry, for purposes of oceanborne trade, of any vessel of a foreign carrier that is identified by the Commission under subsection (e) of this section to any port or place in the United States or the navigable waters of the United States, or shall detain any such vessel at the port or place in the United States from which it is about to depart for any other port or place in the United States.

(g) REPORT.—The Commission shall include in its annual report to Congress—

(1) a list of the twenty foreign countries which generated the largest volume of oceanborne liner cargo for the most recent calendar year in bilateral trade with the United States;

(2) an analysis of conditions described in subsection (b) of this section being investigated or found to exist in foreign countries;

(3) any actions being taken by the Commission to offset such conditions;

(4) any recommendations for additional legislation to offset such conditions; and

(5) a list of petitions filed under subsection (c) of this section that the Commission rejected, and the reasons for each such rejection.

(h) The actions against foreign carriers authorized in subsections (e) and (f) of this section may be used in the administration and enforcement of section 13(b)(5) of the Shipping Act of 1984 (46 App. U.S.C. 1712(b)(5)) or section 19(1)(b) of the Merchant Marine Act, 1920 (46 App. U.S.C. 876).

(i) Any rule, regulation, or final order of the Commission issued under this section shall be reviewable exclusively in the same forum and in the same manner as provided in section 2342(3)(B) of title 28, United States Code.

APPENDIX B

FEDERAL MARITIME COMMISSION
[Circular Letter No. 1-89]

Ocean Common Carriers, Conferences of Such Carriers, Shippers, and Shippers'
Associations in the Foreign Commerce of the United States; Service and Cargo
Commitments in Service Contracts

Section 8(c) of the Shipping Act of 1984 ("1984 Act"), 46 U.S.C. App.
1707(c), requires service contracts between shippers or shippers' associations
and ocean common carriers or conferences to meet certain statutory requirements and to be filed with the Federal Maritime Commission. Section
3(21) of the 1984 Act, 46 U.S.C. App. 1702(21), defines a "service contract" as:

> a contract between a shipper and an ocean common carrier or confer-
> ence in which the shipper makes a commitment to provide a certain mini-
> mum quantity of cargo over a fixed time period, and the ocean common
> carrier or conference commits to a certain rate or rate schedule as well as a
> defined service level—such as, assured space, transit time, port rotation, or
> similar service features; the contract may also specify provisions in the event
> of nonperformance on the part of either party.

The Commission has received service contracts which do not appear to
contain mutually binding commitments by the contract parties sufficient to
meet the definition of "service contract" contained in the 1984 Act.

In addressing the matter of service contract commitments, generally, the
Commission noted in Docket No. 88-7, *Service Contracts—Most-Favored-Shipper*
Provisions ("Docket No. 88-7") that:

> Meaningful minimum quantities of cargo over a fixed time period and
> rate and defined service level commitments between a carrier and a shipper
> are the legislative *quid pro quo* for departing from the published tariff rates
> of the carrier that would otherwise apply. The failure of the contract parties
> to fulfill the basic requirements of this *quid pro quo* not only offends the
> legislative scheme crafted by Congress but also could, as noted above, make
> the service contract but a device to evade the carrier's tariff rates in violation
> of section 10(a)(1) of the 1984 Act. We believe that the Commission is not
> only empowered but also . . . has the responsibility to take whatever regulatory
> action may be necessary and appropriate to ensure against this result.
>
> Accordingly, it is the stated policy of the Commission to require mean-
> ingful rate and volume commitments on the part of the shipper and mean-

ingful service commitments on the part of the carrier in all service contracts
entered into under the authority of section 8(c) of the 1984 Act. The
Commission will scrutinize contracts carefully at the time of filing to ensure
that they contain such commitments, pursuant to the requirements of 46
CFR 581.1(n). Failure to comply with the requirements of 46 CFR 581.1(n),
as herein interpreted, will result in the rejection of the contract pursuant to
46 CFR 581.8 or other appropriate Commission action.

Docket No. 88-7, Proposed Rule, slip op. at 31, 32

In essence, service contracts must, by statute, contain certain definite
commitments by both the carrier and the shipper. Moreover, these commitments must be meaningful, *i.e.,* the contract parties must undertake real
obligations. Service contracts that are indefinite or contain illusory under-
takings simply do not meet the definition of "service contract" under the
1984 Act. A service contract that lacks definite and mutual consideration not
only fails to meet the statutory definition but may also be invalid and
unenforceable at common law.

With respect to carrier or conference commitments in a service contract,
the Commission believes that contract provisions that provide for "regular"
or "frequent" service do not meet the 1984 Act's requirement that the carrier
or conference commit to a "defined service level." Although the Act does
not specifically define the term "service level," it does provide several examples (*e.g.,* assured space, transit time, etc.) sufficient to indicate the scope of
the concept. A mere recitation of a common carrier's obligation under
common law is not adequate.

Moreover, the Commission is aware of some contracts where a carrier
agrees in one provision to specific service commitments (such as assured
space), but in another provision vitiates that commitment by stating that a
shipper's exclusive remedy in the event of a breach of the carrier's commitment is a reduction in the shipper's minimum cargo commitment. Under
such an arrangement, the carrier is in effect committing to nothing. Congress expected both parties to a service contract to make mutual, binding
commitments and anything less is not acceptable.

Similarly, the Commission believes that a service contract that allows a
shipper to default on its cargo commitment while only paying *de minimis*
damages to the carrier may not be a *bona fide* contract. For example, some
service contracts establishing rate levels of over $2,000 per container provide
for liquidated damages of only $40 or $50 per container in the event the
shipper fails to meet its minimum cargo commitment. Such damages provisions do not appear to bear a reasonable relationship to the cargo commitment, the contract rate, or the effects of the loss of cargo to the carrier.
Service contracts embodying *de minimis* liquidated damages provisions may
thus render the shipper's cargo commitment meaningless, and, therefore,
result in a contract that fails to meet the statutory definition. The Commission previously noted:

. . . that although it lacks the authority to directly regulate the use of liquidated damages provisions [this] does not necessarily mean that the Commission is without authority to preclude service contract liquidated damages provisions which may permit evasion of the otherwise applicable tariff rate contrary to the 1984 Act and the policies underlying it, regardless of whether both parties to the contract willingly or unwillingly agree to those provisions.

Docket No. 88-7, Proposed Rule, slip op. at 28, 29. In keeping with this admonition, the Commission will closely scrutinize the levels of liquidated damages for breach of the shipper's cargo commitment and will take appropriate action against service contracts containing damages provisions considered *de minimis.*

The Commission recognizes that liquidated damages provisions in service contracts are permissive and not mandatory under the 1984 Act. Nonetheless, when the parties to a service contract choose to agree on liquidated damages for the breach of a shipper's minimum cargo commitment, that amount must bear some reasonable relation to the actual damages that will otherwise be incurred by a carrier and for which the shipper would be liable absent a liquidated damages provision. Liquidated damages provisions should be legitimate and not be used to give a shipper an unfair benefit even though it did not meet its commitment under the contract.

Ocean common carriers, conferences of such carriers, shippers, and shippers' associations are hereby advised that the Commission expects service contracts to conform to the definitional requirements for service contracts under the 1984 Act. Accordingly, the Commission will begin to take action against any contract filed 45 days after the date of this Circular Letter that does not meet statutory requirements.

April 12, 1989.
Edward P. Walsh,
Managing Director.
[FR Doc. 89-9079 Filed 4-11-89; 8:45 am]
BILLING CODE 6730-01-M

MUTUAL TERMINATION, SETTLEMENT AND
RELEASE AGREEMENT

Agreement made this _____ by and between _____ and _____ .

Whereas _____ and _____ entered into Service Contract No. SC No. _____ (the "Service Contract") on the _____ , 19____ , said contract having been filed with the Federal Maritime Commission, to become effective February 10, 1985; the Service Contract provided for the transportation by _____ of containers placed with it by _____ from specified Far East origins to the United States; and

Whereas _____ sent to _____ an invoice dated _____ , 19____ for the liquidated damages due under the contract because _____did not ship with _____ the number of containers alleged by _____ to be required by the Service Contract; and

Whereas _____ denied _____ entitlement to damages, alleging that the Service Contract, or various of its provisions, were unenforceable, and that _____ was entitled to damages based on _____ allegedly unjustly discriminatory conduct and other actions; and

Whereas _____ and _____ made serious and extensive attempts between themselves and through their attorneys to resolve their dispute without costly litigation or arbitration; and

Whereas _____ served a demand for arbitration on _____ on _____ , 19____, seeking recovery of liquidated damages stated in the Service Contract and other damages arising from _____ alleged breach of the Service Contract, and naming an arbitrator; and

Whereas on _____ , 19____, _____ responded to _____ arbitration demand, seeking damages for _____ alleged breach of the Service Contract and naming an arbitrator; and

Whereas the claim made by _____ and the defenses which have been asserted by _____ on their face present genuine and serious disputes as to their liability to each other, both as a matter of fact and as a matter of law; and resolution of those disputes would necessitate lengthy, time consuming and expensive litigation, in arbitration (the Service Contract calls for arbitration), at the Federal Maritime Commission (to determine _____ assertion that the Service Contract may be in violation of the Shipping Act of 1984), and in court (to enforce or appeal Commission or arbitrators' rulings); and this agreement therefore represents a *bona fide* attempt by the parties to terminate their controversy and avoid the costly delay in resolving their disputes, and is not a device to circumvent the requirements of the Shipping Act of 1984; and

Whereas _____ and _____ wish to fully compromise and settle all their above-mentioned differences, claims, disputes, suits and proceedings;

Now, therefore, the parties agree as follows:

1. The Service Contract, No. _____ between the parties, as identified above, be, and the same hereby is, terminated in all respects.

2. The effective date of the termination of the Service Contract shall be the date set forth above.

3. In consideration of payment in full to _____ of the amount to be paid by _____ to _____ described in Paragraph 4 below, and in consideration of _____ withdrawal, upon such full payment, of its demand to _____ for arbitration described above, _____ and _____ release, remise, and forever discharge each other, their owners, officers, employees, directors, stockholders, partners, subsidiaries and affiliated companies, and their successors and assigns, from any and all liability, claims, causes, actions, suits and demands, whether now known or unknown, which _____ and _____ have had, now have, or may in the future have against each other for damages and reparations of all nature and description and for any other form of legal, equitable, arbitral or administrative relief of all types arising out of the Service Contract and the incidents, circumstances and actions of the parties in connection therewith and pursuant thereto, and out of pleadings and filings in connection therewith; and _____ and _____ further release each other from any and all claims for interest, attorneys' fees, costs, and expenses arising out of the Service Contract, the demand for arbitration and all pleadings and filings in connection therewith and the prosecution and defense of same.

4. _____ shall pay, and _____ shall accept, the sum of $_____ in settlement of any and all claims by _____ under the Service Contract to be paid without interest by _____ as follows: $_____ shall be paid to _____ upon the execution of this Agreement by the parties; $_____ shall be paid on the last day of the month following the execution of this Agreement; and the remaining $_____ shall be paid in equal consecutive monthly installments of $_____ on the last day of each month thereafter.

5. In the event _____ defaults in any of its payments to _____ required by Paragraph 4 above, _____ agrees not to assert any defense in any suit _____ might bring against _____ for collection of the amount past due, and _____ further agrees to pay the expenses and reasonable attorneys' fees of _____ in suit, together with interest of twelve (12) percent on the amount past due calculated from the date payment was to have been made. A default by _____ shall occur if any payment is not received within seven (7) business days after the date on which the payment is due.

6. All payments made by _____ shall be made payable to _____ and shall be delivered to _____.

SHIPPER'S CREDIT AGREEMENT

1. Agreement Designating Forwarder(s)

In consideration of the issuance and release of bills of lading on other than a freight prepaid or collect bill of lading basis by members of the

GULF/MEDITERRANEAN PORTS CONFERENCE

GULF/SCANDINAVIAN AND BALTIC SEA PORTS CONFERENCE

GULF/UNITED KINGDOM CONFERENCE

(If you do NOT elect to participate on all three trade routes please DELETE as per your preference)

at their individual discretion (members as set forth in applicable Conference tariff) at United States ports served by such lines as members of the Conference to us through the following duly authorized forwarders and/or agents:

_____   _____

_____   _____

_____   _____

we hereby agree as follows:

1. To pay (either direct or through the authorized forwarders or agents) to the carrier within fifteen (15) calendar days of the release of the bill of lading or sailing of the vessel, whichever occurs first (and in any case not beyond the date of the vessel's arrival at discharge port), all freight and charges due on bills of lading received by any of the above authorized forwarders or agents in our name and/or due bills signed on our behalf by any of the above authorized forwarders or agents.
2. We will be absolutely and unconditionally responsible to see that all freights and charges due will be paid and guarantee that they will be paid irrespective of whether or not funds for payment have been advanced to the forwarders/agents or otherwise.
3. Credit privileges hereunder may immediately be suspended for any failure to comply with the provisions of this Agreement.
4. This Agreement shall continue in effect until terminated by written notice by the Conference or the shipper; provided, however, that termination shall not extinguish any existing liabilities hereunder.

_____
                    (Shipper)

_____
                    (Address)
        By: _____
                (Signature and Title)

Dated this _____ day of _____, 19____.

2. Agreement Not Designating Forwarder(s)

In consideration of extension of credit to permit the release of bills of lading by member carriers of the River Plate & Brazil Conferences as set forth in the River Plate & Brazil Conferences Tariff, we hereby agree as follows:

1. Receipts for all bills of lading so released shall be signed by us or on our behalf by our duly authorized representative or forwarders.

2. We will be absolutely and unconditionally responsible to the Carrier for payment of all freight and charges due up to fifteen (15) calendar days after the sailing of the vessel from the respective port of loading, and guarantee that the Carrier will be paid within that period, irrespective of whether or not funds for payments have been advanced to the forwarder or otherwise.

3. Credit privileges hereunder will immediately be suspended for any failure to comply with the provisions of this Agreement. It is understood and agreed that the member carrier/s shall notify the Conference office promptly of each instance in which the undersigned fails to pay freight monies and charges within the fifteen (15) day period provided herein and the Conference office shall promptly notify each member carrier of all such instances, whereupon no further credit shall be extended by any member carrier to the undersigned until the Conference office shall have notified each member carrier of the restoration of the right to credit. The right to credit shall not be restored to the undersigned until all freight monies and charges due and owed to any member carrier by the undersigned for a period longer than the fifteen (15) day period herein and above provided shall have been paid.

4. This Agreement shall become effective on its execution and shall continue in effect until terminated by written notice from any party to the other; provided, however, that termination shall not extinguish any existing liabilities hereunder.

5. IT IS UNDERSTOOD AND AGREED THAT NOTHING HEREIN CONTAINED SHALL LIMIT THE RIGHT OF THE MEMBER CARRIER/S NOT TO EXTEND CREDIT TO SHIPPERS AT THEIR DISCRETION. ANY EXTENSION OF CREDIT AT CARRIER'S DISCRETION SHALL NOT PRECLUDE CARRIER'S RIGHT TO COLLECT PAYMENT OF CHARGES PRIOR TO VESSEL'S ARRIVAL AT PORT OF DISCHARGE.

Dated this _____ day of _____, 19____.

_____
                (Shipper)

_____
                (Address)

By:_____
        (Authorized to Sign)

Member Lines of River Plate
& Brazil Conferences
(Listed on reverse hereof)

_____
                CHAIRMAN
Pursuant to Special Authority
from the Individual Member
Lines, 17 Battery Place,
New York, N.Y. 10004

(NOTE: This Agreement is not applicable to freight collect bills
         of lading.)

Before the Federal Maritime Commission
COMPLAINT

_____ v. _____ [Insert without abbreviation exact and complete name of party or parties respondent]

I. The complainant is [State in this paragraph whether complainant is an association, a corporation, firm, or partnership and the names of the individuals composing the same. State also the nature and principal place of business].

II. The respondent is [State in this paragraph whether complainant is an association, a corporation, firm, or partnership and the names of the individuals composing the same. State also the nature and principal place of business].

III. Allegation of jurisdiction. [State in this paragraph a synopsis of the statutory bases for claim(s)].

IV. That [State in this or subsequent paragraphs to be lettered "A," "B," etc., the matter or matters complained of. If rates are involved, name each rate, fare, charge, classification, regulation, or practice, the lawfulness of which is challenged].

V. That by reason of the facts stated in the foregoing paragraphs, complainant has been (and is being) subject to injury as a direct result of the violations by respondent of sections _____ [State in this paragraph the causal connection between the alleged illegal acts of respondent and the claimed injury to complainant, with all necessary statutory sections relied upon.

VI. That complainant has been injured in the following manner: To its damage in the sum of $_____.

VII. Wherefore complainant prays that respondent be required to answer the charges herein; that after due hearing, an order be made commanding said respondent (and each of them): to cease and desist from the aforesaid violations of said act(s): to establish and put in force such practices as the Commission determines to be lawful and reasonable; to pay to said complainant by way of reparations for the unlawful conduct hereinabove described the sum of $_____, with interest and attorney's fees or such other sum as the Commission may determine to be proper as an award of reparation; and that such other and further order or orders be made as the Commission determines to be proper in the premises.

Dated at _____, this _____ day of _____, 19____.

_____
[Complainant's signature}

_____
[Office and post office address]

_____
[Signature of agent or attorney of complainant]

_____
[Post office address]

Verification [See §502.112]

State of _____, County of _____, ss: _____, _____ being first duly sworn on oath deposes and says that he (she) is _____ [The complainant, or, if a firm, association, or corporation, state the capacity of the affiant] and is the person who signed the foregoing complaint; that he (she) has read the complaint and that the facts stated therein, upon information received from others, affiant believes to be true.

Subscribed and sworn to before me, a notary public in and for the State of _____, County of _____, this _____ day _____, A.D. 19____.

[Seal] _____
(Notary Public)
My Commission expires _____.

Answer of Respondent

Before the Federal Maritime Commission
ANSWER

_____ v. _____
[Complainant]   [Respondent]

Docket No. _____

The above-named respondent, for answer to the complaint in this proceeding, states:

I. [State in this and subsequent paragraphs to be numbered II, III, etc., appropriate and responsive admissions, denials and averments, specifically answering the complaint, paragraph by paragraph.]

Wherefore respondent prays that the complaint in this proceeding be dismissed.

_____
[Name of respondent]

By_____
    [Title of Officer]

_____
[Office and post office address]

_____
[Signature of attorney or agent]

_____
[Post office address]

Date _____, 19_____.

Verification

Small Claim Form for Informal Adjudication and Respondent's Affidavit

FEDERAL MARITIME COMMISSION, WASHINGTON, D.C.

Informal Docket No._____

(Claimant)

vs.

(Respondent)

I. The claimant is [state in this paragraph whether claimant is an association, corporation, firm or partnership, and if a firm or partnership, the names of the individuals composing the same. State the nature and principal place of business.]

II. The respondent named above is [state in this paragraph whether claimant is an association, corporation, firm or partnership, and if a firm or partnership, the names of the individuals composing the same. State the nature and principal place of business.]

III. That [state in this and subsequent paragraphs to be lettered A, B, etc., the matters that gave rise to the claim. Name specifically each rate, charge, classification, regulation or practice which is challenged. Refer to tariffs, tariff times or rules, or agreement numbers, if known. If claim is based on the fact that a firm is a common carrier, state where it is engaged in transportation by water and which statute(s) it is subject to under the jurisdiction of the Federal Maritime Commission].

IV. If claim is for overcharges, state commodity, weight and cube, origin, destination, bill of lading description, bill of lading number and date, rate and/or charges assessed, date of delivery, date of payment, by whom paid, rate or charge claimed to be correct and amount claimed as overcharges. [Specify tariff item for rate or charge claimed to be proper].

V. State section of statute claimed to have been violated. (Not required if claim is for overcharges).

VI. State how claimant was injured and amount of damages requested.

VII. The undersigned authorizes the Settlement Officer to determine the above-stated claim pursuant to the informal procedure outlined in subpart S (46 CFR 502.301-502.305) of the Commission's informal procedure for adjudication of small claims subject to discretionary Commission review.

Attach memorandum or brief in support of claim. Also attach bill of lading, copies of correspondence or other documents in support of claim.

(Date)

(Claimant's signature)

(Claimant's address)

(Signature of agent or attorney)

(Agent's or attorney's address)

Verification

State of _____, county of _____, ss: _____, being first duly sworn on oath deposes and says that he or she is

---

The claimant [or if a firm, association, or corporation, state the capacity of the affiant] and is the person who signed the foregoing claim, that he or she has read the foregoing and that the facts set forth without qualification are true and that the facts stated herein upon information received from others, affiant believes to be true.

Subscribed and sworn to before me, a notary public in and for the State of _____, County of _____, this _____ day of _____ 19_____.

(Seal)

(Notary Public)

My Commission expires, _____.

FEDERAL MARITIME COMMISSION, WASHINGTON, DC

Informal Docket No. _____

Respondent's Affidavit

I authorize the Settlement Officer to determine the above-numbered claim in accordance with subpart S (46 CFR 502) of the Commission's informal procedure for adjudication of small claims subject to discretionary Commission Review.

(Date) _____

(Signed) _____

(Capacity) _____

Verification

State of _____, County of _____, ss: _____, being first duly sworn on oath deposes and says that he or she is _____, (Title or Position) and is the person who signed the foregoing and agrees without qualification to its truth.

_____

Subscribed and sworn to before me, a notary public in and for the State of _____, County of _____, this _____ day of _____ 19____.

(Seal)

_____

(Notary Public)
My Commission expires, _____.

Certificate of Service [See § 502.320]

FEDERAL MARITIME COMMISSION NON-VESSEL-OPERATING COMMON CARRIER (NVOCC) BOND (SECTION 23, SHIPPING ACT OF 1984)

_____, as Principal (hereinafter called Principal), and _____, as Surety (hereinafter called Surety) are held and firmly bound unto the United States of America in the sum of $_____ for the payment of which sum we bind ourselves, our heirs, executors, administrators, successors and assigns, jointly and severally.

Whereas, Principal operates as an NVOCC in the waterborne foreign commerce of the United States, has an NVOCC tariff on file with the Federal Maritime Commission, and pursuant to section 23 of the Shipping Act of 1984 has elected to file this bond with the Commission:

Now, Therefore, The condition of this obligation is that the penalty amount of this bond shall be available to pay any judgment for damages against the Principal arising from the Principal's transportation related activities or order for reparations issued pursuant to section 11 of the Shipping Act of 1984, 46 U.S.C. app. 1710, or any penalty assessed against the Principal pursuant to section 13 of the Shipping Act of 1984, 46 U.S.C. app. 1712.

This bond shall inure to the benefit of any and all persons who have obtained a judgment for damages against the Principal arising from its transportation related activities or order of reparation issued pursuant to section 11 of the Shipping Act of 1984, and to the benefit of the Federal Maritime Commission for any penalty assessed against the Principal pursuant to section 13 of the Shipping Act of 1984. However, this bond shall not apply to shipments of used household goods and personal effects for the account of the Department of Defense.

The liability of the Surety shall not be discharged by any payment or succession of payments hereunder, unless and until such payment or payments shall aggregate the penalty of this bond, and in no event shall the Surety's total obligation hereunder exceed said penalty regardless of the number of claims or claimants.

This bond is effective the _____ day of _____, 19___, and shall continue in effect until discharged or terminated as herein provided. The Principal or the Surety may at any time terminate this bond by written notice to the Federal Maritime Commission at its office in Washington, DC. Such termination shall become effective thirty (30) days after receipt of said notice by the Commission. The Surety shall not be liable for any transportation related activities of the Principal after the expiration of the thirty (30) day period but such termination shall not affect the liability of the Principal and Surety for any event occurring prior to the date when said termination becomes effective.

The underwriting Surety will promptly notify the Director, Bureau of Tariffs, Certification and Licensing, Federal Maritime Commission, Washington, DC 20573, of any claim(s) against this bond.

Signed and sealed this _____ day of _____, 19_____.

(Please type name of signer under each signature.)

Individual Principal or Partner

Business Address

Individual Principal or Partner

Business Address

Individual Principal or Partner

Business Address

Trade Name, If Any

Corporate Principal

State of Incorporation

Trade Name, If Any

Business Address

By

Title (Affix Corporate Seal)

Corporate Surety

Business Address

By

Title
(Affix Corporate Seal)

PART 500 — [AMENDED]

Therefore, pursuant to 5 U.S.C. 553 and sections 8 and 17 of the Shipping Act of 1984 (46 U.S.C. app. 1707 and 1716) the Federal Maritime Commission is amending Title 46 CFR Part 580 as follows:

1. The authority citation to Part 580 continues to read:

Authority: 5 U.S.C. 553; 46 U.S.C. app. 1702-1705, 1707, 1709, 1712, 1714-1716 and 1718.

2. Section 580.5 is amended by adding paragraph (d)(14) to read as follows:

§ 580.5 Tariff contents.

(d)

(14) *Special Rules and Regulations applicable to co-loading activities of Non-Vessel-Operating Common Carriers (NVOCCs).*

(i) *Definition.* For the purpose of this section, "Co-loading" means the combining of cargo, in the import or export foreign commerce of the United States, by two or more NVOCCs for tendering to an ocean carrier under the name of one or more of the NVOCCs.

(ii) *Filing Requirements.* All tariffs filed by an NVOCC shall contain a rule describing its co-loading activities as follows:

(A) If an NVOCC does not tender cargo for co-loading, its tariff(s) shall so indicate.

(B) If two or more NVOCCs enter into an agreement which establishes a carrier-to-carrier relationship for the co-loading of cargo, then the existence of such agreement must be noted in each of the NVOCC's tariffs.

(C) If two NVOCCs enter into a co-loading arrangement which results in a shipper-to-carrier relationship, the tendering NVOCC shall describe in its tariff its co-loading practices and specify its responsibility to pay any charges for the transportation of the cargo. A shipper-to-carrier relationship shall be presumed to exist where the receiving NVOCC issues a bill of lading to the tendering NVOCC for carriage of the co-loaded cargo.

(iii) *Documentation Requirements.* NVOCCs which tender cargo to another NVOCC for co-loading whether under a shipper-to-carrier or carrier-to-carrier relationship shall annotate each applicable bill of lading with the identity of any other NVOCC to which the shipment has been tendered for co-loading. Such annotation shall be shown on the face of the bill of lading in a clear and legible manner.

(iv) *Co-Loading Rates.* No NVOCC shall offer special co-loading rates for the exclusive use of other NVOCCs. If cargo is accepted by an NVOCC from another NVOCC which tenders that cargo in the capacity of a shipper, it must be rated and carried under tariff provisions which are available to all shippers.

APPENDIX J

Carrier-to-Carrier Co-loading Agreement

PARTIES TO THE AGREEMENT:

1. _____   2. _____

[Address] _____   [Address] _____

[Telephone] _____   [Telephone] _____

[Facsimile] _____   [Facsimile] _____

PURPOSE OF THE AGREEMENT:

Given the need to consolidate cargoes to provide for efficient and economical transportation and given the need for prompt shipment and periodic shortages of containers and vessel space, the Parties are entering into this Agreement to provide themselves with greater shipping flexibility and more assured transportation arrangements to the end that they may provide better service to their respective customers.

TERMS OF THE AGREEMENT:

(1) This is a cooperative, non-exclusive working agreement between two non-vessel-operating common carriers (NVOCCs), in which one carrier will contract for space in containers loaded by the other carrier on behalf of their respective shippers. This agreement is entered into in accordance with the rules of the Federal Maritime Commission ("FMC") applicable to co-loading on a carrier-to-carrier basis. Both Parties have NVOCC bonds and tariffs on file at the FMC and have provided each other with copies of the respective tariff pages containing their NVOCC bond information.

(2) Each of the Parties agrees that it shall accept for co-loading and shall consolidate cargo tendered to it by the other Party provided that space is available in containers that it is loading or has been reserved or dedicated in advance by such other Party.

(3) The charge for shared space and the name or names in which the containers will be tendered to the vessel-operating carrier will be determined prior to the loading of each container. Payment for the space shall be made on terms as further agreed by the Parties. A receipt for cargo tendered for co-loading will be given upon request. This receipt shall not be, and shall not be considered as, a Bill of Lading. The terms and conditions of this receipt shall govern all claims for loss and damages as between the parties.

(4) Procedures for reserving space, documentation, special handling instructions or requirements, and other administrative matters relating to co-loading provided under this Agreement shall be as the Parties may from time to time agree.

(5) The Parties agree that neither will be liable to the other for loss or damage to cargo in containers co-loaded under this Agreement unless such loss or damage is proximately caused by the negligence of one of the Parties while the cargo is in that Party's possession. In the event that such cargo is lost, damaged or delayed while outside the possession of either Party, the Parties shall look to the vessel-operating carrier or other transportation service provider for compensation. In the event the cargo is tendered to the vessel-operating carrier or other transportation service provider in the name of only one of the Parties, each Party hereby assigns to the other all right, title and interest in any claim, action or damages with respect to co-loaded goods of the other against any carrier or other transportation service provider.

(6) Both Parties agree to note the existence of their carrier-to-carrier co-loading agreements in their respective tariffs filed at the FMC. The NVOCC that tenders cargo for co-loading under this Agreement agrees to annotate the Bill(s) of Lading it issues to its shipper(s) for those shipments with the identity of the receiving NVOCC.

(7) Both Parties agree that this Agreement in no way alters their respective normal commercial and legal responsibilities to their shippers. Each Party will independently solicit cargo under its own tariff, issue its own Bill of Lading and collects its own published tariff rates without regard to the rates of the other carrier. There shall be no revenue pooling or joint rate making.

(8) No freight forwarder compensation shall be payable between the Parties.

(9) Neither Party shall be deemed responsible for its failure to perform any term or condition of this Agreement if such failure is due, without limitation, to civil commotion, invasion, rebellion, sabotage, hostilities, strikes, labor disputes, other work stoppages, governmental acts, regulations or controls, acts of God, inability to obtain materials or services, or any other cause whatsoever, beyond the control of the Party.

(10) This Agreement may be terminated at any time by either Party on ____ days written notice sent by facsimile, telex or letter to the other.

(11) This Agreement shall become effective as of the _____ day of _____, 19____.

Signature _____ Title _____

Date _____ Company _____

Signature _____ Title _____

Date _____ Company _____

Co-Load Cargo Receipt, and Terms and Conditions

CO-LOAD CARGO RECEIPT

[NAME OF CARRIER]   NON-NEGOTIABLE

TENDERING NVOCC	DOCUMENT NO.
DELIVERY PARTY (Name & Address)	CO-LOADING AGREEMENT NO.
NOTIFY PARTY (if any)	AGENT REFERENCES
EXPECTED VESSEL AND/OR CARRIER	CONTAINER NO. AND IDENTIFYING MARKS
PORT OR PLACE OF LOADING	PORT OR PLACE OF DISCHARGE

PARTICULARS FURNISHED BY TENDERING NVOCC

MARKS & NUMBERS	NO. of PKGS.	HAZMAT? "X" if yes	DESCRIPTION OF PACKAGES AND GOODS	Gross Weight	Measurement

Receiving NVOCC's obligations are set forth in the Terms and Conditions on the back of this receipt. Please read them carefully. Without limiting their effect, please note:

1. The undersigned are authorized to enter into contracts with carriers and others involved in the execution of the transport subject to the latter's usual terms and conditions.

2. The undersigned are chartering or leasing space in a container pursuant to a co-loading agreement and take no responsibility for transportation of the co-loading goods in the chartered space. In consequence, they are only responsible for the careful selection of third parties. They are not responsible for the acts or omissions of Carriers involved in the execution of the transport or of other third parties.

3. The undersigned is liable to deliver the co-loaded goods against presentation of this document only or equivalent evidence of entitlement acceptable to the undersigned.

Date: _____

                               [NAME OF CARRIER]

REMARKS:

CO-LOAD CARGO RECEIPT
TERMS AND CONDITIONS

(1) CARRIER TO CARRIER CO-LOADING AGREEMENT:

This Co-load Cargo Receipt (the "Receipt") is issued pursuant to a Carrier-To-Carrier Co-loading Agreement between the tendering non-vessel operating common carrier and receiving non-vessel operating common carrier (both terms as defined below) that has been entered into subject to the Co-loading Regulations of the Federal Maritime Commission of the United States Federal Maritime Commission. The relationship between the parties with respect to the goods for which this receipt is issued shall be governed by the Carrier-To-Carrier Co-loading Agreement and Terms and Conditions.

(2) DEFINITIONS:

2.1 "NVOCC" means a non-vessel operating common carrier as that term is defined in Section 3(17) of the Shipping Act of 1984; 46 U.S.C. app. § 1702(17).

2.2 "Tendering NVOCC" ("T-NVO") means the NVOCC that is leasing the space in a container in which to place the goods covered by this Receipt.

2.3 "Receiving NVOCC" ("R-NVO") means the NVOCC that is providing space pursuant to a co-load lease for the cargo covered by this receipt.

2.4 "Goods" means the articles packed by or on behalf of T-NVO as shown on the front of this Receipt.

2.5 "Co-load" or "co-loading" means to lease or charter space in a container.

2.6 "Package" is the largest individual unit of partially or completely covered or contained cargo made up by or for the T-NVO which is packed or stored in the container of R-NVO, including palletized units and each container stuffed and sealed by the T-NVO or on its behalf, although the T-NVO may have furnished a description of the contents of such sealed container on this Receipt.

2.7 "Container" includes any container, trailer, transportable tank, lift van, flat, pallet, or any similar article of transport used to consolidate the goods.

(3) RESPONSIBILITIES OF RECEIVING NVOCC:

The R-NVO shall:

(a) Provide space in a container such as is ordinarily used in the transportation industry.

(b) Notify T-NVO and the notify party on the face of this Receipt, if any, at the time the container arrives at its destination and is ready to be unloaded.

(c) Notify T-NVO within a reasonable time after actually receiving notice of loss or damage to the container or goods.

(d) Provide reasonable cooperation to T-NVO in tracking the whereabouts of the container.

(4) DISCLAIMER OF CONTRACT OF CARRIAGE:

This Receipt pertains only to a charter of space in a container. Although both R-NVO and T-NVO will be providing carriage of the goods in the container as carriers for their respective shippers, both agree and recognize that R-NVO is not providing carriage for either T-NVO or T-NVO's shippers, but only providing space in the container by co-loading. In this respect, the statements on the face of this Receipt pertaining to the place of loading, destination and means of transport are for information purposes only. R-NVO believes in good faith that the information is true to the best of its knowledge at the time of issue of this Receipt, but makes no representations or warranties as to the absolute truthfulness of those statements.

(5) RESPONSIBILITIES OF TENDERING NVOCC:

The T-NVO shall:

(a) Provide accurate information as to the character, condition, and weight of the commodities in the container.

(b) Know and comply with the marking requirements of the U.S. Customs Service, the regulations of the U.S. Food and Drug Administration, the Hazardous Materials Regulations of the Department of Transportation, and all other requirements, including regulations of Federal, State, and/or local agencies pertaining to its goods.

(c) Indemnify and hold harmless R-NVO against any action taken or fines or penalties assessed by any governmental agency against its cargo because of the failure of T-NVO to comply with the law or the requirements or regulations of any governmental agency or with a notification issued to T-NVO by any such agency.

(d) Be liable for all dues, duties, fines, taxes and charges, including consular fees, levied on its goods, as well as return freight and charges on the goods if they are refused export or import by any government.

(6) CO-LOAD FEES:

6.1 Co-load fees and charges shall be deemed earned on receipt of goods by R-NVO, whether they be intended to be prepaid or collected at destination. Payment shall be in full and in cash, In United States currency, or another currency at R-NVO's option. Interest at 12% shall run from the date when co-load fees and charges are due. Full charges shall be paid on damaged or unsound goods. In any referral for collection or action against T-NVO for monies due to R-NVO, upon recovery by R-NVO, T-NVO shall pay the expenses of collection and litigation, including reasonable attorney's fees.

6.2 T-NVO, and all receiving parties and notify parties named on the face of this Receipt shall be jointly and severally liable to R-NVO for the payment of all co-load fees and charges, including advances.

(7) LIEN:

R-NVO shall have a general lien on any and all property (and documents relating thereto) tendered by or on behalf of T-NVO, in its possession, custody, control or on route, for all claims for charges, expenses or advances incurred by R-NVO in connection with T-NVO's goods and as such claim remains unsatisfied for 30 days after demand for its payment is made, R-NVO may sell at public auction or private sale, upon 10 days written notice, registered mail (R.R.R.) to T-NVO, the goods, wares and/or merchandise, or so much thereof as may be necessary to satisfy such lien, and apply the net proceeds of such sale to the payment of the amount due to R-NVO. Any surplus from such sale shall be transmitted to T-NVO, and T-NVO shall be liable for any deficiency in the sale.

(8) SUBCONTRACTING:

8.1 R-NVO shall be entitled to subcontract directly or indirectly on any terms the whole or any part of the handling, storage or carriage of the container and all duties undertaken by R-NVO in relation to the goods of T-NVO.

8.2 Every servant or agent or subcontractor of R-NVO shall be entitled to the same rights, exemptions from liability, defenses and immunities to which R-NVO is entitled. For these purposes, R-NVO shall be deemed to be acting as agent or trustee for such servants or agents, who shall be deemed to be parties to the contract evidenced in this Receipt.

(9) LIABILITY OF R-NVO:

9.1 R-NVO shall only be liable for negligence in choosing the carriers that will transport the container or for its own negligence during the time when it has physical custody of T-NVO's goods and/or the container.

9.2 Any loss or damage caused while T-NVO's goods and/or the container are outside the physical custody of R-NVO shall be subject to the terms and conditions of any contracts, tariffs or law applicable to the situation in which the damage occurs.

9.3 R-NVO assigns, and T-NVO accepts, all right, title and interest in any claim, action or damages that R-NVO may have against any carrier or other transportation service provider with respect to the goods.

9.4 When any claims are paid to T-NVO by R-NVO, R-NVO shall automatically be subrogated to all rights of T-NVO against all others on account of the losses or damages for which such claims are paid.

(10) COMPENSATION FOR LOSS AND DAMAGES:

10.1 Unless otherwise mandated by compulsory applicable law, R-NVO's liability for compensation for loss of or damage to T-NVO's goods shall in no case exceed the amount of U.S. $500 per package or customary freight unit, unless T-NVO, with the consent of R-NVO, has declared a higher value for the goods in the space provided on the front of this Receipt and paid extra charges per agreement with R-NVO, in which case such higher value shall be the limit of R-NVO's liability. When a container is stuffed by T-NVO or on its behalf, and the container is sealed when received by R-NVO for shipment, R-NVO's liability will be limited to U.S. $500 with respect to the contents of each such container, except when the T-NVO declares the value on the face hereof and pays additional charges on such declared value per agreement with R-NVO. The co-load fees and charges on sealed containers when no higher valuation is declared by T-NVO is based on a value of U.S. $500 per container. However, R-NVO shall not, in any case, be liable for an amount greater than the actual loss to the person entitled to make the claim.

10.2 In any case where R-NVO's liability for compensation may exceed the amount set forth in Clause 10.1 above, compensation shall be calculated by reference to the value of the goods, according to their current market price, at the time and place they are delivered, or should have been delivered. R-NVO shall have the option of replacing lost goods or repairing damaged goods.

10.3 If the value of the goods is less than U.S. $500 per package or per customary freight unit, their value for compensation purposes shall be deemed to be the invoice value, plus co-load charges and insurance, if paid.

(11) NOTICE OF CLAIM AND TIME BAR:

11.1 Written notice of claims for loss of or damage to goods occurring or presumed to have occurred while the goods were in the container must be given to R-NVO before or at the time of removal of the goods by one entitled to them. If such notice is not provided, removal shall be *prima facie* evidence of delivery in good order and condition. If such loss or damage is not apparent, R-NVO must be given written notice within three days of the unloading.

11.2 R-NVO shall be discharged from all liability for loss of or damage to the goods unless suit is brought within nine months after delivery of the goods or the date when the goods should have been delivered.

(12) DANGEROUS GOODS:

12.1 T-NVO may not tender goods of a dangerous nature without written application to R-NVO and R-NVO's acceptance of the same. In the application, T-NVO must identify the nature of the goods with reasonable specificity as well as the names and addresses of the shippers and consignees.

12.2 T-NVO shall distinctly and permanently mark the nature of the goods on the outside of the package and container in a form and manner as required by law and shall submit to R-NVO or to the appropriate authorities all necessary documents required by law or by R-NVO for the transportation of such goods.

12.3 If the goods subsequently, in the judgment of R-NVO, become a danger to R-NVO, the ship, or other cargo, R-NVO may dispose of the goods without compensation to T-NVO and T-NVO shall indemnify R-NVO for any loss or expenses arising from such action.

(13) GENERAL AVERAGE:

13.1 General Average shall be adjusted at New York, or any other port at R-NVO's option, according to the York-Antwerp Rules of 1974 with the exception of Sections 21 and 22. The General Average statement shall be prepared by adjusters appointed by R-NVO.

13.2 In the event of accident, damage, danger or disaster after commencement of the voyage resulting from any cause whatsoever, whether due to negligence or not, for the consequence of which R-NVO is not responsible by statute, contract or otherwise, T-NVO shall contribute with R-NVO in General Average to the payment of any sacrifice, loss or expense of a General Average nature that may be made or incurred, and shall pay salvage or special charges incurred in respect of the goods. If a salving vessel is owned or operated by R-NVO, salvage shall be paid for as fully as if the salving vessel or vessels belonged to strangers.

(14) PERISHABLE CARGO:

14.1 Goods of a perishable nature shall be carried in ordinary containers without special protection, services or other measures unless there is noted on the reverse side of this Receipt that the goods will be carried in a refrigerated, heated, electrically ventilated or otherwise specially equipped container or are to receive special attention in any way.

14.2 T-NVO undertakes not to tender for transportation any goods which require refrigeration without given written notice of their nature and the required temperature setting of the thermostatic controls before receipt of the goods by R-NVO. In case of refrigerated containers packed by or on behalf of T-NVO, T- NVO warrants that the goods have been properly stowed in the container and that the thermostatic controls have been adequately set before receipt of the goods by R-NVO.

14.3 T-NVO's attention is drawn to the fact that refrigerated containers are not designed to freeze down cargo which has not been presented for stuffing at or below its designated carrying temperature. R-NVO shall not be responsible for the consequences of cargo tendered at a higher temperature than that required for the transportation.

14.4 If the above requirements are not complied with, R-NVO shall not be liable for any loss of or damage to the goods whatsoever.

(15) SEVERABILITY:

The terms of this Receipt shall be severable, and, if any part or term hereof shall be held invalid, such holding shall not affect the validity or enforceability of any other part or term hereof.

(16) VARIATION OF THE CONTRACT:

No servant or agent of R-NVO shall have power to waive or vary any of the terms hereof unless such variation is in writing and is specifically authorized or ratified in writing by R-NVO.

(17) JURISDICTION:

This Receipt is to be governed by the law of the State of _____. All suits with respect to the lease or charter of space for which this Receipt is issued shall be bought in the courts of the State of _____. For this purpose, T-NVO and R-NVO agree to submit themselves to the jurisdiction and venue of such courts.

Terms and Conditions of Service by Forwarders and Customs Brokers

TERMS AND CONDITIONS

Recommended for Use by NCBFAA Members

The recommended *Terms and Conditions of Service* for use by members of the Association are reproduced on the reverse side of this sheet. These *Terms and Conditions* set forth conditions under which the forwarder/broker agrees to render services on behalf of a client.

This version includes certain copyright provisions that protect a broker who, as an innocent third party, enters merchandise that may be subject to restrictions, claims and possible lawsuits under copyright and trademark laws.

These recommended *Terms and Conditions* should be reproduced on the reverse side of the broker/forwarder invoice. If used in this manner, the front of the invoice must then bear a legend stating that all shipments are handled pursuant to the *Terms and Conditions of Service* on the reverse side. The *Terms and Conditions* also may be shown on the reverse side of other documents — such as letterheads — with the same legend on the front side.

Before reproducing this document for your own use, the name of your company should be inserted in the blank space on the third line and the state and city should be inserted in paragraph 18.

The use of the *Terms and Conditions* is at your discretion and is not required by reason of your membership in the Association. It is furnished solely as a convenience to the members and you are not under any obligation to adopt it.

TERMS AND CONDITIONS OF SERVICE

(Please Read Carefully)

All shipments to or from the Customer, which term shall include the exporter, importer, sender, receiver, owner, consignor, transferor or transferee of the shipments, will be handled by:

(herein called the Company) on the following terms and conditions:

1. Services by Third Parties. Unless the Company carries, stores or otherwise physically handles the shipment, and loss, damage, expense or delay occurs during such activity, the Company assumes no liability as a carrier and is not to be held responsible for any loss, damage, expense or delay to the goods to be forwarded or imported except as provided in paragraph 8 and subject to the limitations of paragraph 9 below, but undertakes only to use reasonable care in the selection of carriers, truckmen, lightermen, forwarders, customs brokers, agents, warehousemen and others to whom it may entrust the goods for transportation, cartage, handling and/or delivery and/or storage or otherwise. When the company carries, stores or otherwise physically handles the shipment, it does so subject to the limitation of liability set forth in paragraph 8 below unless a separate bill of lading, air waybill or other contract of carriage is issued by the Company, in which event the terms thereof shall govern.

2. *Liability Limitations of Third Parties.* The Company is authorized to select and engage carriers, truckmen, lightermen, forwarders, customs brokers, agents, warehousemen and others, as required, to transport, store, deal with and deliver the goods, all of whom shall be considered as the agents of the Customer, and the goods may be entrusted to such agencies subject to all conditions as to limitation of liability for loss, damage, expense or delay and to all rules, regulations, requirements and conditions, whether printed, written or stamped, appearing in bills of lading, receipts or tariffs issued by such carriers, truckmen, lightermen, forwarders, customs brokers, agents, warehousemen and others. The Company shall under no circumstances be liable for any loss, damage, expense or delay to the goods for any reason whatsoever when said goods are in custody, possession or control of third parties selected by the Company to forward, enter and clear, transport or render other services with respect to such goods.

3. *Choosing Routes or Agents.* Unless experts instructions in writing are received from the Customer, the Company has complete freedom in choosing the means, route and procedure to be followed in the handling, transportation and delivery of the goods. Advice by the Company to the Customer that a particular person or firm has been selected to render services with respect to the goods shall not be construed to mean that the Company warrants or represents that such person or firm will render such services.

4. *Quotations Not Binding.* Quotations as to fees, rates of duty, freight charges, insurance premiums or other charges given by the Company to the Customer are for informational purposes only and are subject to change without notice and shall not under any circumstances be binding upon the Company unless the Company in writing specifically undertakes the handling or transportation of the shipment at a specific rate.

5. *Duty to Furnish Information.* (a) On an import at a reasonable time prior to entering of the goods for U.S. Customs, the Customer shall furnish to the Company invoices in proper form and other documents necessary or useful in the preparation of the U.S. Customs entry and, also, such further information as may be sufficient to establish, inter alia, the dutiable value, the

classification, the country of origin, the genuineness of the merchandise and any mark or symbol associated with it, the Customer's right to import and/or distribute the merchandise, and the merchandise's admissibility, pursuant to U.S. law or regulation. If the Customer fails in a timely manner to furnish such information or documents, in whole or in part, as may be required to complete U.S. Customs entry or comply with U.S. laws or regulations, or if the information or documents furnished are inaccurate or incomplete, the Company shall be obligated only to use its best judgment in connection with the shipment and in no instance shall be charged with knowledge by the Customer of the true circumstances to which such inaccurate, in-complete, or omitted information or document pertains. Where a bond is required by U.S. Customs to be given for the production of any document or the performance of any act, the Customer shall be deemed bound by the terms of the bond notwithstanding the fact that the bond has been executed by the Company as principal, it being understood that the Company entered into such undertaking at the instance and on behalf of the Customer, and the Customer shall indemnify and hold the Company harmless for the consequences of any breach of the terms of the bond. (b) On an export at a reasonable time prior to the exportation of the shipment the Customer shall furnish to the Company the commercial invoice in proper form and number, a proper consular declaration, weights, measures, values and other information in the language of and as may be required by the laws and regulations of the U.S. and the country of destination of the goods. (c) On an export or import the Company shall not in any way be responsible or liable for increased duty, penalty, fine or expense unless caused by the negligence or other fault of the Company, in which event its liability to the Customer shall be governed by the provisions of paragraphs 8-10 below. The Customer shall be bound by and warrant the accuracy of all invoices, documents and information furnished to the Company by the Customer or its agent for export, entry or other purposes and the Customer agrees to indemnify and hold harmless the Company against any increased duty, penalty, fine or expense including attorneys' fees, resulting from any inaccuracy, incomplete statement, omission or any failure to make timely presentation, even if not due to any negligence of the Customer.

6. *Declaring Higher Valuation.* Inasmuch as truckers, carriers, warehouse-men and others to whom the goods are entrusted usually limit their liability for loss or damage unless a higher value is declared and a charge based on such higher value is agreed to by said truckers, etc., the Company must receive specific written instructions from the Customer to pay such higher charge based on valuation and the trucker, etc. must accept such higher declared value; otherwise the valuation placed by the Customer on the goods shall be considered solely for export or customs purposes and the goods will be delivered to the truckers, etc. subject to the limitation of liability set forth

herein in paragraphs 8-10 below with respect to any claim against the Company and subject to the provisions of paragraph 2 above.

7. *Insurance.* The Company will make reasonable efforts to effect marine, fire, theft and other insurance upon the goods only after specific written instructions have been received by the Company in sufficient time prior to shipment from point of origin, and the Customer at the same time states specifically the kind and amount of insurance to be placed. The Company does not undertake or warrant that such insurance can or will be placed. Unless the Customer has its own open marine policy and instructs the Company to effect insurance under such policy, insurance is to be effected with one or more insurance companies or other underwriters to be selected by the Company. Any insurance placed shall be governed by the certificate or policy issued and will only be effective when accepted by such insurance companies or underwriters. Should an insurer dispute its liability for any reason, the insured shall have recourse against the insurer only and the Company shall not be under any responsibility or liability in relation thereto, notwithstanding that the premium upon the policy may not be at the same rates as that charged or paid to the Company by the Customer, or that the shipment was insured under a policy in the name of the Company. Insurance premiums and the charge of the Company for arranging the same shall be at the Customer's expense. If for any reason the goods are held in warehouse, or elsewhere, the same will not be covered by any insurance, unless the Company receives written instructions from the Customer. Unless specifically agreed in writing, the Company assumes no responsibility to effect insurance on any export or import shipment which it does not handle.

8. *Limitation of Liability for Loss, etc.* (a) The Customer agrees that the Company shall only be liable for any loss, damage expense or delay to the goods resulting from the negligence or other fault of the Company; such liability shall be limited to an amount equal to the lesser of fifty dollars ($50.00) per entry or shipment or the fee(s) charged for services, provided that, in the case of partial loss, such amount will be adjusted, *pro rata;*

(b) Where the Company issues its own bill of lading and receives freight charges as its compensation, Customer has the option of paying a special compensation and increasing the limit of Company's liability up to the shipment's actual value; however, such option must be exercised by written agreement, entered into prior to any covered transaction(s), setting forth the limit of the Company's liability and the compensation received;

(c) In instances other than in (b) above, unless the Customer makes specific written arrangements with the Company to pay special compensation and declare a higher value and Company agrees in writing, liability is limited to the amount set forth in (a) above;

(d) Customer agrees that the Company shall, in no event, be liable for consequential, punitive, statutory or special damages in excess of the monetary limit provided for above.

9. Presenting Claims. Company shall not be liable under paragraph 8 for any claims not presented to it in writing within 90 days of either the date of loss or incident giving rise to the claim; no suit to recover for any claim or demand hereunder shall be maintained against the Company unless instituted within six (6) months after the presentation of the said claim or such longer period provided for under statute(s) of the State having jurisdiction of the matter.

10. Advancing Money. The Company shall not be obliged to incur any expense, guarantee payment or advance any money in connection with the importing, forwarding, transporting, insuring, storing or coopering of the goods, unless the same is previously provided to the Company by the Customer on demand. The Company shall be under no obligation to advance freight charges, customs duties or taxes on any shipment, nor shall any advance by the Company be construed as a waiver of the provisions hereof.

11. Indemnification for Freight, Duties. In the event that a carrier, other person or any governmental agency makes a claim or institutes legal action against the Company for ocean or other freight, duties, fines, penalties, liquidated damages or other money due arising from a shipment of goods of the Customer, the Customer agrees to indemnify and hold harmless the Company for any amount the Company may be required to pay such carrier, other person or governmental agency together with reasonable expenses, including attorneys' fees, incurred by the Company in connection with defending such claim or legal action and obtaining reimbursement from the Customer. The confiscation or detention of the goods by any governmental authority shall not affect or diminish the liability of the Customer to the Company to pay all charges or other money due promptly on demand.

12. C.O.D. Shipments. Goods received with Customer's or other person's instructions to Collect on Delivery (C.O.D.) by drafts or otherwise, or to collect on any specified terms by time drafts or otherwise, are accepted by the Company only upon the express understanding that it will exercise reasonable care in the selection of a bank, correspondent, carrier or agent to whom it will send such item for collection, and the Company will not be responsible for any act, omission, default, suspension, insolvency or want of care, negligence, or fault of such bank, correspondent, carrier or agent, nor for any delay in remittance lost in exchange, or during transmission, or while in the course of collection.

13. General Lien on Any Property. The Company shall have a general lien on any and all property (and documents relating thereto) of the Customer, in its possession, custody or control or en route, for all claims for charges, expenses or advances incurred by the Company in connection with any shipments of the Customer and if such claim remains unsatisfied for thirty (30) days after demand for its payment is made, the Company may sell at public auction or private sale, upon ten (10) days written notice, registered mail (R.R.R.), to the Customer, the goods, wares and/or merchandise, or so much thereof as may be necessary to satisfy such lien, and apply the net proceeds of such sale to the payment of the amount due to the Company. Any surplus from such sale shall be transmitted to the Customer, and the Customer shall be liable for any deficiency in the sale.

14. Compensation of Company. The compensation of the Company for its services shall be included with and is in addition to the rates and charges of all carriers and other agencies selected by the Company to transport and deal with the goods and such compensation shall be exclusive of any brokerage, commissions, dividends or other revenue received by the Company from carriers, insurers, and others in connection with the shipment. On ocean exports, upon request, the Company shall provide a detailed breakout of the components of all charges assessed and a true copy of each pertinent document relating to these charges. In any referral for collection or action against the Customer for monies due the Company, upon recovery by the Company, the Customer shall pay the expenses of collection and/or litigation, including a reasonable attorney fee.

15. No Responsibility for Governmental Requirements. It is the responsibility of the Customer to know and comply with the marking requirements of the U.S. Customs Service, the regulations of the U.S. Food and Drug Administration, and all other requirements, including regulations of Federal, state and/or local agencies pertaining to the merchandise. The Company shall not be responsible for action taken or fines or penalties assessed by any governmental agency against the shipment because of the failure of the Customer to comply with the law or the requirements or regulations of any governmental agency or with a notification issued to the Customer by any such agency.

16. Indemnity Against Liability Arising from the Importation of Merchandise. The Customer agrees to indemnify and hold the Company harmless from any claims and/or liability arising form the importation of merchandise which violates any Federal, state and/or other laws or regulations and further agrees to indemnify and hold the Company harmless against any and all liability, loss, damages, costs, claims and/or expenses, including but not limited to attorney's fees, which the Company may hereafter incur, suffer or be required to pay by reason of claims by any government agency or private party. In the event that any action, suit or proceeding is brought against the Company by an government agency or any private party, the Company shall give notice in writing to the Customer by mail at its address on file with the Company. Upon receipt of such notice, the Customer at its own expense shall defend against such action and take all steps as may be necessary or proper to prevent the obtaining of a judgment and/or order against the Company.

17. Loss, Damage or Expense Due to Delay. Unless the services to be performed by the Company on behalf of the Customer are delayed by reason of the negligence or other fault of the Company, the Company shall not be responsible for any loss, damage or expense incurred by the Customer because of such delay. In the event the Company is at fault, as aforesaid, its liability is limited in accordance with the provisions of paragraphs 8-9 above.

18. Construction of Terms and Venue. The foregoing terms and conditions shall be constructed according to the laws of the State of:

_____

Unless otherwise consented to in writing by the Company, no legal proceeding against the Company may be instituted by the Customer, its assigns, or subrogee except in the City of _____.

Approved by the National Customs Brokers & Forwarders Association of America, Inc. (Revised 6/94)

APPENDIX M

1986 Amendment 19 U.S.C. 1641 re Independent Action
on Compensation to Forwarder/Customs Broker and Compensation
on Surcharges

I-886

(8) Section 641 (19 U.S.C. 1641) is amended by adding at the end thereof the following new subsection:

"(i) COMPENSATION OF OCEAN FREIGHT FORWARDERS.—

"(1) IN GENERAL.—Notwithstanding any other provision of law, no conference or group of two or more ocean common carriers in the foreign commerce of the United States that is authorized to agree upon the level of compensation paid to ocean freight forwarders may—

"(A) deny to any member of such conference or group the right, upon notice of not more than 10 calendar days, to take independent action on any level of compensation paid to an ocean freight forwarder who is also a customs broker, and

"(B) agree to limit the payment of compensation to an ocean freight forwarder who is also a customs broker to less than 1.25 percent of the aggregate of all rates and charges applicable under the tariff assessed against the cargo on which the forwarding services are provided.

"(2) ADMINISTRATION.—The provisions of this subsection shall be enforced by the agency responsible for administration of the Shipping Act of 1984 (46 U.S.C. 1701, et seq.).

"(3) REMEDIES.—Any person injured by reason of a violation of paragraph (1) may, in addition to any other remedy, file a complaint for reparation as provided in section 11 of the Shipping Act of 1984 (46 U.S.C. 1710), which may be enforced pursuant to section 14 of such Act (46 U.S.C. 1713).

"(4) DEFINITIONS.—For purposes of this subsection, the terms 'conference,' 'ocean common carrier,' and 'ocean freight forwarder' have the respective meaning given to such terms by section 3 of the Shipping Act of 1984 (46 U.S.C. 1702)."

b. Customs broker's freight forwarding

The conferees also clarified Congressional intent with respect to the compensation of customs brokers for certain services. The conference agreement provides licensed customs brokers, when performing ocean freight forwarder services on export shipments from the United States, with the benefits of the right of independent action with respect to the level of forwarder compensation in a shipping conference's freight tariff. Under present law, a conference may prohibit its members from taking independent action on forwarder compensation. This amendment makes clear that a conference must allow its members to take independent action on compensation to the extent that compensation is or will be paid to a forwarder who is also a licensed customs broker under the Tariff Act of 1930.

This provision also benefits customs brokers when they act in the capacity of a licensed freight forwarder on shipments exported from the United States. Despite the requirement of current law that conferences not deny forwarders a reasonable percentage of the carrier's freight charges as compensation for the forwarder's service, some conferences are limiting forwarders' compensation to a percentage of some, but not all, of the rates and charges assessed against the cargo in their tariffs. The purpose of this amendment is to make clear that when compensation is paid to a forwarder who is also a licensed customs broker, the compensation must be based on all the freight charges, including, but not limited to, surcharges, handling charges, service charges, terminal charges, supplements, currency adjustment factors, and any and all other charges required to be paid by the shipper or consignee under the tariff.

These amendments do not in any way modify or diminish the existing scope or protections of the Shipping Act of 1984 as applied to ocean freight forwarders in general. Their sole purpose is to impose additional requirements on conferences or carrier groups in their concerted dealings with forwarders who are also licensed customs brokers.

APPENDIX N

FEDERAL MARITIME COMMISSION REGULATION OF OCEAN FREIGHT FORWARDERS—PART 510

SUBCHAPTER B—REGULATIONS AFFECTING OCEAN FREIGHT FORWARDERS, MARINE TERMINAL OPERATIONS AND PASSENGER VESSELS

PART 510—LICENSING OF OCEAN FREIGHT FORWARDERS

AUTHORITY: 5 U.S.C.553; 46 U.S.C. app. 1702, 1707, 1709, 1710, 1712, 1714, 1716, and 1718.

SOURCE: 49 FR 36297, Sept. 14, 1984, unless otherwise noted.

Subpart A—General

§ 510.1 Scope

(a) This part sets forth regulations providing for the licensing as ocean freight forwarders of persons, including individuals, corporations and partnerships, who wish to carry on the business of freight forwarding. This part also prescribes the bonding requirements and the duties and responsibilities of ocean freight forwarders, regulations concerning practices of freight forwarders and common carriers, and the grounds and procedures for revocation and suspension of licenses.

(b) Information obtained under this part is used to determine the qualifications of freight forwarders and their compliance with shipping statutes and regulations. Failure to follow the provisions of this part may result in denial, revocation or suspension of a freight forwarder license. Persons operating without the proper license may be subject to civil penalties not to exceed $5,000 for each such violation unless the violation is willfully and knowingly committed, in which case the amount of the civil penalty may not exceed $25,000 for each violation; for other violations of the provisions of this part, the civil penalties range from $5,000 to $25,000 for each violation (46 U.S.C. app. 1712). Each day of a continuing violation shall constitute a separate violation.

§ 510.2 Definitions.

The terms used in this part are defined as follows:

(a) *"Act"* means the Shipping Act of 1984 (46 U.S.C. app. 1701–1720).

(b) *"Beneficial interest"* includes a lien or interest in or right to use, enjoy, profit, benefit, or receive any advantage, either proprietary or financial, from the whole or any part of a shipment of cargo where such interest arises from the financing of the shipment or by operation of law, or by agreement, express or implied. The term "beneficial interest" shall not include any obligation in favor of a freight forwarder arising solely by reason of the advance of out-of-pocket expenses incurred in dispatching a shipment.

(c) *"Branch office"* means any office established by or maintained by or under the control of a licensee for the purpose of rendering freight forwarding services, which office is located at an address different from that of the licensee's designated home office. This term does not include a separately incorporated entity.

(d) *"Brokerage"* refers to payment by a common carrier to an ocean freight broker for the performance of services as specified in paragraph (m) of this section.

(e) *"Common carrier"* means any person holding itself out to the general public to provide transportation by water of passengers or cargo between the United States and a foreign country for compensation that:

(1) Assumes responsibility for the transportation from the port or point of receipt to the port or point of destination, and

(2) Utilizes, for all or part of that transportation, a vessel operating on the high seas or the Great Lakes between a port in the United States and a port in a foreign country.

(f) *"Compensation"* means payment by a common carrier to a freight forwarder for the performance of services as specified in §510.23(c) of this part.

(g) *"Freight forwarding fee"* means charges billed by a freight forwarder to a shipper, consignee, seller, purchaser, or any agent thereof, for the performance of freight forwarding services.

(h) *"Freight forwarding services"* refers to the dispatching of shipments on behalf of others, in order to facilitate shipment by a common carrier, which may include, but are not limited to, the following:

(1) Ordering cargo to port;

(2) Preparing and/or processing export declarations;

(3) Booking, arranging for or confirming cargo space;

(4) Preparing or processing delivery orders or dock receipts;

(5) Preparing and/or processing ocean bills of lading;

(6) Preparing or processing consular documents or arranging for their certification;

(7) Arranging for warehouse storage;

(8) Arranging for cargo insurance;

(9) Clearing shipments in accordance with United States Government export regulations;

(10) Preparing and/or sending advance notifications of shipments or other documents to banks, shippers, or consignees, as required;

(11) Handling freight or other monies advanced by shippers, or remitting or advancing freight or other monies or credit in connection with the dispatching of shipments;

(12) Coordinating the movement of shipments from origin to vessel; and

(13) Giving expert advice to exporters concerning letters of credit, other documents, licenses or inspections, or on problems germane to the cargoes' dispatch.

(i) *"From the United States"* means oceanborne export commerce from the United States, its Territories, or possessions to foreign countries.

(j) *"Licensee"* is any person licensed by the Federal Maritime Commission as an ocean freight forwarder.

(k) *"Non-vessel-operating common carrier"* means a common carrier that does not operate the vessels by which the ocean transportation is provided, and is a shipper in its relationship with an ocean common carrier.

(l) *"Ocean common carrier"* means a vessel-operating common carrier but the term does not include one engaged in ocean transportation by ferry boat or ocean tramp.

(m) *"Ocean freight broker"* is an entity which is engaged by a carrier to secure cargo for such carrier and/or to sell or offer for sale ocean transportation services and which holds itself out to the public as one who negotiates between shipper or consignee and carrier for the purchase, sale, conditions and terms of transportation.

(n) *"Ocean freight forwarder"* means a person in the United States that:

(1) Dispatches shipments from the United States via common carriers and books or otherwise arranges space for those shipments on behalf of shippers; and

(2) Processes the documentation or performs related activities incident to those shipments.

(o) *"Principal,"* except as used in Surety Bond Form FMC 59, Rev., refers to the shipper, consignee, seller, or purchaser of property, and to anyone acting on behalf of such shipper, consignee, seller, or purchaser of property, who employs the services of a licensee to facilitate the ocean transportation of such property.

(p) *"Reduced forwarding fees"* means charges to a principal for forwarding services that are below the licensee's usual charges for such services.

(q) *"Shipment"* means all of the cargo carried under the terms of a single bill of lading.

(r) *"Shipper"* means an owner or person for whose account the ocean transportation of cargo is provided or the person to whom delivery is to be made.

(s) *"Small shipment"* refers to a single shipment sent by one consignor to one consignee on one bill of lading which does not exceed the underlying common carrier's minimum charge rule.

(t) *"Special contract"* is a contract for freight forwarding services which provides for a periodic lump sum fee.

(u) *"United States"* includes the several States, the District of Columbia, the Commonwealth of Puerto Rico, the Commonwealth of the Northern Marianas, and all other United States territories and possessions.

§ 510.3 License; when required.

Except as otherwise provided in this part, a person must hold a valid ocean freight forwarder license in order to perform freight forwarding services, and, except as provided in § 510.4, no person shall perform, or hold out to perform such services unless such person holds a valid license issued by the Commission to engage in such business. A separate license is required for each branch office that is separately incorporated.

§ 510.4 License; when not required.

A license is not required in the following circumstances:

(a) *Shipper.* Any person whose primary business is the sale of merchandise may, without a license, dispatch and perform freight forwarding services on behalf of its own shipments, or on behalf of shipments or consolidated shipments of a parent, subsidiary, affiliate, or associated company. Such person shall not receive compensation from the common carrier for any services rendered in connection with such shipments.

(b) *Employee or branch office of licensed forwarder.* An individual employee or unincorporated branch office of a licensed ocean freight forwarder is not required to be licensed in order to act solely for such licensee, but each licensed ocean freight forwarder will be held strictly responsible hereunder for the acts or omissions of any of its employees rendered in connection with the conduct of the business.

(c) *Common carrier.* A common carrier, or agent thereof, may perform ocean freight forwarding services without a license only with respect to cargo carried under such carrier's own bill of lading. Charges for such forwarding services shall be assessed in conformance with the carrier's published tariffs on file with the Commission.

(d) *Ocean freight brokers.* An ocean freight broker is not required to be licensed to perform those services specified in § 510.2(m).

Subpart B—Eligibility and Procedure for Licensing; Bond Requirements

§ 510.11 Basic requirements for licensing; eligibility.

(a) *Necessary qualifications.* To be eligible for an ocean freight forwarder's license, the applicant must demonstrate to the Commission that:

(1) It possesses the necessary experience, that is, its qualifying individual has a minimum of three (3) years experience in ocean freight forwarding duties in the United States, and the necessary character to render forwarding services; and

(2) It has obtained and filed with the Commission a valid surety bond in conformance with § 510.14.

(b) *Qualifying individual.* The following individuals must qualify the applicant for a license:

(1) *Sole proprietorship*—The applicant sole proprietor.

(2) *Partnership*—At least one of the active managing partners, but all partners must execute the application.

(3) *Corporation*—At least one of the active corporate officers.

(c) *Affiliates of forwarders.* An independently qualified applicant may be granted a separate license to carry on the business of forwarding even though it is associated with, under common control with, or otherwise related to another ocean freight forwarder through stock ownership or common directors or officers, if such applicant submits: (1) A separate application and fee, and (2) a valid surety bond in the form and amount prescribed under § 510.14. The proprietor, partner or officer who is the qualifying individual of one active licensee shall not also be designated the qualifying proprietor, partner or officer of an applicant for another ocean freight forwarder license.

(d) *Common carrier.* A common carrier or agent thereof which meets the requirements of this part may be licensed to dispatch shipments moving on other than such carrier's own bill of lading subject to the provisions of § 510.23(g).

[49 FR 36297, SEPT. 14, 1984; 49 FR 38544, OCT. 1, 1984]

§ 510.12 Application for license.

(a) (1) *Application and forms.* Any person who wishes to obtain a license to carry on the business of forwarding shall submit, in duplicate, to the Director of the Commission's Bureau of Tariffs, a completed application Form FMC–18 Rev. ("Application for a License as an Ocean Freight Forwarder") and a completed anti-rebate certification in the format prescribed under § 510.25. Copies of Form FMC–18 Rev. may be obtained from the Director, Bureau of Tariffs, Federal Maritime Commission, Washington, D.C. 20573, or from any of the Commission's offices at other locations. Notice of filing of such application shall be published in the FEDERAL REGISTER and shall state the name and address of the applicant. If the applicant is a corporation or partnership, the names of the officers or partners thereof shall be published.

(2) An individual who is applying for a license in his or her own name must complete the following certification.

I, _____(Name) _____, certify under penalty of perjury under the laws of the United States, that I have not been convicted, after September 1, 1989, of any Federal or State offense involving the distribution or possession of a controlled substance, or that if I have been so convicted, I am not ineligible to receive Federal benefits, either by court order or operation of law, pursuant to 21 U.S.C. 853a.

(b) *Fee.* The application shall be accompanied by a money order, certified check or cashier's check in the amount of $350 made payable to the "Federal Maritime Commission."

(c) *Rejection.* Any application which appears upon its face to be incomplete or to indicate that the applicant fails to meet the licensing requirements of the Shipping Act of 1984, or the Commission's regulations, shall be returned by certified U.S. mail to the applicant without further processing, together with an explanation of the reason(s) for rejection, and the application fee shall be refunded in full. All other applications will be assigned an application number, and each applicant will be notified of the number assigned to its application. Persons who have had their applications returned may reapply for a license at any time thereafter by submitting a new application, together with the full application fee.

(d) *Investigation.* Each applicant shall be investigated in accordance with § 510.13.

(e) *Changes in fact.* Each applicant and each licensee shall submit to the Commission, in duplicate, an amended Form FMC–18 Rev. advising of any changes in the facts submitted in the original application, within thirty (30) days after change(s) occur. In the case of an application for a license, any unreported change may delay the processing and investigation of the application and may result in rejection or denial of the application. No fee is required when reporting changes to an application for initial license under this section.

§ 510.13 Investigation of applicants.

The Commission shall conduct an investigation of the applicant's qualifications for a license. Such investigations may address:

(a) The accuracy of the information submitted in the application;

(b) The integrity and financial responsibility of the applicant;

(c) The character of the applicant and its qualifying individual; and

(d) The length and nature of the qualifying individual's experience in handling freight forwarding duties.

§ 510.14 Surety bond requirements.

(a) *Form and amount.* No license shall be issued to an applicant who does not have a valid surety bond (FMC–59 Rev.) on file with the Commission in the amount of $30,000. The amount of such bond shall be increased by $10,000 for each of the applicant's unincorporated branch offices. Bonds must be issued by a surety company found acceptable by the Secretary of the Treasury. Surety Bond Form FMC–59 Rev. can be obtained in the same manner as Form FMC–18 Rev. under § 510.12(a).

(b) *Filing of bond.* Upon notification by the Commission by certified U.S. mail that the applicant has been approved for licensing, the applicant shall file with the Director of the Commission's Bureau of Tariffs, a surety bond in the form and amount prescribed in § 510.14(a). No license will be issued until the Commission is in receipt of a valid surety bond from the applicant. If more than six (6) months elapse between issuance of the notification of qualification and receipt of the surety bond, the Commission shall, at its discretion, undertake a supplementary investigation to determine the applicant's continued qualification. The fee for such supplementary investigation shall be $100 payable by money order, certified check or cashier's check to the "Federal Maritime Commission." Should the applicant not file the requisite surety bond within two years of notification, the Commission will consider the application to be invalid.

(c) *Branch offices.* A new surety bond, or rider to the existing bond, increasing the amount of the bond in accordance with § 510.14(a), shall be filed with the Commission prior to the date the licensee commences operation of any branch office. Failure to adhere to this requirement may result in revocation of the license.

(d) *Termination of bond.* No license shall remain in effect unless a valid surety bond is maintained on file with the Commission. Upon receipt of notice of termination of a surety bond, the Commission shall notify the concerned licensee by certified U.S. mail, at its last known address, that the Commission shall, without hearing or other proceeding, revoke the license as of the termination of the date of the bond, unless the licensee shall have submitted a valid replacement surety bond before such termination date. Replacement surety bonds must bear an effective date no later than the termination date of the expiring bond.

§ 510.15 Denial of license.

If the Commission determines, as a result of its investigation, that the applicant:

(a) Does not possess the necessary experience or character to render forwarding services;

(b) Has failed to respond to any lawful inquiry of the Commission; or

(c) Has made any willfully false or misleading statement to the Commission in connection with its application,

A letter of intent to deny the application shall be sent to the applicant by certified U.S. mail, stating the reason(s) why the Commission intends to deny the application. If the applicant submits a written request for hearing on the proposed denial within twenty (20) days after receipt of notification, such hearing shall be granted by the Commission pursuant to its Rules of Practice and Procedure contained in Part 502 of this chapter. Otherwise, denial of the application will become effective and the applicant shall be so notified by certified U.S. mail. Civil penalties for violations of the Act or any Commission order, rule or regulation may be assessed in accordance with subpart W of part 502 of this chapter in any proceeding on the proposed denial of a license or may be compromised for any such violation when a proceeding has not been instituted.

[58 FR 27208; MAY 7, 1993]

§ 510.16 Revocation or suspension of license.

(a) *Grounds for revocation.* Except for the automatic revocation for termination of a surety bond under § 510.14(d), or as provided in § 510.14(c), a license may be revoked or suspended after notice and hearing for any of the following reasons:

(1) Violation of any provision of the Act, or any other statute or Commission order or regulation related to carrying on the business of forwarding;

(2) Failure to respond to any lawful order or inquiry by the Commission;

(3) Making a willfully false or misleading statement to the Commission in connection with an application for a license or its continuance in effect;

(4) Where the Commission determines that the licensee is not qualified to render freight forwarding services;

(5) Failure to honor the licensee's financial obligations to the Commission, such as for civil penalties assessed or agreed to in a settlement agreement under subpart W of part 502 of this chapter; or

(6) Failure to file an anti-rebate certification as required by § 510.25 and part 582 of this chapter. Any licensed freight forwarder who fails to file an anti-rebate certification will be notified by FEDERAL REGISTER publication and by certified mail that if within forty-five (45) days from the date the certified notice is mailed the licensee does not either establish that the required anti-rebate certification was filed in accordance with § 510.25 and part 582 of this chapter or file the required anti-rebate certification, its license will be suspended until such time as it is reinstated by the Commission after an anti-rebate certification is filed. The license of any freight forwarder who files an anti-rebate certification after December 31 but before the end of the forty-five (45) days notice period will not be suspended; however, the licensee will be subject to civil penalties as provided in part 582 of this chapter. After the forty-five days, any licensee that still does not have an anti-rebate certification on file with the Commission will be notified by FEDERAL REGISTER publication and certified mail, return receipt requested, that its license has been suspended.

(b) *Civil penalties.* As provided for in subpart W of part 502 of this chapter, civil penalties for violations of the Act or any Commission order, rule, or regulation may be assessed in any proceeding to revoke or suspend a license and may be compromised when such a proceeding has not been instituted.

(c) *Notice of revocation.* The Commission shall publish in the FEDERAL REGISTER a notice of each revocation.

[55 FR 35316, AUGUST 29, 1990; 57 FR 39622, SEPT. 1, 1992; 58 FR 27208, MAY 7, 1993]

§ 510.17 Application after revocation or denial.

Whenever a license has been revoked or an application has been denied because the Commission has found the licensee or applicant to be not qualified to render forwarding services, any further application within 3 years of the date of the most recent conduct on which the Commission's notice of revocation or denial was based, made by such former licensee or applicant or by another applicant employing the same qualifying individual or controlled by persons on whose conduct the Commission based its determination for revocation or denial, shall be reviewed directly by the Commission.

§ 580.18 Issuance and use of license.

(a) *Qualification necessary for issuance.* The Commission will issue a license if it determines, as a result of its investigation, that the applicant possesses the necessary experience and character to render forwarding services and has filed the required surety bond.

(b) *To whom issued.* The Commission will issue a license only in the name of the applicant, whether the applicant be a sole proprietorship, a partnership, or a corporation, and the license will be issued to only one legal entity. A license issued to a sole proprietor doing business under a trade name shall be in the name of the sole proprietor, indicating the trade name under which the licensee will be conducting business. Only one license shall be issued to any applicant regardless of the number of names under which such applicant may be doing business.

(c) *Use limited to named licensee.* Except as otherwise provided in this part, such license is limited exclusively to use by the named licensee and shall not be transferred without approval to another person.

§ 510.19 Changes in organization.

(a) The following changes in an existing licensee's organization require prior approval of the Commission:

(1) Transfer of a corporate license to another person;

(2) Change in ownership of an individual proprietorship;

(3) Addition of one or more partners to a licensed partnership;

(4) Change in the business structure of a licensee from or to a sole proprietorship, partnership, or corporation, whether or not such change involves a change in ownership;

(5) Any change in a licensee's name; or

(6) Change in the identity or status of the designated qualifying individual, except as discussed in paragraphs (b) and (c) of this section.

(b) *Operation after death of sole proprietor.* In the event the owner of a licensed sole proprietorship dies, the licensee's executor, administrator, heir(s), or assign(s) may continue operation of such proprietorship solely with respect to shipments for which the deceased sole proprietor had undertaken to act as an ocean freight forwarder pursuant to the existing license, if the death is reported within thirty (30) days to the Commission and to all principals for whom services on such shipments are to be rendered. The acceptance or solicitation of any other shipments is expressly prohibited until a new license has been issued. Applications for a new license by the said executor, administrator, heir(s), or assign(s) shall be made on Form FMC–18 Rev., and shall be accompanied by the transfer fee set forth in paragraph (e) of this section.

(c) *Operation after retirement, resignation, or death of qualifying individual.* When a partnership or corporation has been licensed on the basis of the qualifications of one or more of the partners or officers thereof, and such qualifying individual(s) shall no longer serve in a full-time, active capacity with the firm, the licensee shall report such change to the Commission within thirty (30) days. Within the same 30-day period, the licensee shall furnish to the Commission the name(s) and detailed ocean freight forwarding experience of other active managing partner(s) or officer(s) who may qualify the licensee. Such qualifying individual(s) must meet the applicable requirements set forth in § 510.11(a) of this part. The licensee may continue to operate as an ocean freight forwarder while the Commission investigates the qualifications of the newly designated partner or officer.

(d) *Incorporation of branch office.* In the event a licensee's validly operating branch office undergoes incorporation as a separate entity, the licensee may continue to operate such office pending receipt of a separate license, provided that:

(1) The separately incorporated entity applies to the Commission for its own license within ten (10) days after incorporation, and

(2) The continued operation of the office is carried on as a *bona fide* branch office of the licensee, under its full control and responsibility, and not as an operation of the separately incorporated entity.

(e) *Application form and fee.* Applications for Commission approval of status changes or for license transfers under paragraph (a) of this section shall be filed in duplicate with the Director, Bureau of Tariffs, Certification and Licensing, Federal Maritime Commission, on Form FMC–18, Rev., together with a processing fee of $100, made payable by money order, certified check, or cashier's check or personal check to the Federal Maritime Commission. Should a personal check not be honored when presented for payment, the processing of the application shall be suspended until the processing fee is paid.

(f) *Acquisition of one or more additional licensees.* In the event a licensee acquires one or more additional licensees, for the purpose of merger, consolidation, or control, the acquiring licensee shall advise the Commission of such change within thirty days after such change occurs by submitted in duplicate, an amended Form FMC–18, Rev. No application fee is required when reporting this change.

[57 FR 40129, SEPT. 2, 1992]

Subpart C—Duties and Responsibilities of Freight Forwarders; Forwarding Charges; Reports to Commission

§ 510.21 General duties.

(a) *License; name and number.* Each licensee shall carry on the business of forwarding only under the name in which its license is issued and only under its license number as assigned by the Commission. Wherever the licensee's name appears on shipping documents, its FMC license number shall also be included.

(b) *Stationery and billing forms; notice of shipper affiliation.* (1) The name and license number of each licensee shall be permanently imprinted on the licensee's office stationery and billing forms. The Commission may temporarily waive this requirement for good cause shown if the licensee rubber stamps or types its name and FMC license number on all papers and invoices concerned with any forwarding transaction.

(2) When a licensee is a shipper or seller of goods in international commerce or affiliated with such an entity, the licensee shall have the option of: (i) Identifying itself as such and/or, where applicable, listing its affiliates on its office stationery and billing forms, or (ii) including the following notice on such items:

> *This company is a shipper or seller of goods in international commerce or is affiliated with such an entity. Upon request, a general statement of its business activities and those of its affiliates, along with a written list of the names of such affiliates, will be provided.*

(c) *Use of license by others; prohibition.* No licensee shall permits its license or name to be used by any person who is not a *bona fide* individual employee of the licensee. Unincorporated branch offices of the licensee may use the license number and name of the licensee if such branch offices: (1) Have been reported to the Commission in writing; and (2) are covered by an increased bond in accordance with § 510.14(c).

(d) *Arrangements with forwarders whose licenses have been revoked.* Unless prior written approval from the Commission has been obtained, no licensee shall, directly or indirectly:

(1) Agree to perform forwarding services on export shipments as an associate, correspondent, officer, employee, agent, or sub-agent of any person whose license has been revoked or suspended pursuant to § 510.16;

(2) Assist in the furtherance of any forwarding business of such person;

(3) Share forwarding fees or freight compensation with any such person; or

(4) Permit any such person, directly or indirectly, to participate, through ownership or otherwise, in the control or direction of the freight forwarding business of the licensee.

(e) *Arrangements with unauthorized persons.* No licensee shall enter into an agreement or other arrangement (excluding sales agency arrangements not prohibited by law or this part) with an unlicensed person so that any resulting fee, compensation, or other benefit inures to the benefit of the unlicensed person. When a licensee is employed for the transaction of forwarding business by a person who is not the person responsible for paying the forwarding charges, the licensee shall also transmit to the person paying the forwarding charges a copy of its invoice for services rendered.

(f) *False or fraudulent claims, false information.* No licensee shall prepare or file or assist in the preparation or filing of any claim, affidavit, letter of indemnity, or other paper or document concerning a forwarding transaction which it has reason to believe is false or fraudulent, nor shall any such licensee knowingly impart to a principal, common carrier or other person, false information relative to any forwarding transaction.

(g) *Response to requests of Commission.* Upon the request of any authorized representative of the Commission, a licensee shall make available promptly for inspection or reproduction all records and books of account in connection with its forwarding business, and shall respond promptly to any lawful inquiries by such representative.

(h) *Policy against rebates.* The following declaration shall appear on all invoices submitted to principals:

> (Name of firm) has a policy against payment, solicitation, or receipt of any rebate, directly or indirectly, which would be unlawful under the United States Shipping Act of 1984.

§ 510.22 Forwarder and principal; fees.

(a) *Compensation or fee sharing.* No licensee shall share, directly or indirectly, any compensation or freight forwarding fee with a shipper, consignee, seller, or purchaser, or an agent, affiliate, or employee thereof; nor with any person advancing the purchase price of the property or guaranteeing payment therefor; nor with any person having a beneficial interest in the shipment.

(b) *Withholding information.* No licensee shall withhold any information concerning a forwarding transaction from its principal.

(c) *Due diligence.* Each licensee shall exercise due diligence to ascertain the accuracy of any information it imparts to a principal concerning any forwarding transaction.

(d) *Errors and omissions.* Each licensee shall comply with the laws of the United States and any involved State, Territory, or possession thereof, and shall assure that to the best of its knowledge there exists no error, misrepresentation in, or omission from any export declaration, bill of lading, affidavit, or other document which the licensee executes in connection with a shipment. A licensee who has reason to believe that its principal has not, with respect to a shipment to be handled by such licensee, complied with the laws of the United States or any state, Commonwealth or Territory thereof, or has made any error or misrepresentation in, or omission from, any export declaration, bill of lading, affidavit, or other paper which the principal executes in connection with such shipment, shall advise its principal promptly of the suspected noncompliance, error, misrepresentation or omission, and shall decline to participate in any transaction involving such document until the matter is properly and lawfully resolved.

(e) *Express written authority.* No licensee shall endorse or negotiate any draft, check, or warrant drawn to the order of its principal without the express written authority of such principal.

(f) *Receipt for cargo.* Each receipt issued for cargo by a licensee shall be clearly identified as "Receipt for Cargo" and be readily distinguishable from a bill of lading.

(g) *Invoices; documents available upon request.* A licensee may charge its principal for services rendered. Upon request of its principal, each licensee shall provide a complete breakout of the components of its charges and a true copy of any underlying document or bill of charges pertaining to the licensee's invoice. The following notice shall appear on each invoice to a principal:

> *Upon request, we shall provide a detailed breakout of the components of all charges assessed and a true copy of each pertinent document relating to these charges.*

(h) *Special contracts.* To the extent that special arrangements or contracts are entered into by a licensee, the licensee shall not deny equal terms to other shippers similarly situated.

(i) *Reduced forwarding fees.* No licensee shall render, or offer to render, any freight forwarding service free of charge or at a reduced fee in consideration of receiving compensation from a common carrier or for any other reason. *Exception:* A licensee may perform freight forwarding services for recognized relief agencies or charitable organizations, which are designated as such in the tariff of the common carrier, free of charge or at reduced fees.

(j) *Accounting to principal.* Each licensee shall account to its principal(s) for overpayments, adjustments of charges, reductions in rates, insurance refunds, insurance monies received for claims, proceeds of c.o.d. shipments, drafts, letters of credit, and any other sums due such principal(s).

§ 510.23 Forwarder and carrier; compensation.

(a) *Disclosure of principal.* The identity of the shipper must always be disclosed in the shipper identification box on the bill of lading. The licensee's name may appear with the name of the shipper, but the licensee must be identified as the shipper's agent.

(b) *Certification required for compensation.* A common carrier may pay compensation to a licensee only pursuant to such common carrier's tariff provisions. Where a common carrier's tariff provides for the payment of compensation, such compensation shall be paid on any shipment forwarded on behalf of others where the licensee has provided a written certification as prescribed in paragraph (c) of this section and the shipper has been disclosed on the bill of lading as provided for in paragraph (a) of this section. The common carrier shall be entitled to rely on such certification unless it knows that the certification is incorrect. The common carrier shall retain such certification for a period of five (5) years.

(c) *Form of certification.* Where a licensee is entitled to compensation, the licensee shall provide the common carrier with a signed certification which indicates that the licensee has performed the required services that entitle it to compensation. The certification shall read as follows:

> *The undersigned hereby certifies that neither it nor any holding company, subsidiary, affiliate, officer, director, agent or executive of the undersigned has a beneficial interest in this shipment; that it is the holder of valid FMC License No._____, issued by the Federal Maritime Commission and has performed the following services:*
>
> *(1) Engaged, booked, secured, reserved, or contracted directly with the carrier or its agent for space aboard a vessel or confirmed the availability of that space; and*
>
> *(2) Prepared and processed the ocean bill of lading, dock receipt, or other similar document with respect to the shipment.*

The required certification may be placed on one copy of the relevant bill of lading, a summary statement from the licensee, the licensee's compensation invoice, or as an endorsement on the carrier's compensation check. Each licensee shall retain evidence in its shipment files that the licensee, in fact, has performed the required services enumerated on the certification.

(d) *Compensation pursuant to tariff provisions.* No licensee, or employee thereof, shall accept compensation from a common carrier which is different than that specifically provided for in the carrier's effective tariff(s) lawfully on file with the Commission. No conference or group of common carriers shall deny in the export commerce of the United States compensation to an ocean freight forwarder or limit that compensation to less than a reasonable amount.

(e) *Compensation; services performed by underlying carrier; exemptions.* No licensee shall charge or collect compensation in the event the underlying common carrier, or its agent, has, at the request of such licensee, performed any of the forwarding services set forth in § 510.2(h) unless such carrier or agent is also a licensee, or unless no other licensee is willing and able to perform such services.

(f) *Duplicative compensation.* A common carrier shall not pay compensation for the services described in § 510.23(c) more than once on the same shipment.

(g) *Licensed non-vessel-operating common carriers; compensation.* (1) A non-vessel-operating common carrier or person related thereto licensed under this part may collect compensation when, and only when, the following certification is made together with the certification required under paragraph (c) of this section:

> *The undersigned certifies that neither it nor any related person has issued a bill of lading or otherwise undertaken common carrier responsibility as a non-vessel-operating common carrier for the ocean transportation of the shipment covered by this bill of lading.*

(2) Whenever a person acts in the capacity of a non-vessel-operating common carrier as to any shipment, such person shall not collect compensation, nor shall any underlying ocean common carrier pay compensation to such person for such shipment.

(h) A freight forwarder may not receive compensation from a common carrier with respect to any shipment in which the forwarder has a beneficial interest or with respect to any shipment in which any holding company, subsidiary, affiliate, officer, director, agent, or executive of such forwarder has a beneficial interest.

[48 FR 36297, SEPT. 14, 1984; 49 FR 38544, OCT.1, 1984; 57 FR 40129, SEPT. 2, 1992]

§ 510.24 Records required to be kept.

Each licensee shall maintain in an orderly and systematic manner, and keep current and correct, all records and books of account in connection with its business of forwarding. These records must be kept in the United States in such manner as to enable authorized Commission personnel to readily determine the licensee's cash position, accounts receivable and accounts payable. The licensee must maintain the following records for a period of five years:

(a) *General financial data.* A current running account of all receipts and disbursements, accounts receivable and payable, and daily cash balances, supported by appropriate books of account, bank deposit slips, cancelled checks, and monthly reconciliation of bank statements.

(b) *Types of services by shipment.* A separate file shall be maintained for each shipment. Each file shall include a copy of each document prepared, processed, or obtained by the licensee, including each invoice for any service arranged by the licensee and performed by others, with respect to such shipment.

(c) *Receipts and disbursements by shipment.* A record of all sums received and/or disbursed by the licensee for services rendered and out-of-pocket expenses advanced in connection with each shipment, including specific dates and amounts.

(d) *Special contracts.* A true copy, or if oral, a true and complete memorandum, of every special arrangement or contract with a principal, or modification or cancellation thereof, to which it may be a party. Authorized Commission personnel and *bona fide* shippers shall have access to such records upon reasonable request.

§ 510.25 Anti-rebate certifications.

(a) Every licensed ocean freight forwarder shall file an anti-rebating certification or before December 31, 1992, and thereafter, on or before December 31 of each succeeding even-numbered calendar year.

(b) Every applicant for an ocean freight forwarder license shall file an anti-rebating certificate with its license application. Any application for an ocean freight forwarder license that does not include an anti-rebate certification in accordance with § 510.12 and part 582 of this chapter shall be rejected. Certificates filed with license applications shall be valid from the granting of an ocean freight forwarder license through the first succeeding December 31 of an even-numbered calendar year.

(c) The anti-rebating certificate shall comply with the requirements of part 582 of this chapter.

[51 FR 30863, AUG. 29, 1986; 55 FR 35316, AUGUST 29, 1990; 57 FR 39622, SEPT. 1, 1992]

§ 510.91 OMB control numbers assigned pursuant to the Paperwork Reduction Act.

This section displays the control numbers assigned to information collection requirements of the Commission in this part by the Office of Management and Budget pursuant to the Paperwork Reduction Act of 1980, Pub. L. 96-511. The Commission intends that this part comply with the requirements of section 3507(f) of the Paperwork Reduction Act, which requires that agencies display a current control number assigned by the Director of the Office of Management and Budget (OMB) for each agency information collection requirement:

Section	Current OMB Control No.
510.12: (Form FMC-18)	3072-0018
510.14	3072-0018
510.15	3072-0018
510.19: (Form FMC-18)	3072-0018
510.21 through 510.25	3072-0018

FEDERAL MARITIME COMMISSION ORGANIZATIONAL CHART

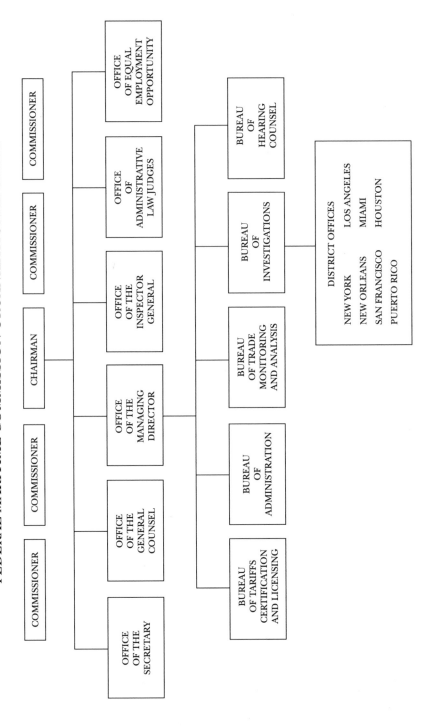

NOTES

Chapter I: History of U.S. Ocean Shipping Regulation

1. M. D. A. Azuni. *The Maritime Law of Europe,* published by George Forman (N.Y.), Vol. II (1806).
2. Railway and Canal Traffic Act, 1854 (17 & 18 Vict. c. 31), s.2.
3. Railway and Canal Traffic Act, 1888 (51 & 52 Vict. c. 25), s.28.
4. 46 U.S.C.A. §815.
5. 46 App. U.S.C.A. §1709(b)(11) & (12).
6. 46 U.S.C.A. 814.
7. *F.M.C. v. Isbrandtsen Co.,* 356 U.S. 481 (1958).
8. 46 U.S.C.A. 813a.
9. *F.M.C. v. Aktiebolaget Svenska Amerika Linien,* 390 U.S. 238 (1968).
10. See Ullman,"The Intermodal Movement of LCL Freight: The Problem Areas," *Denver Transportation Law Journal,* Vol. XII, No. 1, 1981, p. 95.
11. 46 App. U.S.C.A. §1701 *et seq.*
12. 46 App. U.S.C.A. §1705(c)(1) and (2).
13. 46 App. U.S.C.A. §1706(a)(2).
14. 46 App. U.S.C.A. §§1703(a)(1) and 1707(a).
15. 46 App. U.S.C.A. §1709(e).
16. *Bernhard Ulmann, Inc. v. Porto Rican Express Co.,* 3 F.M.B. 771 (1952); *Common Carriers by Water, Etc.,* 6 F.M.C. 245 (1961).
17. 46 App. U.S.C.A. §1702(17).
18. 46 App. U.S.C.A. §1707(b) and (c).
19. 46 App. U.S.C.A. §1702(24)
20. 46 App. U.S.C.A. §1709(b)(13).
21. As of the spring of 1994, the FMC oversees the practices of 1,750 ocean freight forwarders, 2,160 non-vessel-operating common carriers (NVOCCs), 437 marine terminal operators, and 580 vessel-operating common carriers. *American Shipper,* June 1994, p.23.

Chapter II: Ocean Common Carriers

1. Pub. L. 98–237, Mar. 20, 1984, 98 Stat. 67.
2. 46 App. U.S.C.A. §1701.
3. H. Rept. 98–600, 98th Cong., 2nd Sess., p. 27, 2/23/84, (hereinafter "Conf. Rept.")
4. 46 App. U.S.C.A. §1701(1).
5. 46 App. U.S.C.A. §1702.
6. *Publication of Inactive Tariffs, Etc.,* 20 F.M.C. 433 (1978).
7. 46 App. U.S.C.A. §1702(6).
8. *Determination of Common Carrier Status,* 6 F.M.B. 245 (1961).
9. *Austasia Intermodal Lines v. F.M.C.,* 580 F.2d 642 (D.C. Cir. 1978).
10. *Ship's Overseas Service v. F.M.C.,* 670 F.2d 304 (D.C. Cir. 1981).
11. *Transshipment Agreement, Etc.,* 10 F.M.C. 199 (1966).
12. 46 App. U.S.C.A. §1701(2).
13. Conf. Rept. p.13.

14. 46 App. U.S.C.A. §1701(3).
15. *See* n. 13.
16. 46 App. U.S.C.A. §1703.
17. 46 App. U.S.C.A. §1702(6). See Appendix A for the full definition. A more concise definition is set forth in Part 582.2 of the F.M.C. Regulations, 46 C.F.R. 580.2.
18. *Determination of Common Carrier Status,* 6 F.M.B. 245 (1961).
19. *Absorption or Equalization, Etc.,* 6 F.M.B. 138 (1960).
20. *Tariff Filing Practices, Etc., of Containerships, Inc.,* 9 F.M.C. 56 (1965).
21. *Id.* at 63.
22. *Id.* at 64.
23. *Id.* at 65.
24. *McAllister Bros., Inc. v. Norfolk & Western Ry.,* 20 F.M.C. 63 (1977).
25. *Publication of Inactive Tariffs, Etc.,* 20 F.M.C. 433 (1978).
26. *Zima Corp. v. M. Roman Pazinsky,* 493 F. Supp. 268 (D.C. S.D. N.Y. 1980).
27. *Ships Overseas Service v. F.M.C.,* 670 F. 2d 304 (D.C. Cir. 1981).
28. *Grace Line, Inc. v. Skips Viking, Etc.,* 7 F.M.C. 432 (1962).
29. *Rates of General Atlantic S.S. Corp.,* 2 U.S.M.C. 681 (1943).
30. *Isbrandtsen Co., Inc. v. American Export Lines, Inc.,* 4 F.M.B. 772 (1956).
31. *Puerto Rican Rates,* 2 U.S.M.C. 117 (1939); *Philips R. Consolo v. Grace Line, Inc.,* 4 F.M.B. 293 (1953).
32. *Puget Sound Tug and Barge Co. v. Foss Launch & Tug Co.,* 7 F.M.C. 611 (1963).
33. *Agreement—Gulf Mediterranean Conf.,* 8 F.M.C. 703 (1965).
34. 46 App. U.S.C.A. §1702(7).
35. Report of Advisory Commission on Conferences in Ocean Shipping, (hereinafter "ACCOS") established pursuant to Section 18(d) of the 1984 Act; 46 App. U.S.C.A. 1717(d).
36. 46 App. U.S.C.A. §1703(a). See Appendix A.
37. 46 App. U.S.C.A. §1704(a) and (b).
38. 46 App. U.S.C.A. §1702(3).
39. S.Rept. No. 98-3, 98th Cong., 1st Sess., 2/14/83, p.20.
40. 46 App. U.S.C.A. §1702(23).
41. ACCOS p.53, n.22.
42. 46 App. U.S.C.A. §1702(24).
43. ACCOS, p.23.
44. 46 App. U.S.C.A. §1703.
45. 46 App. U.S.C.A. §§1704, 1705, 1706.
46. For the full text, *see* Appendix A.
47. *Isbrandtsen Co., Inc. v. States Marine,* 6 F.M.B. 422 (1961).
48. *Unapproved Sect. 15 Agreements, Etc.,* 7 F.M.C. 22 (1961).
49. *Transshipment Agreement, Etc.,* 10 F.M.C. 183 (1966).
50. *North Atlantic Mediterranean Frt. Conf., Etc.,* 9 F.M.C. 431 (1966).
51. *Boston Shipping Assn. v. Port of Boston, Etc.,* 11 F.M.C. 1 (1967).
52. 46 C.F.R. 572.202.
53. *Intercoastal Rate Investigation,* 1 U.S.S.B. 108 (1926).
54. *Intercoastal Rate Investigation,* 1 U.S.S.B. 400 (1935).
55. *Joint Committee, Etc. v. Pac. W/B Conf.,* 4 F.M.B. 166 (1953).
56. *Agreement No. 8905, Etc.,* 7 F.M.C. 792, (1964).
57. *Unapproved Section 15 Agreements, Etc.,* 8 F.M.C. 596,(1965).
58. 46 C.F.R. 572.104(w).
59. *West Coast Line, Inc. v. Grace Line,* 3 F.M.B. 586 (1951).
60. *Nopal v. Moore-McCormack,* 8 F.M.C. 213 (1964).
61. *Inter-American Frt. Conf., Etc.,* 14 F.M.C. 58 (1970).
62. *P/S Ivarans Rederi v. U.S.,* 895 F.2d 1441 (D.C. Cir. 1990).

63. 46 CFR 572.104(y).
64. *York Forwarding Corp., Etc.*, 15 F.M.C. 114 (1972).
65. *F.M.C. v. Seatrain Line Inc.*, 411 U.S. 726 (1973).
66. 44 U.S.C.A. §814.
67. H. Rept. 97-611, Part 1, 97th Cong., 2nd Sess., 6/16/82, p.29.
68. *Id.* at p. 34–35.
69. 46 App. U.S.C.A. §1703(a)(7).
70. ACCOS, p.133.
71. *See* ACCOS, p.145.
72. H. Rept. No. 98-53, Part 1, 98th Cong., 1st Sess., 4/12/83, p.17.
73. *See* ACCOS, p.137.
74. *See* S. Rept. No. 98-3, 98th Cong., 1st Sess., 2/14/83, p.22, stating the objective to be "to assure protection against abuses of concerted shipping activity."
75. For the full text of this section, see Appendix A.
76. 46 U.S.C.A. §814.
77. H.R. Rept. 98-53, Part 1, 98th Cong., 1st Sess., 4/12/82, p.30.
78. Section 15 of the 1916 Act permitted such agreements.
79. 46 App. U.S.C.A. §1703(c).
80. S. Rept. No. 98-3 on S.504, 98th Cong., 1st Sess., 2/14/83, p.24.
81. 46 U.S.C.A. §814.
82. *F.M.C. v. Seatrain, Inc.*, 411 U.S. 726 (1973)
83. *American Mail Line Ltd. v. F.M.C.*, 503 F.2d 157 (D.C. Cir. 1974); *cert. denied*, 419 U.S. 1070.
84. 46 App. U.S.C.A. §1704.
85. 46 App. U.S.C.A. §1702(1).
86. 46 C.F.R. 572.104(a).
87. 46 U.S.C. §814.
88. 46 App. U.S.C.A. §1715.
89. 46 C.F.R. 572.302(a)(1) and (2).
90. *Id.* at 303–309, incl.
91. Conf. Rept., p.28.
92. 46 App. U.S.C.A. §1702(6).
93. Agreement No. 9955-1, 18 F.M.C. 426 (1975).
94. Docket No. 83-39, *Armada/GLTL I.D.*, ____ F.M.C. ____, 22 S.R.R. 500 (I.D.) final through operation of law (1983).
95. *Isbrandtsen Co., Inc. v. States Marine*, 6 F.M.B. 422 (1961).
96. *Unapproved Section 15 Agreements*, 7 F.M.C. 22 (1961).
97. *Boston Shipping Assn. v. Port of Boston Marine Term.*, 11 F.M.C. 1 (1967).
98. *Practices and Agreement of Common Carriers*, 7 F.M.C. 51 (1962)
99. *Transpacific v. F.M.C.*, 938 F.2d 1025 (9th Cir. 1991).
100. Docket No. 83-52, *Status of Matson Agencies, Etc.*, ____ F.M.C. ____, 22 S.R.R. 752, 1984.
101. 46 C.F.R. 572.406(a).
102. *Seatrain Lines, Inc. v. F.M.C.*, 460 F.2d (D.C. Cir. 1972), 932 *aff'd.* 411 U.S. 726 (1972).
103. *Square D Co. v. Niagara Frontier*, 760 F.2d 1347 (2nd Cir. 1985), *aff'd.*, 476 U.S. 409 (1985).
104. 46 App.U.S.C.A. §1704(b)(2).
105. ACCOS, p.18.
106. 46 App. U.S.C.A. §1717(f).
107. H. Rept. 97-611, Part I, 99th Cong., 2nd Sess., 6/10/82, p.35.
108. *Sprague v. Ivarans*, 2 U.S.M.C. 72 (1939).
109. *Waterman S.S. Corp. v. Bernstein Line*, 2 U.S.M.C. 238 (1939).
110. *American-Hawaiian S.S. Co. v. Intercontinental Marine Lines, Inc.*, 4 F.M.B. 160 (1953).
111. *Conference Agreement No. 9218*, 8 F.M.C. 170 (1964).
112. *North Atlantic French Atlantic Frt. Conf.*, 14 F.M.C. 46 (1970).

113. *Agreement No. 5200-26*, Etc., 13 F.M.C. 16 (1969).
114. 46 App. U.S.C.A. §1704(b)(4).
115. S. Rept. No. 97-414, 97th Cong., 2nd Sess., 5/25/82, p.30.
116. H. Rept. 98-53, Part I, 98th Cong., 1st Sess, Etc. 4/12/82, pp.31–32.
117. The procedure for dealing with a failure by a carrier to comply, absent a neutral body, is contained in Section 13(b)(4); 46 App. U.S.C.A. §1712(b)(4).
118. Docket 85-4, *Miscellaneous Modifications, Etc.*, 23 S.R.R. 134 (1985).
119. *Trans-Pacific Frt. Conf. Etc.*, 7 F.M.C. 653 (1962).
120. *States Marine Lines v. F.M.C.*, 376 F.2d 230 (D.C. Cir. 1967).
121. *Modification of Agreements, Etc.*, 11 F.M.C. 434 (1968).
122. *States Marine Line, Inc. v. Pac. Coast European Conf.*, 12 F.M.C. 1 (1968).
123. *Modification of Agreements, No. 150, Etc.*, 11 F.M.C. 434, (1968).
124. 46 App.U.S.C.A. §1710(g).
125. *Id.* at 1712(b)(1).
126. Conf. Rept., pp.28–29.
127. *Id.* at 29.
128. 46 App. U.S.C.A. §1706(a)(2).
129. Section 11(c); 46 App. U.S.C.A. §1710(c).
130. *Delaware River Port Authority v. U.S. Lines, Inc.*, 331 F. Supp. 441 (D.C.E.D. Pa. 1971).
131. Docket No. 76-44, *Order of Hearing, Berthing of Seatrain Vessels, Etc.*, 16 S.R.R. 1395, 1397 (1976), not officially reported.
132. *Id.*
133. Conf. Rept., p.29.
134. *Id.*
135. 46 App. U.S.C.A. §1704(b)(6).
136. S. Rept. No. 97-414, 97th Cong., 2nd Sess., 5/25/82, p.30.
137. Docket No. 92-32, *Amendments to Agreement Recordkeeping Regulations*, 46 C.F.R. Parts 560 & 572, 26 S.R.R. 474 (1992).
138. 46 App. U.S.C.A. §1704(b)(7).
139. *Caterpillar Overseas, S.A. v. South African Marine Corp. N.Y.*, 19 F.M.C. 31 (1976).
140. 46 App. U.S.C.A. §1704(b)(8).
141. Docket 86-3, *Modification of Trans-Pacific Frt. Conf. of Japan Agreement*, _____ F.M.C. _____, 23 S.R.R. 1390 (1986).
142. *Id.*
143. 46 App. U.S.C.A. §1707(a)(1)(c).
144. Docket No. 85-8, *Matter of Independent Action, Etc.*, _____ F.M.C. _____, 23 S.R.R. 390, (1985).
145. *See* 19 U.S.C.A. §1641(i).
146. *Chemical Manufacturers N.F.R.S. Ass'n. v. F.M.C.*, 900 F.2d 311 (D.C.C. Cir. 1990).
147. Docket No. 92-16, *Conference Independent Action Provisions*, 26 S.R.R. 620 (1992).
148. 46 C.F.R. 572.801.
149. H. Rept., 97-611, Part I, 97th Cong., 2nd Sess., 6/16/82, p. 36.
150. S. Rept., No. 98-3, 98th Cong., 1st Sess., 2/14/83, p. 24.
151. 46 App. U.S.C.A. §1704(d).
152. 46 App. U.S.C.A. §1702(3).
153. 46 App. U.S.C.A. §1710(g).
154. H. Rept., 97-611, Part I, 97th Cong., 2nd Sess., 6/16/82, p.36.
155. H.R. 97-600, 98th Cong., 2nd Sess., 2/23/84, p.30.
156. Docket No. 84-6, *Port Auth. of N.Y. & N.J. v. N.Y. Shipping Assn.*, _____ F.M.C. ____, 23 S.R.R. 228, (1985).
157. Docket 82-1, *California Cartage Co. Inc. v. Pacific Maritime Assn.*, _____ F.M.C. ____, 23 S.R.R. 420 (1985); *affd., California Cartage Co. v. U.S.*, 802 F.2d 353 (1986).
158. 46 App. U.S.C.A. §1702(16). See Appendix A for a definition in Section 3(16).

159. "50-Mile Container Rules" ____ F.M.C. ____, 24 S.R.R. 411 (1987), *petition for review denied, sub nom. N.Y. Shipping Ass'n. v. FMC,* 854 F.2d 1338 (D.C. Cir. 1988), *cert. denied,* 488 U.S. 1041 (1989).
160. S. Rep. No. 98-3, 98th Cong., 1st Sess., 1983, p.25.
161. N.Y. Shipping Assn., Inc. v. F.M.C., 854 F.2d 1338, (D.C. Cir. 1988), *cert. denied,* 477 U.S. 1041 (1989).
162. 46 App. U.S.C.A. 1705.
163. S. Rept. No. 98-3, 98th Cong., 1st Sess., 2/23/84, p.26.
164. Conf. Rept., p.30.
165. S. Rept. 98-53, Part 2, 98th Cong., 1st Sess., 2/23/84, p.10.
166. Conf. Rept. pp.30–31.
167. *Id.* at p.31.
168. 46 C.F.R. 572.603(a) and (b).
169. H. Rept.98-53, Part 2, 98th Cong., 1st Sess., 7/1/83, p.11.
170. S. Rept. No. 98-3, 98th Cong., 1st Sess., 2/14/83, p.27.
171. Conf. Rept., p.34.,
172. *Id.* at pp. 34–35.
173. *Id.* at p.35.
174. *Id.*
175. *Id.* at pp.35–36.
176. *Id.* at p.36.
177. *Id.* at p.37.
178. ACCOS, p.25.
179. 46 U.S.C.A. §1705(h).
180. H. Rept. 98-53, Part 2, 98th Cong., 1st Sess., 4/12/82, p.12.
181. *Id.*
182. *Id.*
183. Conf. Rept., p.32.
184. *See,* e.g., *L.S.B. Industries, Inc. v. Prudential Lines, Inc.,* 736 F.2d 10 (2nd Cir., 1984).
185. 46 C.F.R. 502.181.
186. H. Rept. 98-53, Part 2, 98th Cong., 1st Sess., 6/1/83, p.12.
187. 46 App. U.S.C.A. §1706.
188. 46 U.S.C.A. §814.
189. S. Rept. No. 98-3, 98th Cong., 1st Sess., 4/12/83, p.6, *See FMC v. Svenska, Etc.,* 390 U.S. 238 (1968).
190. S. Rept. No. 98-3, op. cit., p.29.
191. Conf. Rept., p.37.
192. *Carnation Co. v. Pacific Westbound Conf.,* 383 U.S. 213 (1966).
193. Senate Rept. No. 98-3, n.3, *supra,* p.7.
194. S. Rept. No. 97-414, 97th Cong., 2nd Sess., 5/25/82, p.34.
195. S. Rept. No. 98-3, n.3, *supra,* p.29.
196. *Id.* at p.30.
197. *See F.M.C. v. Seatrain Lines, Inc.,* 411 U.S. 726 (1973).
198. 46 App. U.S.C.A. §1707.
199. S. Rept. 98-3, 98th Cong., 1st Sess., 2/14/83, p.30.
200. For full text of §8(a)(1), see Appendix A.
201. 46 App. U.S.C.A. §1707(a)(1).
202. 46 C.F.R. 580.2(b).
203. *Id,* §580.2(h).
204. Conf. Rept., p.38.
205. 46 C.F.R. 580.2(c).
206. *Id.* at 580.2(d).
207. *Id.* at 580.2(i).

208. *Id.* at 580.2(j).
209. *Id.* at 580.2(o).
210. *Id.* at 580.2(r).
211. 46 C.F.R. 580.7 (a)(1) and (2).
212. 46 C.F.R. 580.1(a).
213. Docket No. 85-6, *Notice of Inquiry, Etc.*, 24 S.R.R. 131 (1987).
214. Docket No. 92-35, *Notice of Inquiry, Etc.*, 26 S.R.R. 610 (1992).
215. *Id.* at p.12.
216. *Bills of Lading, Etc.*, 3 U.S.M.C. 111 (1949).
217. *Leather's Best Inc. v. S.S.* Mormaclynx, 313 F.Supp. 137 (2nd Cir. 1989).
218. Docket No. 80-9, *Schenkers International Forwarders, Inc. v. Sea Land Services Inc.*, 23 F.M.C. 370 (1980).
219. *Intercoastal Investigation,* 1 U.S.S.B. 400 (1935).
220. *U.S. v. Pan American Mail Line, Inc.*, 359 F. Supp. (D.C.S.D. N.Y. 1972).
221. *States S.S. Co., Etc.*, 19 F.M.C. 793 (1977).
222. *Sugar from Virgin Islands,* 1 U.S.M.C., 695 (1938).
223. *Sea-Land, Inc. Etc.*, 10 F.M.C. 395 (1967).
224. *International Packers, Ltd. v. North Pier Terminal Co.*, 11 F.M.C. 525 (1968).
225. *See* n. 23, *supra.*
226. *See* n. 24.
227. *Trucker and Lighter Loading, Etc.*, 9 F.M.C. 157 (1966).
228. *Carton-Print, Inc. v. Austasia Container Express,* 20 F.M.C. 31 (1977).
229. *West Coast of Italy, Etc.*, 21 F.M.C. 121 (1981).
230. Docket 85-14, *Cari Cargo Int'l., Etc. I.D.*, ____ F.M.C. ____, 23 S.R.R. 1007 (1986), administratively final.
231. *La Salle Mach. Tool, Inc. v. Maher Terminals Inc.*, 611 F.2d 56 (4th Cir. 1979).
232. *Bratti v. Prudential, et al.*, 8 F.M.C. 375 (1964).
233. *F. Powers Co. Inc. v. Orient Overseas Container Lines,* 19 F.M.C. 219 (1976).
234. *First Int.'l.Development. Corp. v. Ships Overseas Services, Inc.*, 21 F.M.C. 899 (1980).
235. *Johns–Manville Products Corp.*, 13 F.M.C. 192 (1970).
236. *Aleutian Homes, Inc. v. Coastwise Line,* 5 F.M.B. 602 (1959).
237. *Lykes Bros. S.S. Co., Inc.*, 20 F.M.C. 552 (1978).
238. *Crestline Supply Corp. v. Concordia Line,* 19 F.M.C. 207 (1978).
239. *Los Angeles By-Products Co. v. Barber Line,* 2 U.S.M.C. 106 (1939).
240. *W. Gulf Maritime Assn. v. Port of Houston Authority,* 652 F.2d 197 (1981).
241. *See* n. 23, *supra.*
242. *Misclassification, Etc.*, 6 F.M.B. 289 (1961).
243. Docket No. 87-19, *Atlantis Lines, Ltd. v. APL,* ____ F.M.C. ____, 24 S.R.R. 1391 (1988).
244. *Bulkley Dunton Etc. v. Blue Star Shipping Corp.*, 8 F.M.C. 137 (1964).
245. *Corn Products Co. v. Hamburg-Amerika Lines,* 10 F.M.C. 388 (1967).
246. *Transocean Van Service v. U.S.*, 426 F.2d, 329 (U.S. Ct. Cl. 1970).
247. Docket No. 91-14, *Inquiry Concerning Use and Effect of Surcharges, Etc.*, ____ F.M.C. ____, 24 S.R.R. 108 (1992).
248. *Id.*
249. *Id.*
250. As of July 1994 the surcharge problem had not been alleviated. A shipper representative has said that "[t]he bunker surcharge starts out modestly but tends to increase faster than the cost of fuel and decreases more slowly, and it is rolled into the rates periodically to start a few months later, applied to a higher base rate." Michael B. Berzon, "The Only Way to Win," *American Shipper,* July 1994, p.44.
251. 10 U.S.C. §2305(b)(3).
252. *Id.* at §2631.
253. *Rates on U.S. Government Cargoes,* 11 F.M.C. 263 (1967).

254. *In the Matter of the Carriage of Military Cargo,* 10 F.M.C. 69 (1966).
255. *Proposed Rule—Time Limit Etc.,* 12 F.M.C. 298 (1969).
256. *Dept. of Defense v. Matson Navigation Co.,* 20 F.M.C. 24 (1977).
257. Docket No. 92-25, *Regulation of Military Rates Under the Shipping Act of 1984,* 1992.
258. 46 C.F.R. 580.1(d).
259. Docket No. 92-25, *Order of Discontinuance,* 26 S.R.R. 599 (1992).
260. Docket No. 89-04, *Tariff Publication of Free Time and Detention Charge, Etc.,* 25 S.R.R. 778 (1990).
261. 46 C.F.R. 580.1(c)(8).
262. 46 C.F.R. 550, 580 and 581.
263. 25 S.R.R. at 782.
264. *Chiselli Bros. v. Micronesia Int. Line,* 13 F.M.C. 179 (1970).
265. *Antilles Ins. Co. v. Transcommex,* 672 F.Supp. 61 (D.C.P.R. 1987).
266. 46 App. U.S.C.A. §8(f).
267. *See Isbrandtsen Co., Petition of,* 201 F.2d 281 (2nd Cir. 1953).
268. *See Commonwealth of PA v. F.M.C.,* 392 F.Supp.(D.C.C. Cir. 1975) 795; and *Mitsui v. Glory River,* 1981 AMC 1237 (W.D. Wash.).
269. *Comm. of Penn v. F.M.C.,* 392 F.2d 795 (D.C. Cir. 1975).
270. 46 App. U.S.C.A. §1708; For the full text, *see* Appendix A.
271. 46 App. U.S.C.A. §1702(8).
272. S.Rept. 98-3, 98th Cong., 1st Sess., 2/14/83, p.33.
273. H.Rept. 98-53, Part I, 98th Cong., 1st Sess. 4/12/82, p.7.
274. *Rates of Far Eastern Shipping Co.,* 22 F.M.C. 651 (1980).
275. Docket No. 79-104, *Specific Commodity Rates of Far Eastern Shipping Co. Etc.,* 23 F.M.C. 87, *reconsideration denied,* 23 F.M.C. 406 (1980).
276. 46 App. U.S.C.A. §1709. *See* Appendix A for complete text.
277. S. Rept. No. 98-3, 98th Cong., 1st Sess., 2/14/83, p.34.
278. ACCOS, p.28.
279. 46 App. U.S.C.A. §1709(a)(1). The term "no person" replaced "any shipper, consignor, consignee, forwarder, broker, or other person" in Section 16 of the 1916 Act; 46 U.S.C.A. §815.
280. *Misclassification of Tissue Paper, Etc.,* 4 F.M.B., 483 (1954).
281. *Hazel-Atlas Glass Co., Etc.,* 5 F.M.B. 515 (1958).
282. *Raymond Int'l., Inc. v. Venezuelan Line,* 6 F.M.B. 189 (1961).
283. *In re Rubin, Etc.,* 6 F.M.B. 235 (1961).
284. *Id.*
285. *Ocean Freight Consultants v. Royal Netherland S.S.,* 17 F.M.C. 143 (1973).
286. *Union Carbide Corp. v. American Etc. Line,* 17 F.M.C.177 (1973).
287. *European Trade, Etc. v. Prudential-Grace Lines, Inc.,* 19 F.M.C. 148 (1976).
288. *CSC Int'l. Inc. v. Orient Overseas,* 19 F.M.C. 465 (1977).
289. Informal Docket 681(F), *Saniro Co. Ltd. v. Maersk Line,* 23 S.R.R. 150 (1980).
290. *Stackpole Corp. v. Sea-Land, Etc.,* I.D. 24 F.M.C. 26 (1981).
291. Docket 85-14, *I.D. Cari Cargo Int'l. Inc.,* ____ F.M.C. ____, 29 S.R.R. 1607 (1986), *administratively final.*
292. Docket 80-63, *West Coast of Italy, Etc.,* 24 F.M.C. 121 (1981).
293. *Beaumont Port Commission v. Seatrain Lines, Inc.,* 3 F.M.B. 556 (1951).
294. *Hohenberg Bros. Co. v. F.M.C.,* 316 F.2d 381 (D.C. Cir. 1963).
295. *Prince Line v. American Paper Exports Inc.,* 55 F.2d 1053 (2nd Cir. 1932).
296. *U.S. v. Open Bulk Carriers,* 727 F.2d 1061 (11th Cir. 1984).
297. *Brokerage on Ocean Freight, Etc.,* 5 F.M.B. 435 (1958).
298. *Misclassification and Misbilling, Etc.,* 6 F.M.B. 155 (1960).
299. *U.S. Gulf-Atlantic Conf., Etc.,* 2 U.S.M.C. 749 (1945).
300. *Malpractices, Brazil U.S. Trade, Etc.,* 15 F.M.C. 55 (1971).

301. 46 U.S.C.A. §814.
302. *Pennsylvania Motor Truck Assn. v. Port of Philadelphia, Etc.*, 183 F.Supp. 910 (D.C. Pa. 1960).
303. 46 App.U.S.C.A. §1709(b)(1).
304. *U.S. Borax, Etc. v. Pac. Coast Europ. Conf.*, 11 F.M.C. 451 (1968).
305. *Colgate Palmolive v. Grace Lines*, 17 F.M.C. 279 (1974).
306. *Trane Co. v. South African Marine Corp. (N.Y.)*, 19 F.M.C. 375) (1976).
307. *Caterpillar Overseas S.A. v. South African Marine Corp.*, 19 F.M.C. 316 (1976).
308. *Madeplac, Etc. v. L. Figueriedo*, 20 F.M.C. 578 (1978).
309. Docket No. 86-17, *Mobile Law Corp. v. Barber Blue Sea Lines*, 24 S.R.R. 1059, I.D. (1988).
310. *Muller v. Peralta Shipping Corp.*, 8 F.M.C. 361 (1965).
311. *Malpractices, Etc.*, 15 F.M.C. 55 (1971).
312. Docket No. 87-19, *Atlantic Lines Ltd. v. American President Lines Ltd.*, ___ F.M.C. ___, 24 S.R.R. 1391 (1988).
313. *Freight Forwarder Investigation, Etc.*, 6 F.M.C. 327 (1961).
314. *General Investigation, Etc.*, 16 F.M.C. 344 (1973).
315. *Rates, Hong Kong, Etc.*, 11 F.M.C. 168 (1967.
316. *CHR. Salveson & Co., Etc. v. W. Mich. Dock, Etc.*, 12 F.M.C. 135 (1968).
317. *General Investigation, Etc.*, 16 F.M.C. 344 (1973).
318. *See* Section 3(6); 46 App. U.S.C.A. 1702(3)
319. *Investigation of Storage Practices*, 6 F.M.B. 301 (1961).
320. *Misclassification, Etc.*, 6 F.M.B. 155 (1960).
321. *First Int'l. Devel. Corp. v. Ships Overseas, Etc.*, 21 F.M.C. 899 (1980).
322. *Isbrandtsen Co. v. U.S.*, 356 U.S. 481 (1958).
323. For full text, *see* Appendix A.
324. S. Rept. 98-3, 98th Cong., 1st Sess., 2/14/83, p.35.
325. *Eden Mining Co. v. Bluefields Fruit & S.S. Co.*, 1 U.S.S.B. 41 (1922).
326. *Port Util. Comm. Etc. v. Carolina Co.*, 1 U.S.S.B. 61 (1925).
327. *Intercoastal Investigation*, 1 U.S.S.B.B. 400 (1935).
328. *Agreement 8765, Etc.*, 7 F.M.C. 495 (1963).
329. *Violations of Secs. 14, Etc.*, 15 F.M.C. 92 (1972); *N.Y. Freight Forwarders, Etc. v. F.M.C.*, 337 F.2d 289 (2nd Cir. 1964).
330. *Stockton Port Dist. v. Pac. Westbound Conf.*, 9 F.M.C. 12 (1965).
331. *Volkswagenwerk v. F.M.C.*, 390 U.S. 261 (1968).
332. *Commodity Credit v. Lykes Bros. S.S. Co. Inc.*, 18 F.M.C. 50 (1974).
333. *Household Goods Etc. v. Amer. Export Lines*, 20 F.M.C. 496 (1978).
334. *Misclassification Etc.*, 6 F.M.B. 289 (1961).
335. *Corn Products Co. v. Hamburg-Amerika Lines*, 10 F.M.C. 388 (1967).
336. *European Trade Specialists Inc., Etc. v. Prudential-Grace Lines Inc.*, 19 F.M.C. 148 (1976).
337. *Johns-Manville Products Corp., Etc.*, 13 F.M.C. 192 (1970).
338. *Sugar from Virgin Islands*, 1 U.S.M.C. 695 (1938).
339. *Patrick L.B.R. Co. v. Calmar S.S. Corp.*, 2 U.S.M.C. 494 (1941).
340. *Phillip R. Consolo v. Flota Mercant*, 7 F.M.C. 635 (1963).
341. *Arthur Schwartz v. Grace Line, Inc.*, 12 F.M.C. 253 (1969).
342. "50-Mile Container Rules", 24 S.R.R. 411 (1987), *petition for review denied*, 854 F.2d 1338 (D.C. Cir. 1988), *cert. denied*, 488 U.S. 1041 (1989).
343. Docket No. 89-27, *Martyn Merrit et al., Order Adopting Initial Decision*, 25 S.R.R. 1495 (1991).
344. *Charges, Delivery, Etc.*, 11 F.M.C. 222 (1967).
345. *Practices, Etc.*, 2 U.S.M.C. 588 (1941).
346. *Gulf Puerto Rico Line v. Assoc. Food Co.*, 366 F.Supp. 631 (D.C. P.R. 1973).
347. *Los Angeles Traffic, Etc., S. Calif., Etc.*, 3 F.M.B. 569 (1951).
348. *Remis v. Moore-McCormick*, 2 U.S.M.C. 687 (1945).
349. *Waterman v. Stockhoms, Etc.*, 3 F.M.B. 248 (1950).
350. *Swift & Co. v. Gulf and S. Atl. Havana Conf.*, 6 F.M.B. 215 (1961).

351. *Phillip Consolo v. Flota Mercante, Etc.*, 6 F.M.B. 262 (1961).
352. *J.M. Altieri v. Puerto Rico Port Auth.*, 7 F.M.C. 416 (1962).
353. Docket No. 92-46, *Unpaid Freight Charges,* ____ F.M.C. ____, 26 S.R.R. 735 (1993).
354. 46 U.S.C.A. §812 (Second).
355. *Grace Line, Inc. v. Skips, Etc.*, 7 F.M.C. 432 (1962).
356. *Seas Shipping Co. v. American South African Line*, 1 U.S.S.B.B. 568 (1936).
357. S. Rept. No. 97-414, 87th Cong., 2nd Sess., 5/25/82, p.40.
358. *Transshipment Agreement,* 10 F.M.C. 183 (1966).
359. *Rates on U.S. Government Cargoes,* 11 F.M.C. 263 (1967).
360. Section 18(b)(5); 46 U.S.C.A. 817(b)(5).
361. The conferees felt that the "prohibited acts" in the Shipping Act of 1984 will continue the protections of the present law against predation, Conf. Rept., p.33.
362. Section 3(9); 46 App. U.S.C.A. 1702(9). For the full definition, *see* Appendix A.
363. *Investigation, Practices, Etc.,* 10 F.M.C. 95 (1966).
364. *Isbrandtsen Co. v. States Marine,* 6 F.M.B. 422   (1961).
365. *U.S. Lines, Etc.,* 7 F.M.C. 464 (1962).
366. Section 3(14), 46 App. U.S.C.A. §1702(14).
367. Docket No. 87-26, *Transpacific Westbound Rate Agreement, Etc.,* _____ F.M.C. _____, 24 S.R.R. 1395 (1988), *affd.*, 900 F.2d 311 (D.C. Cir. 1990).
368. *F.M.C. v. Isbrandtsen Co.*, 354 U.S. 481 (1958).
369. Pub. L. 87-346 (1961); 46 U.S.C.A. §813a.
370. *In Re Agreement Nos. 150 DR-7, Etc.*, 22 F.M.C. 378 (1979).
371. 28 C.F.R. 50.6.
372. S.Rept. No. 97-414, 99th Cong. 2nd Sess., 5/28/82, pp.39–40.
373. *Id.*
374. *See* n. 97.
375. *Sea-Land Services, Inc. v. S. Atl. & Carribean Line, Inc.*, 9 F.M.C. 338 (1966).
376. Docket No. 78-32, *Pac. Westbound Conf., Etc.,* ____ F.M.C. ____, 22 S.R.R. 946 (1984).
377. *See* n. 100.
378. *Investigation of Overland/OCP Rates,* 12 F.M.C. 184 (1969).
379. *Delaware River Port Auth. v. Transamerican Trailer Etc.*, 17 F.M.C. 234, *affd.*, 536 F.2d 391 (D.C. Cir. 1976).
380. *Pac. Westbound-Conf.-Equalization Rules,* 21 F.M.C. 937 (1979).
381. *Id.*
382. 46 U.S.C.A. §815.
383. *Amer. Tobacco Co. v. C.G.T.*, 1 U.S.S.B. 3 (1919).
384. *Intercoastal Investigation,* 1 U.S.S.B.B. 400 (1935).
385. *West Indies Fruit Co. v. Flota Mercante,* 7 F.M.C. 66 (1962).
386. *Valley Evaporating Co. v. Grace Line,* 14 F.M.C. 16, *affd on reconsideration,* (1970).
387. *Freight Forwarder Bids, Etc.,* 19 F.M.C. 619 (1977).
388. Violations of §§14(4), 16(1) and 17, 15 F.M.C. 92 (1972).
389. 46 App. U.S.C.A. §1709(b)(12).
390. Docket No. 89-14, *Credit Practices of the North Europe - U.S. Atlantic Conference, Order to Show Cause,* ____ F.M.C. ____, 25 S.R.R. 288 (1989).
391. 49 App. U.S.C.A. §2(24).
392. ACCOS, p.23.
393. *Id.*, pp.53–54 n.37.
394. For further exceptions and full text, *see* Appendix A.
395. 46 U.S.C.A. §819.
396. *Practices, Etc. of San Francisco Bay Terminals,* 2 U.S.M.C. 588 (1941).
397. H. Rept. 98-53, Part I, 98th Cong., 1st Sess., 4/12/82 pp.23–24. The four prohibited acts referred to were enlarged to six in the 1984 Act.
398. S. Rept., No. 97-414, 97th Cong., 2nd Sess., 5/25/82, pp.40–41.

399. Docket No. 77-23, *Agreement No. 10294*, 19 S.R.R. 1113 (I.D. 1979), discontinued.
400. S.Rept. No. 98-3, 98th Cong., 1st Sess., 2/14/83, p.37.
401. *Japan/Korea Atl. & Gulf Conf.*, 22 F.M.C. 56, (1981).
402. S.Rept. No. 98-3, 98th Cong., 1st Sess, 2/14/83, p.30.
403. *Id.* at p.38.
404. 46 App. U.S.C.A. §1709(e).
405. 46 C.F.R. 572 104(n).
406. Conf. Rept., p.36.
407. S.Rept. No. 98-3, 98th Cong., 1st Sess., 4/14/83, p.39.
408. Conf. Rept., p.40.
409. *Far East Conf. v. U.S.*, 342 U.S. 570 (1952).
410. 46 C.F.R. 502.62(a), (c).
411. *Id.* at 502.64(a).
412. *Isthmian S.S. Co. v. U.S.*, 53 F.2d 251 (D.C.S.D. N.Y. 1931); *Anglo-Canadian Ship Co., Ltd. v. Mitsui S.S. Co., Ltd.*, 4 F.M.B. 535 (1955).
413. *Pacific Coast Europ. Conf., Etc.*, 5 F.M.B. 247 (1957).
414. *Trane Co. v. S. African Marine Corp. (N.Y.)*, 19 F.M.C., 375 (1976).
415. Op. cit.
416. Informal Docket No. 439(I), *Mine Safety, Etc. v. S. African Marine Corp.*, 21 F.M.C. 619 (1978).
417. *Old Ben Coal Co. v. Sea-Land Service, Inc.*, 21 F.M.C. 506 (1978).
418. 46 C.F.R. 502.91.
419. 46 C.F.R. 502.93.
420. Public Law 101-552.
421. Docket No. 93-06, *Alternative Dispute Resolution*, 26 S.R.R. 1032 (1993).
422. 46 C.F.R. 502.91.
423. 46 C.F.R. 502.91(d).
424. 46 C.F.R. 502.147(a).
425. *Imposition of Surcharge, Etc.*, 9 F.M.C. 129 (1965).
426. *Alaska S.S. Co., Etc.*, 11 F.M.C. 314 (1968).
427. *Pacific Coast Europ. Conf., Etc.*, 4 F.M.B. 696 (1955).
428. *Parsons & Whittemore, Inc. v. Johnson Line*, 7 F.M.C. 721 (1964).
429. *Eden Mining Co. v. Bluefields Fruit & S.S. Co.*, 1 U.S.S.B. 41 (1922).
430. *Reliance Mtr. Car. v. G.L.T.C.*, 1 U.S.M.C. 794 (1938).
431. *Fiat-Allis, Etc. v. Atlantic Ctr. Line*, 22 F.M.C. 544 (1980).
432. *Tyler Pipe, Etc. v. Lykes Bros.*, 15 F.M.C. 29 (1971).
433. *U.S.A. v. Isbrandtsen Lines, Inc.*, 11 F.M.C. 11 (1968).
434. *See* n. 25.
435. *Firearms Import, Etc. v. Lykes Bros.*, 458 F.Supp. 88 (S.D. FL. 1978). This decision appears questionable. If the overcharge action would not be barred by a federal statute of limitations, the fact that an FMC action seeking reparations for overcharges would be barred by the FMC under Section 11(g) of the 1984 Act seems inapplicable.
436. *West Indies Fruit Co. v. Flota Mercante*, 7 F.M.C. 66 (1962).
437. Docket No. 71-53, *Sea-Land Service, Inc.*, 13 S.R.R. 907 (1975), not officially reported.
438. *Consolidated Int'l. Corp. v. Concordia Line, Etc.*, 18 F.M.C. 181 (1975).
439. *U.S. Borax, Etc. v. Pac. Coast Europ. Conf.*, 11 F.M.C. 451 (1968).
440. 46 C.F.R. 502.253.
441. Conf. Rept., p.41.
442. 46 C.F.R. 502.254(b).
443. Allowing, but not mandating double damages, recognized that private suits under the antitrust laws will no longer be allowed under Section 7(c)(2). Conf. Rept. pp. 40–42.
444. *Delaware River Port Authority v. U.S. Lines, Inc.*, 331 F.Supp. 441 (D.C.E.D. Pa. 1971); Agreement 7700, Etc., 10 F.M.C. 61 (1966).

445. Conf. Rept., p.41.

446. *Id.*

447. *See* 46 CFR 61-76, incl.

448. 46 C.F.R. 502.181-184, incl.

449. 46 C.F.R. 502.311-321 incl.

450. *Mueller v. Peralta Shipping Corp.,* 8 F.M.C. 361 (1965).

451. 46 C.F.R. 304(g). See Appendix G for appropriate forms for adjudication under Subpart S.

452. 46 C.F.R. 502.304(f).

453. Pub. L. 100-418, Title X, Aug. 23, 1988; this law has been incorporated as section 11a., in the 1984 Act in the West Publishing Co. 1992 Cumulative Docket Part. Appendix A, however, contains the 1984 Act and the Foreign Shipping Practices Act as separate publications.

454. 46 U.S.C.A. §861 et. seq.

455. 46 U.S.C.A. §876.

456. 46 C.F.R. 585.301 (Subpart C).

457. Docket No. 92-42, *Conditions Unfavorable to Shipping in U.S. Korean Trade,* sl.op., 11/13/92. In the spring of 1994 after the complaining parties advised that objectionable conditions no longer exist, the proceeding was discontinued. *Am. Shipper,* June 1994, p.21.

458. 46 App. U.S.C.A. §1710a.(b).

459. 46 C.F.R. 585.601.

460. Docket No. 91-31, *Adverse Conditions in the U.S./China Trade,* 20 S.R.R. 163 (1992).

461. 46 App. U.S.C.A. §1711. For the full text, *see* App. A.

462. *Agreements, Etc.,* 7 F.M.C. 228 (1962).

463. *F.M.C. v. De Smedt,* 268 F.Supp., 972 (S.D.N.Y. 1967).

464. 46 C.F.R. 502.201.

465. *Id.* at 502-201(h).

466. *Id.* at 502.201(i).

467. 46 U.S.C.A. §821(b).

468. 46 U.S.C.A. §826.

469. *Takazato v. F.M.C.,* 633 F.2d 1276 (9th Cir. 1980).

470. S.Rept. 98-3, 98th Cong., 1st Sess., 4/12/82, p.40.

471. 46 C.F.R. 502.131 & 132.

472. 46 App. U.S.C.A. §1712. For the full text, see Appendix A.

473. 46 U.S.C.A. §831(b).

474. 46 U.S.C.A. §831(a) and (c).

475. 46 App. U.S.C.A. §1712(a).

476. Docket No. 85-14, *Cari Cargo Int'l., Inc., Etc. Initial Dec.,* _____ F.M.C. _____, 23 S.R.R. 1007 (1986); *In re Rubin,* 6 F.M.B. 235 (1961).

477. 46 App. U.S.C.A. §1712(c).

478. 46 C.F.R. 587.

479. *See U.S. v. Hutto,* No. 1, 256 U.S. 524 (1921).

480. Docket No. 80-5, *Certified Corporation, Etc.,* Order of Partial Adoption, 21 S.R.R. 468 (1982).

481. Docket No. 84-13, *Artic Gulf Marine, Inc.,* Order of Partial Adoption, _____ F.M.C. _____, 245 S.R.R. 159 (1987).

482. Docket No. 84-38, *Ariel Maritime Group et al.,* _____ F.M.C. _____, 24 S.R.R. 517 (1987).

483. Docket No. 81-5, *Int'l. Assn. of NVOCCs v. Atlantic Container Line,* _____ F.M.C. _____, 25 S.R.R. 734 (1990).

484. *See* 46 App. U.S.C.A §1712(b)(3).

485. 46 App. U.S.C.A. §1713. For the full text, see Appendix A.

486. 46 U.S.C.A. §§822, 824, 828 & 829.

487. *Swayne & Hoyt v. Kerr Gifford & Co.,* 14 F.Supp. 805 (D.C.E.D. La. 1935).

488. *Persian Gulf Outward Fr. Conf. v. F.M.C.,* 375 F.2d 335 (D.C. Cir. 1967).

489. *Crown Steel Sales, Inc. v. Port of Chicago,* 12 F.M.C. 353 (1967).

490. *Transamerican Trailer Transport, Inc. v. F.M.C.*, 492 F.2d, 617 (D.C. Cir. 1974).

491. *Anchor Line Ltd. v. F.M.C.*, 299 F.2d, 124, (D.C. Cir. 1962), *cert. denied*, 370 U.S. 922 (1962).

492. *F.M.C. v. Port of Seattle*, 521 F.2d, 431 (9th Cir. 1975).

493. *F.M.C. v. Transoceanic Terminal Corp.*, 252 F.Supp., 743 (1966).

494. *D.L. Piazza Co. v. West Coast Line*, 210 F.2d 947 (2nd Cir. 1954), cert. denied 348 U.S. 839 (1954).

495. *Roberto Hernandez, Inc. v. Arnold Bernstein, Etc.*, 116 F.2d, 849 (2nd Cir. 1941), *cert. denied*, 313 U.S. 582 (1941). Query whether either party in an enforcement action in the district court may "introduce" new evidence, as the court appears to have indicated.

496. *F.M.C. v. Caragher*, 364 F.2d, 696 (D.C. Cir. 1966).

497. 40 C.F.R. 502.68.

498. *Petition for Declaratory Order, Etc.*, 21 F.M.C. 187 (1978).

499. *Compensation, Etc. of Forwarders*, 22 F.M.C. 740 (1980).

500. Senate Rept. No. 98-3, 98th Cong., 1st Sess., 2/4/83, p.41.

501. 46 U.S.C.A. §820.

502. 46 App. U.S.C.A. §1714(a).

503. 46 C.F.R. 502.288.

504. *Pac. Coast European Conf. v. F.M.C.*, 350 F.2d 41 (1960).

505. *Montship Lines, Ltd. v. F.M.B.*, 295 F.2d, 147 (D.C. Cir. 1961).

506. *Isbrandtsen, Etc. v. U.S.*, 300 U.S. 139 (1937).

507. *Trailer Marine Transport Corp. v. F.M.C.*, 602 F.2d, 379 (D.C. Cir. 1979).

508. *Montship Lines, Ltd. v. F.M.B.*, 205 F.2d 147 (D.C. Cir. 1961).

509. 46 App. U.S.C.A. §1714(b).

510. 46 C.F.R. 510.16(6).

511. 46 C.F.R. 514.1 (iii)(C).

512. 46 C.F.R. 580.5(c)(ii)(B).

513. 46 C.F.R. 582.3(e).

514. Docket No. 92-27, *Filing Requirements for Anti-Rebate Certifications*, 26 S.R.R. 478 (1992).

515. 46 C.F.R. 572.703.

516. 46 App. U.S.C.A. §1715. *See* Appendix A for full text.

517. 46 U.S.C.A. §833(a).

518. S.Rept. No. 98-3, 98th Cong., 1st Sess., 2/14/83, p.41.

519. *E.g., see* Docket No. 75-56, *Canadian-American Working Arrangement*, 16 S.R.R. 737 (1976), not officially reported.

520. 46 C.F.R. 580.1(b).

521. *Id.* at 580.1(c).

522. *Id.* at 580.1(e).

523. *New Orleans S.S. Assn. v. Bunge Corp.*, 8 F.M.C. 687 (1965).

524. Docket No. 83-23, *Central Nat'l. Corp., Etc. v. Port of Houston*, order adopting Initial Decision, _____ F.M.C. _____, 22 S.R.R. 795 (1984).

525. Docket No. 85-10, *Marine Terminal Agreements*, 24 S.R.R. 192 (1987).

526. 46 App. U.S.C.A. §1716. For full text, *see* Appendix A.

527. 46 U.S.C.A. §841(a).

528. *Carrier-Imposed Time Limits, Etc.*, 4 F.M.B. 29 (1952).

529. *Actions To Adjust Or Meet Conditions*, 21 F.M.C., 719 (1979), citing *N.Y. Foreign Freight Forwarders, Etc. v. F.M.C.*, 337 F.2d, 289, (2nd Cir. 1964), *cert. denied*, 380 U.S. 910 (1965).

530. *Alcoa Steamship Co. v. F.M.C.*, 348 F.2d 756 (D.C. Cir. 1965).

531. *Pacific Coast European Conf. v. F.M.C.*, 376 F.2d 785 (D.C. Cir. 1967).

532. *Austasia Intermodal Lines, Ltd. v. F.M.C.*, 580 F.2d 642 (D.C. Cir. 1978).

533. Docket No. 81-5, *International Ass'n. of NVOCCs v. Atlantic Container Line, et al.*, 25 S.R.R. 734 (1990).

534. Pub. Law No. 101-648.

535. Docket No. 93-06, *Alternative Dispute Resolution*, 26 S.R.R. 1032 (1993).

536. 46 C.F.R. 502.56.
537. 46 App. U.S.C.A. §1717; *See* Appendix A for the full text.
538. Conf. Rept., pp.42-43.
539. ACCOS, Executive Summary, p. i.
540. *Id.*
541. *Id.* at xii.
542. Conf. Rept., p.43.
543. 46 App. U.S.C.A. §1718, et seq. *See* Appendix A for the full text.
544. 46 App. U.S. 1719.
545. *Application of Shipping Act of 1984 to Formal Proceedings Pending before Federal Maritime Commission,* 46 Fed. Reg. 21798 5/15/84.
546. *California Cartage Co., Inc. v. U.S.,* 802 F.2d 353 (9th Cir. 1986).
547. *Seawinds Ltd. v. Nedlloyd Lines, B.V.,* 80 B.R. 181 (N.D. Cal. 1987), *aff'd,* 846 F.2d 586, (9th Cir. 1988), *cert. denied,* 484 U.S. 891.
548. *Bradley v. Richmond School Board,* 416 U.S. 696 (1984).
549. *Taub, Hummel & Schnall v. Atlantic Container Line,* 864 F.2d (2nd Cir. 1990).
550. *Id.* at 529-530.
551. H.Rept. No. 88-53, 98th Cong., 1st Sess., 4/12/82, p.39.
552. S.Rept. No. 98-3, 98th Cong., 1st Sess., 2/14/83, p.42.
553. 46 App. U.S.C.A. §1721. *See* Appendix A for the full text.

Chapter III: Shippers

1. 46 App. U.S.C.A. §1702(23).
2. *International Maritime Dictionary* by R. deKerchove, New York: Van Nostrand Co., 1948, p.65.
3. ACCOS, p.53, n. 22.
4. *Intercoastal Rate Investigation,* 1 U.S.S.B. 108 (1926).
5. *Intercoastal Investigation,* 1 U.S.S.B.B. 400 (1935).
6. *Agreement No. 8905, Etc.,* 7 F.M.C. 792 (1964).
7. *Joint Committee, Etc. v. Pac. Westbound Conf.,* 4 F.M.B. 166 (1953).
8. *Unapproved Sec. 15 Agreements, Etc.,* 8 F.M.C. 596 (1965).
9. *U.S. v. Hellenic Lines Ltd.,* 14 F.M.C. 254 (1971).
10. *Lykes-Harrison Pooling Ag't,* 4 F.M.B. 515 (1954).
11. *Investigation of Rate Practices, Etc.,* 7 F.M.C. 118 (1962).
12. 46 U.S.C.A. §817.
13. Docket No. 1757(F), *Elinel Corp. v. Sea-Land,* ____F.M.C.____, 26 S.R.R. 1399 (1994).
14. *Beaumont Port Comm. v. Seatrain Lines, Inc.,* 3 F.M.B. 556 (1951).
15. 46 U.S.C.A. §817(b)(5).
16. Pub.L. 98-237, 3/20/84, 98 Stat. 88.
17. *Frt. Forwarder Investigation, Etc.,* 6 F.M.B. 327 (1961).
18. *Alaskan Rates,* 2 U.S.M.C. 558 (1941).
19. *Bills of Lading Etc.,* 3 U.S.M.C., 111 (1949).
20. *West India Industries v. Tradex,* 664 F.2d 946 (5th Cir. 1982).
21. *Allstate Ins. Co. v. Int'l. Shipping Corp.,* 703 F.2d, 497 11th Cir. 1983).
22. *Continental Ore Corp. v. U.S.,* 423 F.2d 1248 (1st Cir. 1970).
23. *American Tobacco Co. v. French Line,* 1 U.S.S.B. 53 (1923).
24. *Sea-Land Services, Inc. v. Acme Fast Frt. Etc.,* 21 F.M.C. 561 (1978), *petition for review denied,* 612 F.2d 1312 (1st Cir. 1979).
25. *Intercoastal Investigation,* 1 U.S.S.B.B. (1935).
26. *Misclassification of Tissue Paper, Etc.,* 4 F.M.B. 483 (1954). *See also* heading "I. Misclassification of Goods," *infra.*

27. *American Union Transport v. River Plate and Brazil Conf.*, 5 F.M.B. 171 (1956).
28. *Intercoastal Segregation Rules*, 1 U.S.M.C. 725 (1938).
29. *Terminal Rate Increase, Etc.*, 3 U.S.M.C. 21 (1948).
30. *Terminal Rate Structure, Etc.*, 5 F.M.B. 53 (1956).
31. *Levantino & Sons, Inc. v. Prudential-Grace Lines, Inc.*, 18 F.M.C. 82 (1974).
32. *Assembling & Distribution Charge*, 1 U.S.S.B. 380 (1935).
33. *Investigation of Free Time Practices, Etc.*, 9 F.M.C. 525 (1966).
34. *Loading & Unloading Rates, Etc.*, 13 F.M.C. 51 (1969).
35. *Storage Practices, Etc.*, 6 F.M.B. 178 (1960).
36. *Free Time, Etc.*, 13 F.M.C. 207 (1970).
37. *Free Time, Etc.*, 3 U.S.M.C. 89 (1948).
38. *Id.*
39. *See* n. 35.
40. *Boston Shipping Assn. v. Port of Boston*, 10 F.M.C. 409 (1967).
41. *Investigation of Free Time Practices*, 9 F.M.C. 525 (1966).
42. *Practices of San Francisco, Etc.*, 2 U.S.M.C. 588 (1941).
43. *City of Galveston v. Kerr S.S. Co.*, 362 F.Supp. 289, (D.C.S.D. Tex. 1973).
44. *Gulf Puerto Rico Lines v. Assoc. Food Co.*, 366 F.Supp. 631 (D.C.P.R. 1973).
45. *Free Time, Etc.*, 3 U.S.M.C. 89 (1948).
46. *Free Time & Demurrage Practices, Etc.*, 11 F.M.C. 238 (1967).
47. *Midland Metals Corp. v. Mitsui*, 15 F.M.C. 193 (1972).
48. *Boston Wool Trade Ass'n. v. Merchants and Miners Transportation Co.*, 1 U.S.S.B. 32 (1921).
49. *McCormack S.S. Co. v. U.S.*, 16 F.Supp. 45 (D.C.N.D. Cal. 1936).
50. *Plum Tool Co. v. American-Hawaiian*, 2 U.S.M.C. 523 (1941).
51. *Lykes Bros. S.S. Co., Etc.*, 7 F.M.C. 602 (1963).
52. *Trane Co. v. S. African Marine Corp. (N.Y.)*, 19 F.M.C. 375 (1976).
53. *Madeplac, Etc. v. L. Figueriedo, Etc.*, 20 F.M.C. 578 (1978).
54. *Colgate Palmolive Co. v. Grace Line*, 17 F.M.C. 279 (1974).
55. Docket No. 86-17, *Mobile Oil Co. v. Barber Blue Sea Lines*, (ALJ), 24 S.R.R. 633 (1987).
56. Section 11(g); 46 App. U.S.C.A. §1710(g).
57. 46 C.F.R. 502.253.
58. *Id.* at 502.254(a),(b).
59. 46 App. U.S.C.A. §1707(e). For the full text, *see* Appendix A.
60. *Application of Columbus Line, Etc.*, 24 S.R.R. 210 (1987).
61. *Application of Inter-Am. Fr. Conf.*, 22 S.R.R. 1572 (1985).
62. *Application of Am. President Lines, Etc.*, 24 S.R.R. 887 (1988).
63. 46 U.S.C.A. 1707 (l)(2).
64. Special Docket 1826, *Applic. of OOCL (USA), Etc.*, _____ F.M.C._____, 25 S.R.R. 1064 (1990).
65. Docket No. 78-6, *Adel Int'l., Etc. v. P.R. Maritime Shpng. Authority*, Order Adopting Initial Decision, _____ F.M.C._____, 20 S.R.R. 687 (1980).
66. *Nepera Chem. v. F.M.C.*, 662 F.2d 18 (D.C.C. Cir. 1981).
67. ACCOS at pp. 23, 54 (n.37), 62.
68. 46 App. U.S.C.A. §1707(c).
69. H.Rept. 97-611, Part I, 97th Cong., 2nd Sess. 6/16/82 p.38.
70. S.Rept. No. 97-14, 97th Cong., 2nd Sess. 5/25/92 pp.36–37.
71. *Id.* at p.37.
72. Conf. Rept., p.40
73. Docket No. 84-21, Service Contracts, 22 S.R.R. 1424 (1984).
74. *Id.*
75. *Id.*
76. *Id.*
77. *Id.*
78. *Id.*

79. Op. cit; In Docket No. 94-3, a line is defending a claim of a violation by a shipper asserting status as a "similarly situated" shipper on the ground that the line's West African service used Rotterdam as a transshipment port and because the line has "limited capacity" from that port it could not service additional business "without experiencing long delays in Rotterdam." Hearing counsel of the FMC has argued that the line is in violation of section 8(c) and sections 10(b)(3) and (12). As of this writing, an initial decision by the ALJ is anticipated.

80. Docket 88-15, *CA Shipping Line, Inc. v. Yangming,* _____F.M.C._____, 25 S.R.R. 1213 (1990).

81. Docket No. 92-38, *Transportation Services, Etc. v. Coex Coffee Int'l., Inc.,* _____F.M.C._____, 26 S.R.R. 646 (1992); *See also Vinmar, Inc. v. China Ocean Shipping Co.,* _____ F.M.C. _____, 26 S.R.R. 130, (1992); *Western Trade, Etc. v. ANERA Ag't.,* _____ F.M.C. _____, 26 S.R.R. 1239 (1994); and Informal Docket No. 1758(I), *Uniroyal, Etc. v. Nedlloyd Lines,* _____F.M.C._____, 26 S.R.R. 1369 (1994).

82. Docket No. 91-17, *Consumer Electronics Shippers' Ass'n. v. Anera,* _____F.M.C._____, 26 S.R.R. 766 (1993).

83. Docket No. 92-06, *Western Overseas Trade, Etc. v. Asia N. America East-bound,* ____ F.M.C. ____, 26 S.R.R. 1066 (ALJ)(1993)

84. See also, *Supplemental Report,* above docket, ____ F.M.C. ____, 26 S.R.R. 1239 (1994), on petition for review (filed 3/14/94), *sub nom. All Trading Co. v. F.M.C.,* D.C. Cir. 94-1165.

85. FMC Circular Letter No. 1-89, Service and Cargo Commitments in Service Contracts, 64 Fed. Reg. p.15256, 4/17/89.

86. *Id.*

87. 46 C.F.R. 581.7(c).

88. 46 U.S.C.A. §812 Fourth.

89. *Ball Mill Lumber v. Port of N.Y. Authority,* 11 F.M.C. 494 (1968); *see also American Export Isbrandtsen Lines v. F.M.C.,* 380 F.2d 609 (D.C. Cir., 1967).

90. 46 App. U.S.C.A. §1707(b).

91. 46 C.F.R. 580.12(a).

92. S.Rept. No. 98-3, 98th Cong. 1st Sess., 2/14/83 p.32.

93. Docket No. 83-31, *Volume Incentive Program, Etc.,* _____F.M.C._____, 22 S.R.R. 686 (1984).

94. *Id.*

95. A copy of such an agreement is attached hereto as Appendix D.

96. *Nedlloyd v. Uniroyal, Inc.,* 433 F.Supp. 121 (S.D.N.Y. 1977).

97. *Strachan Shipping Co. v. Dresser Industries, Inc.,* 701 F.2d, 483 (5th Cir. 1983).

98. *Id.* at 485-486.

99. *NLRB v. Int'l Longshoremen's Assoc. (ILA II),* 473 U.S. 61 (1985).

100. Docket No. 81-11, *"50-Mile Container Rules,"* ____ F.M.C. ____, 21 S.R.R 411 (1987).

101. *N.Y. Shipping Assoc. v. F.M.C.,* 854 F.2d 1338 (D.C.Cir. 1988), *cert. denied,* 488 U.S. 1041 (1989).

102. *Misclassification of Glassware,* 5 F.M.B. 509 (1958).

103. *Misclassification of Tissue Paper, Etc.,* 4 F.M.B. 483 (1954).

104. Docket No. 283(I), *Western Publ. Co. v. Hapag Lloyd,* sl. op, 4/4/72.

105. *Carpoundum Co. v. Royal Netherland S.S. Co.,* 19 F.M.C. 431 (1977).

106. *In re Rubin,* 6 F.M.B. 235 (1961).

107. Informal Docket 681(F), *Sanrio C. Ltd. v. Maersk Line,* sl.op. 4/21/80, adopted 9/5/80.

108. *C.S.C. Int'l. Co. v. Lykes Bros.,* 20 F.M.C. 551 (1978).

Chapter IV: Marine Terminal Operators

1. 46 App. U.S.C.A. §1702(3)(15).

2. 46 U.S.C.A. §801.

3. 46 C.F.R. 515.3.

4. *Bethlehem Steel Corp. v. Indiana Port Comm.*, 21 F.M.C. 629 (1979), *aff'd.*, 642 F.2d 1215 (D.C. Cir. 1980).
5. *Plaquemines Port District v. F.M.C.*, 838 F.2d 536 (D.C. Cir. 1988).
6. Docket 77-5, *Port of Ponce v. P.R. Ports Authority*, ____ F.M.C. ____, 25 S.R.R. 883 (1990).
7. *Puerto Rico Ports Authority v. F.M.C.*, 919 F.2d 799 (1st Cir. 1990).
8. *See* n. 3.
9. *Gillen's Sons Lighterage v. American Stevedores*, 12 F.M.C. 325 (1969).
10. *Status of Carloaders and Unloaders*, 2 U.S.M.C. 761 (1946).
11. 46 App. U.S.C.A. §1701.
12. Docket No. 79-9, *Richmond Transfer & Storage Co., Etc.*, I.D. 23 F.M.C. 362 (1980); *Marine Terminal Practices of Port of Seattle*, 21 F.M.C. 397 (1978). But see *Investigation of Certain Storage Practices, Etc.*, 6 F.M.B. 301 (1961) where the FMC indicated that the service involved should be "within the geographical confines of an ocean terminal facility, such as a warehouse adjacent to a dock or pier . . ." Query whether a consolidator located away from the pier complies with this requirement.
13. 46 App. U.S.C.A. 1709(d)(1).
14. Docket No. 79-45, *Louis Dreyfus Corp. v. Plaquemines Port, Etc.*, sl. op. Order adopting Initial Decision, ____ F.M.C. ____, 21 S.R.R. 1072 (1982).
15. Docket 84-28, *Petchem, Inc. v. Canaveral Port Auth.*, ____ F.M.C. ____, 23 S.R.R. 974 (1968), *petition for review denied*, 853 F.2d, 958 (D.C. Cir. 1988).
16. *Portlatin, Etc. v. Sea-land Services*, 10 F.M.C. 362 (1967).
17. *A.P. St. Philip, Inc. v. Atlantic Land & Improvement Co.*, 13 F.M.C. 166 (1969).
18. *Bethlehem Steel Corp. v. Indian Port Commission.*, 17 F.M.C. 266 (1969).
19. *Marine Terminal Practices, Seattle*, 21 F.M.C. 397 (1978).
20. Docket No. 79-82, *Pier Services Inc. v. Portside Refrigerated Terminals*, 23 F.M.C. 306 (1980).
21. *See* n. 12.
22. ACCOS, p. 24.
23. S. Rept. No. 98-3, 98th Cong., 1st Sess., 2/14/83 p.22.
24. H. Rept 98-53, Part 2, 98th Cong., 1st Sess., 7/1/83, p.21.
25. 46 App. U.S.C.A. §1706(a)(1).
26. Docket No. 62-33, *Marine Terminal Facilities Agreement Exemptions*, 26 S.R.R. 709 (1993).
27. Docket 79-72, *Cargill v. Waterman S.S. Corp., Order of Partial Adoption*, 24 F.M.C. 442 (198).
28. *Practices, Etc., San Francisco*, 2 U.S.M.C., 588 (1991).
29. *Boston Shipping Ass'n. v. Port of Boston*, 11 F.M.C. 1 (1967).
30. *CHR. Salveson v. West Mich. Dock*, 12 F.M.C. 135 (1968).
31. *Id.*
32. *Id.*
33. *Id.*
34. *See* 46 C.F.R. 515.
35. Conf. Rept., p. 39.
36. 46 C.F.R. 515.3.
37. 46 C.F.R. 515.4.
38. Docket 83-2, *New Orleans S.S. Ass'n v. Plaquemines Port, Etc.*, Order Adopting Initial Decision, ____ F.M.C. ____, 23 S.R.R. 1365 (1985), *petition for review denied*, 838 F.2d 536 (D.C. Cir. 1988).
39. Docket No. 77-56, *W. Gulf Maritime Ass'n. v. City of Galveston, Etc.*, 22 F.M.C. 101 (1979).
40. *Id.*
41. *Plaquemines Port, Etc. v. F.M.C.*, 838 F.2d 536 (D.C. Cir. 1988).
42. *Ferrex Int'l. v. M/V Rico Chone*, 718 F.Supp. 451 (D.C. Cir. 1988).
43. *Wharfage Charges, Etc.*, 2 U.S.M.C. 245 (1940).
44. *West Coast Maritime Ass'n. v. Port of Houston Auth.*, 21 F.M.C. 24; *aff'd*, 610 F.2d 1001; *cert. denied*, 449 U.S. 822 (1980).
45. Docket 74-15, *W. Gulf Maritime Ass'n. Port of Houston Auth.*, 22 F.M.C. 426 (1980), *aff'd.*, 652 F.2d, 197 (1981).

46. *Practices, Etc., San Francisco,* 2 U.S.M.C. 588 (1941).

47. *Intercoastal S.S. Frt. Ass'n. v. Northwest Marine Terminal Ass'n.,* 4 F.M.B. 387 (1953).

48. *Id.*

49. *See* n. 39, *supra.*

50. 46 C.F.R. 515.6.

51. *Contract Rates, Etc.,* 2 U.S.M.C. 727 (1945).

52. *Terminal Rate Increase, Etc., Puget Sound,* 3 U.S.M.C. 21 (1948).

53. *Investigation of Free Time - San Diego,* 9 F.M.C. 525 (1960).

54. 46 C.F.R. 515.6(d)(3).

55. *Terminal Rate Increases, Etc.,* 3 U.S.M.C. 21 (1948).

56. *Free Time and Demurrage Charges, New York, Etc.,* 3 U.S.M.C. 89 (1948).

57. *Penna. Motor Truck Assn. v. Phila. Piers,* 3 F.M.B. 789 (1952).

58. *Free Time and Demurrage Charges on Export Cargo,* 13 F.M.C. 207 (1970).

59. *Id.*

60. *Id.*

61. *See* n. 30.

62. 46 C.F.R. 515.6(d)(4).

63. *Midland Metals Corp. v. Mitsui,* 15 F.M.C. 193 (1972).

64. *Id.*

65. *Boston Shipping Ass'n. v. Port of Boston,* 10 F.M.C. 409 (1967).

66. *Free Time and Demurrage Practices, New York, Etc.,* 11 F.M.C. 238 (1967).

67. 46 C.F.R. 515.6(d)(5).

68. *Storage Charges, Etc.,* 2 U.S.M.C. 48 (1939).

69. *Storage Practices at Longview, WA,* 6 F.M.B. 178 (1960).

70. *See* n. 51.

71. *See* n. 58.

72. *Volkswagon v. F.M.C.,* 392 U.S. 901 (1968).

73. *International Maritime Dictionary,* op cit., p.727.

74. *Calif. S. & B. Co. v. Stockton Port District,* 7 F.M.C. 75 (1962).

75. *See* n. 26.

76. *McCab Etc. v. C. Brewer Corp.,* 16 F.M.C. 49 (1972).

77. *Pittson Stevedoring Corp. v. New Haven Terminal,* 13 F.M.C. 33 (1969).

78. 46 C.F.R. 515.6(d)(6).

79. *Los Angeles Managers' Conf. v. Southern Calif. Carloading, Etc.,* 3 F.M.B. 569 (1951).

80. *See* n. 70.

81. 46 C.F.R. 515.6(d)(7).

82. *Status of Carloaders, Etc.,* 2 U.S.M.C. 761 (1946).

83. *Charges, Delivery, Etc.,* 11 F.M.C. 222 (1967).

84. *Truck and Lighter Loading and Unloading Practices,* 12 F.M.C. 166 (1969); *aff'd.,* 444 F.2d 824 (D.C. Cir. 1970).

85. 46 C.F.R. 515.6(d)(8-10).

86. *Int'l. Maritime Dictionary,* op. cit., p. 416.

87. *Rates Between Places In Alaska,* 3 U.S.M.C. 7 (1947).

88. *Truck & Lighter Loading & Unloading, N.Y. Harbor,* 9 F.M.C. 505 (1966).

89. *Int'l Packers Ltd. v. N. Pier Terminal Co.,* 11 F.M.C. 525 (1968).

90. 46 U.S.C.A. §814.

91. 46 App. U.S.C.A. §1706(a)(1); the FMC has recommended that antitrust immunity for MTOs be eliminated. ACCOS, p. 81.

92. 46 C.F.R. 572.307.

93. Docket No. 90-16, *Seacon Terminals, Inc. v. The Port of Seattle,* ____ F.M.C. ____, 26 S.R.R. 886 (1993).

94. 46 App. U.S.C.A. §§1709(d)(1) and (3) and 1709(b)(11, 12, and 16).

95. *See* n. 93.

96. *Id.*
97. *Petchem, Inc. v. Canaveral Port Authority,* ____ F.M.C. ____, 23 S.R.R. 974 (1986).
98. *Agreement No. 2598,* 17 F.M.C. 286 (1974).
99. *See* n. 93.
100. *Agreement Nos. T-953, Etc.,* 11 F.M.C. 156 (1967).
101. *San Francisco Port Authority, Etc.,* 14 F.M.C. 233 (1971); Supplemental Rept., 14 F.M.C. 247 (1971).
102. *W. Gulf Maritime Ass'n. v. City of Galveston Etc.,* 22 F.M.C. 101 (1979).
103. *Id.*
104. *U.S. Lines v. MD Port Administration,* Order adopting Initial Decision, 23 F.M.C. 441 (1980).

Chapter V: Non-Vessel-Operating Common Carriers by Water

1. 46 App. U.S.C.A. §1702(17).
2. 2.H. Rept. 97-611, Part 1, 97th Cong., 1st Sess., 6/16/82, p.34.
3. *Determination of Common Carrier Status,* 6 F.M.B. 245 (1961). NVOCCs may be (1) controlled by a forwarder, (2) be associated with a U.S. trucker, or (3) handle FCL loads only as a selling arm of a vessel operator.
4. *Charging Higher Rates Than Tariff,* 19 F.M.C. 44 (1975). The FMC noted therein that the Interstate Commerce Commission operated under a similar concept under Part IV of the Interstate Commerce Act, now repealed, dealing with the domestic freight forwarder.
5. ACCOS, p. 22.
6. *Id.,* p. 53, n. 32.
7. *See* n. 3
8. *Universal Transcontinental Corp., Etc.,* 265 I.C.C. 726 (1950); *See* Ullman, "The Intermodal Movement of LCL Freight," *Denver College Transportation Law Journal,* Vol. XII, No. 1, 1981.
9. *U.S. v. American Union Transport, Inc.,* 327 U.S. 437 (1946).
10. 46 C.F.R. 510.22(g).
11. *See* 18 U.S.C. 371; *U.S. v. Hutto, No. 1,* 256 U.S. 524 (1921).
12. *Austasia Container Express Etc.,* 19 F.M.C. 512 (1977).
13. *Austasia Intermodal Lines v. F.M.C.,* 580 F.2d 642 (D.C. Cir. (1978).
14. *Puerto Rico Maritime Shipping Authority v. ICC,* 602 F.2d 379 (D.C. Cir. 1979).
15. *California Frt. Specialists, Etc.,* 24 F.M.C. 288 (1981).
16. 46 C.F.R. 583.7(c).
17. Pub. L. 101-595, §710(e) (104 Stat. 2997).
18. 46 App. U.S.C.A. §1721.
19. Congressional Record, E 2210, 6/28/90.
20. Docket No. 91-1, *Bonding of Non-Vessel-Operating Common Carriers,* 25 S.R.R. 1679 (1991).
21. *Id.*
22. Pub. L. 102-251 (106 Stat. 60). For the full text *see* Appendix A.
23. 46 C.F.R. Parts 514, 580, 581 and 583 (1/15/93).
24. 46 C.F.R. 583.4(a), (b), and (c).
25. 46 C.F.R. 583.4(d)(2).
26. 46 C.F.R. 583.5(b).
27. *Id.* at 583.5(d).
28. 46 C.F.R. 583.6(a).
29. *Sea-Land Service, Inc. et al. v. Acme Fast Freight,* 21 F.M.C. 194 (1978); *See also States Marine Lines, et al. v. PCFC et al.,* 12 F.M.C. 1 (1968).
30. *Ship's Overseas Service, Inc. v. F.M.C.,* 670 F.2d 304 (D.C. Cir. 1981).
31. Docket No. 84-27, *Co-loading Practices by NVOCCs,* 23 S.R.R. 350 (1985); 46 C.F.R. §580.5(c)(14).

32. *Id.*
33. This document, as well as the following one, was prepared by the Washington firm of Galland, Kharasch, Morse & Garfinkle, P.C. to whom the author is grateful.
34. In November, 1993, the FMC in Docket No. 93-22, *Co-Loading Practices of Non-Vessel-Operating Common Carriers,* proposed extensive changes in its co-loading regulations. In October 1994, the F.M.C. in an open session voted to hold this docket in obeyance and issue a Notice of Intent stating that it was inclined to eliminate the curent co-loading rules as having no legal basis. Before doing so, it will consider comments as to whether it should, under section 16, grant an exemption for co-loading.
35. *California Shipping Line, Inc. v. Yangming Marine Transport Corp.,* 25 S.R.R. 1213 (1990).

Chapter VI: Ocean Freight Forwarders

1. 46 App. U.S.C.A. §1702(19).
2. For a detailed list of forwarder services, *see* 46 C.F.R. 510.2(h).
3. *See* 46 App. U.S.C.A. §§1709(c)(5) and 1718(d).
4. The FMC has defined an ocean freight broker as "an entity which is engaged by a carrier to secure cargo for such carrier, etc." 46 C.F.R. 510.2(m). While this definition is correct for a ship's broker, it omits the cargo broker engaged by the exporter to secure space from a tramp or contract carrier.
5. *Freight Forwarder Investigation, Etc.,* 6 F.M.B. 327 (1961).
6. S.Rept. No. 691, 87th Cong., 1st Sess., 1961, p.3.
7. *N.Y. For. Fr. F'drs., Etc. v. U.S.,* 337 F.2d 289 (2nd Cir. 1964), *cert. denied,* 380 U.S. 910.
8. *U.S. v. American Union Transport, Inc.,* 327 U.S. 437 (1946).
9. *Farrell Lines, Inc. v. Titan Industrial Group,* 306 F.Supp. 1348 (S.D.N.Y. 1969); *Nedloyd v. Uniroyal, Inc.,* 433 F.Supp. 121 (S.D.N.Y. 1977); *Neptune v. All International Fr. F'drs., Inc.,* 709 F.2d 663 (11th Cir. 1983).
10. *Norman G. Jensen, Inc. v. F.M.C.,* 497 F.2d 1053 (8th Cir. 1974).
11. *Independent Ocean Fr. F'dr. License Application,* 15 F.M.C. 127 (1972).
12. *N.Y. Frt. Fg. Investigation,* 3 U.S.M.C. 157 (1949).
13. *See N.Y. Central R.R.V. Ross Lumber Co.,* 234 N.Y. 261 (1922).
14. *See N.Y. Central R.R. v. Sharp,* 124 Misc. 265 (N.Y. 1924).
15. *See Dart v. Ensign,* 47 N.Y. 619 (1872).
16. H. Rept. No. 1214, 69th Cong., 1st Sess., pp.2–3.
17. 3 C.J.S., Agency, §243.
18. *Alcoa S.S. Co. v. Graver Tank Mfg. Co., Inc.,* 124 N.Y.S. 2d 77 (N.Y. 1953). *See also: Farrell Lines, Inc. v. Titan Industrial, Inc.,* 306 F.Supp. 1348 (S.D.N.Y. 1969), *aff'd,* 419 F.2d 835 (1969); *Venezuela Lines v. Mandy,* 171 F.Supp. 290 (D.C.E.D. La. 1959).
19. *Nat'l. Customs Brokers, Etc. v. U.S.,* 883 F.2d 93 (D.C. Cir. 1989).
20. *Venezuelan Lines v. A.J. Perez Export Co.,* 303 F.2d 692 (5th Cir. 1962).
21. 46 C.F.R. 510.14(a).
22. 46 U.S.C.A. 190.
23. *Chicago, M., P. Etc. v. Acme Fast Freight,* 336 U.S. 465 (1949).
24. *See* n. 8.
25. *J.C. Penney v. American Express Co., Inc.,* 102 F.Supp. 742 (S.D.N.Y. 1951), *aff'd,* 201 F.2d 846 (2nd Cir. 1953).
26. *See Princess Pat Ltd. v. Judson Sheldon Div.,* 223 F.2d 916 (7th Cir. 1955).
27. *See* Appendix L.
28. *See Tankers Tramps Corp. v. Tugs Jane McAllister, Etc.,* 358 F.2d 896 (2nd Cir. 1966).
29. *Consolidation Int'l. Corp. v. S.S. Falcon,* 1983 American Maritime Cases 270; *Windsor Trading Corp. v. Schenkers Int'l. Fdrs.,* Civil Ct., N.Y. County, Index No. 1180/82, 11/29/83.
30. *See* n. 17.

31. So too, when the services of a forwarder at another port are used the outport forwarder should look to the shipper for payment unless otherwise agreed.
32. *See* n. 8.
33. 46 U.S.C.A. §841(b).
34. 46 App. U.S.C.A. §1702(19).
35. 46 App. U.S.C.A. §1718(d)(4).
36. *See Ocean Fr. Fdr. License,* 10 F.M.C. 281 (1967).
37. S.Rept. No. 97-414, 97th Cong., 2nd Sess., 5/25/82, p.38.
38. 46 C.F.R. 510.21(b)(2).
39. 46 U.S.C.A. §814.
40. *Consolidated Forwarders Intermodal Corporation,* 21 F.M.C. 553 (1978).
41. The assistant attorney general furnishing this business review letter in May 1986 is now Judge Douglas H. Ginsberg of the U.S. Court of Appeals, D.C. Circuit, the author of that court's later decision holding the 50-Mile Rule unlawful.
42. *Misclassification of Tissue Paper, Etc.,* 4 F.M.B. 483 (1954).
43. *Id.*
44. *In re Ruben, Etc.,* 6 F.M.B. 235 (1961).
45. *Misclassification, Etc.,* 6 F.M.B. 289 (1961).
46. *Aleutian Homes, Inc. v. Coastline Line,* 5 F.M.B. 602 (1959).
47. *U.S. v. Missouri R.R. Co.,* 250 F.2d 805 (5th Cir. 1958).
48. *Atlantic Coastline R. Co. v. Atlantic Bridge Co.,* 57 F.2d 654 (5th Cir. 1932).
49. *U.S. v. Gulf Refining Co.,* 268 U.S. 542 (1925).
50. *Pure Oil Co. v. Alton & S.R.,* 284 I.C.C. 461 (1952).
51. *Continental Can Co. v. U.S.,* 272 F.2d 312 (2nd Cir. 1959).
52. *Hazel-Atlass Glass Co., Etc.,* 5 F.M.B. 515 (1958).
53. *Continental Can Co. v. U.S.,* 272 F.2d 312 (2nd Cir. 1959).
54. *Royal Netherland St. Co. v. F.M.B.,* 304 F.2d 938 (D.C. Cir. 1962).
55. *Hasman & Baxt, Etc. v. Misclassification, Etc.,* 8 F.M.C. 453 (1965).
56. 46 App. U.S.C.A. 1707(a)(2).
57. 46 App. U.S.C.A. 1709(b)(2).
58. *Malpractices—Brazil/U.S. Trade,* 15 F.M.C. 55 (1971).
59. 18 U.S.C. §371.
60. *U.S. v. Hutto.,* No. 1, 256 U.S. 524 (1921).
61. 46 App. U.S.C.A. §1709(a)(1).
62. *See U.S. Lines, Etc., Sec. 16 Violation,* 7 F.M.C. 464 (1962).
63. Neither the 1984 Act nor Part 510 regulating forwarders authorizes the FMC to fix the amount of brokerage.
64. Further, the provisions of Section 10, Prohibited Acts, is overall, to "restrain the abuses of concerted power. . . ." S.Rept. No. 98-3, 98th Cong., 1st Sess., 1983, p. 34. Paying brokerage in excess of the tariff amount is the individual act of a single carrier and not "concerted" action by two or more carriers.
65. 46 App. U.S.C.A. §1718.
66. 46 App. U.S.C.A. §19(a)(1).
67. S.Rept. No. 98-3, 98th Cong., 1st Sess., 1983, p.33.
68. 46 C.F.R. 510.11(a).
69. *Anthony G. O'Neill,* 12 F.M.C. 68 (1968).
70. *Carlos H. Cabezas,* 8 F.M.C. 130 (1964).
71. *Harry Kaufman,* Initial Decision, 16 F.M.C. 264 (1973).
72. 46 C.F.R. 510.13.
73. 46 C.F.R. 510.15.
74. 46 App. U.S.C.A. §1718(a)(2).
75. 46 C.F.R. 510.14(a).

76. Disputes between forwarders and carriers, particularly with respect to the proper freight charge, are not uncommon.

77. 46 App. U.S.C.A. §718(b).

78. 46 C.F.R. 510.16. Perhaps the mandatory "shall" in Section 19(b) should be changed to "may."

79. *E.L. Mobley, Inc.*, 21 F.M.C. 845 (1979).

80. 46 C.F.R. 510.14(d).

81. 46 App. U.S.C.A. 1718(c).

82. 46 C.F.R. 510.4(a).

83. Revised American Foreign Trade Definition, 1941, National Foreign Trade Council Inc., New York, N.Y., 1941, p.4.

84. 46 C.F.R. 510.4(c). Such charges, however, may be nominal to attract patronage.

85. 46 C.F.R. 510.11(d). The use of the word "may" appears confusing. Since the exception to licensing in Part 510.4(e) applies only to cargo moving under the NVOCC's bill of lading, it should be clear in the rule that it is mandatory to obtain a license for the forwarding of shipments not moving under the NVOCC's bill of lading.

86. *National Customs Brokers & Forwarders Ass'n of America v. U.S.*, 883 F.2d 93 (D.C. Cir. 1989).

87. H.Rept. No. 1096, 87th Cong., 1st Sess., 1961, p.3.

88. *Chevron U.S.A. v. Natural Resources Defense Counsel*, 467 U.S. 837 (1984).

89. *Volkswagen v. F.M.C.*, 390 U.S. 261 (1968). This view by the Supreme Court is not easily reconciled with the D.C. Circuit's position (n. 86 above) that the authority to review FMC decisions was "expressly limited" and that the Court must be "highly deferential" to the agency ruling. Faced with such judicial obeisance, it seems that one seeking a reversal of an agency ruling faces a difficult, if not virtually impossible, task on an appeal.

90. *Freight Forwarder Investigation, Etc.*, 6 F.M.B. 327 (1961).

91. S.Rept. No. 691, 87th Cong., 1st Sess. (1961).

92. 46 App. U.S.C.A. §1718(d).

93. H.Rept. 798, 86th Cong., 1st Sess. (1959).

94. H.Rept. No. 1096, 87th Cong., 1st Sess. (1961).

95. *See Bush v. Springall*, 36 N.Y.S. 2d 708, N.Y. (1942).

96. 46 C.F.R. 510.23(b).

97. 46 C.F.R. 510.23(g)(1) and (2).

98. 46 App. U.S.C.A. §1718(d)(2).

99. 46 C.F.R. 510.2(d).

100. 46 App. U.S.C.A. §1718(d)(3).

101. 46 C.F.R. 510.23. The heading of the rule is "Forwarder and carrier compensation."

102. *Agreements and Practice re Brokerage*, 3 U.S.M.C. 170, (1949), *aff'd.; Atlantic & Gulf/West Coast Etc. v. U.S.*, 94 F.Supp. 138 (S.D.N.Y., 1950); and *Pacific Westbound Conf. v. U.S.*, 94 F.Supp. 649 (N.D. CA. 1950).

103. *Joint Committee Etc. v. Pacific W/B Conference*, 4 F.M.B. 166 (1953).

104. *See* Appendix M for the statute amending 19 U.S.C. 1641 (P.Law 99-514, 10(22 1986) and an extract from H.Rept. 99-841, 99th Cong., 2nd Sess., (1986).

105. 46 App. U.S.C.A. §1709(c)(5).

106. Conf. Rept., p.40.

107. 46 App. U.S.C.A. §1718(d)(4).

108. *Memphis F'dg. Co., Inc., Etc.*, _____ F.M.C. _____, 265 S.R.R. 833 (1993).

109. 46 C.F.R. 510.23(h).

110. 46 C.F.R. 510.2(b).

111. *Bolton & Mitchell, Inc. Etc.*, 15 F.M.C. 248 (1972); and at 17 F.M.C. 151 (1973).

112. BMI at 17 F.M.C. 155, n. 5.

113. *Norman G. Jensen, Inc. v. F.M.C.*, 497 F.2 1053 (8th Cir. 1974).

114. *See Ansonia National Bank v. U.S.*, 147 Fed. Supp. 864 (D.C. Conn. 1956).

115. *See Thomas v. U.S.*, 189 F.2d 494 (6th Cir. 1951), *cert. denied*, 342 U.S. 850.

116. *N.Y. For. Fr. Fds., Etc. v. U.S.*, 337 F. 2d 289, (2nd Cir. 1964), *cert. denied*, 380 U.S. 910.

117. S.Rept. 691, 87th Cong., 1st Sess., 1961, p.4.

118. *See Los Angeles By-Products Co. v. Barber S.S. Lines*, 2 U.S.M.C. 106 (1959); *Heavy Lift Practices, Etc.*, 21 F.M.C. 237 (1979).

119. *Nat'l. Customs Brokers, Etc. v. U.S.*, 883 F.2d 93 (D.C. Cir. 1989).

120. *U.S. v. American Union Transport, Inc.*, 327 U.S. 437 (1946).

121. *See* the discussion, *supra*, of the FMC's rule-making authority under Section 17 (46 App. U.S.C.A. §1716).

122. 46 C.F.R. Part 510 et seq. *See* Appendix N for a copy of this part.

123. 46 C.F.R. 510.22(a).

124. *General Increases in Alaskan Rates and Charges*, 7 F.M.C. 563 (1963).

125. 46 C.F.R. 510.22(g).

126. 46 Fed. Reg. 36296, 9/14/84.

127. *See* Appendix K, par. 154.

128. 46 C.F.R. 510.22(i).

129. 46 C.F.R. 510.2(p).

130. *See* n. 119.

131. *American Union Transport, Inc. v. River Plate & Brazil Conf.*, 5 F.M.B. 216 (1957), *aff'd.*, 257 F.2d 607 (D.C. Cir., 1958), *cert. denied*, 358 U.S. 828.

132. *Freight Forwarders Bids on Gov't. Shipments*, 19 F.M.C. 619 (1977).

133. *See* Appendix O for a current copy of the organization chart of the FMC.

INDEX

ABOUT THE AUTHOR

Gerald H. Ullman practiced law in New York City for forty-two years and was head of his own firm since 1948, specializing in international ocean transportation. He represented many firms, both large and small, engaged in various activities related to our export-import commerce.

A graduate of Dartmouth College and Harvard Law School, Mr. Ullman was a Captain in the Transportation Corps of the U.S. Army during World War II serving in various legal capacities and on a troop transport operating in the European Theater.

During his distinguished career Mr. Ullman was counsel to a New York Assembly Committee; Assistant Counsel to U.S. Senator Irving M. Ives in Washington, D.C.; and General Counsel to the National Customs Brokers & Forwarders Association of America. He appeared before many congressional committees, drafted the 1961 amendment on the licensing of ocean freight forwarders and participated in the drafting of sections of the Shipping Act of 1984 and other legislation.

Mr. Ullman played a pivotal role in the lengthy litigation on the 50-Mile Rule, acting as lead counsel in the Supreme Court, and succeeded in obtaining a ruling that held unlawful the restrictive and costly union requirements that severely impeded the containerization of U.S. exports and imports.

Mr. Ullman, the author in 1967 of a treatise on forwarder law, has written extensively on legal issues, including the restrictions on intermodal movement of traffic, as a contributor to the *Journal of Maritime Law and Commerce* and other publications.

Mr. Ullman retired in 1990 and resides in Scottsdale, Arizona, with his wife Susie. He has two children and two grandchildren.

ISBN 0-87033-470-0

54500